Parting Shots
from My
Brittle Bow

Parting Shots
from My
Brittle Bow

Reflections on American Politics and Life

EUGENE J. MCCARTHY

 Fulcrum Publishing
Golden, Colorado

Library of Congress Cataloging-in-Publication Data

McCarthy, Eugene J., 1916-
  Parting shots from my brittle bow / Eugene McCarthy.
    p. cm. — (Speaker's corner books)
  Includes bibliographical references.
  ISBN 1-55591-528-0
  1. United States—Politics and government—1945-1989. 2. United States—Politics and government—1989- 3. Democracy—United States. 4. Political culture—United States. 5. Political parties—United States. 6. United States—Foreign relations—20th century. 7. McCarthy, Eugene J., 1916- I. Title. II. Series.
  E838.5.M3772 2004
  320.973—dc22

                                                        2004020650

ISBN 1-55591-528-0

Printed in the United States of America
0 9 8 7 6 5 4 3 2 1

Editorial: Faith Marcovecchio, Katie Raymond, Haley Groce
Design: Jack Lenzo

Cover image: © Leonard McCombe/Getty Images

Fulcrum Publishing
16100 Table Mountain Parkway, Suite 300
Golden, Colorado 80403
(800) 992-2908 • (303) 277-1623
www.fulcrum-books.com

Also by Eugene McCarthy

Frontiers in American Democracy
Dictionary of American Politics
A Liberal Answer to the Conservative Challenge
The Limits of Power: America's Role in the World
The Year of the People
The Hard Years: A Look at Contemporary America and American Institutions
America Revisited: 150 Years After Tocqueville
A Political Bestiary (with James J. Kilpatrick)
The Ultimate Tyranny: The Majority over the Majority
Complexities and Contraries: Essays of Mild Discontent
The View from Rappahannock
The View from Rappahannock II
Up 'Til Now
A Colony of the World: The United States Today
Nonfinancial Economics (with William McGaughey)
No-Fault Politics: Modern Presidents, the Press and Reformers

Poetry

Other Things and the Aardvark
Ground Fog and Night
Gene McCarthy's Minnesota: Memories of a Native Son
Collected Poems

Children's Books

Mr. Raccoon and His Friends

Table of Contents

Editor's Foreword

In early 2004, I came across an interview with former Senator Eugene McCarthy in the *New Yorker*. In the piece, McCarthy decried the Bush administration's policy in Iraq. More compelling to me was his statement that the *New York Times* and *Washington Post* were no longer interested in his views on politics, and that he instead was publishing new material in small journals such as *Minnesota Law and Politics*. I was shocked that a figure of such intellect and insight was being "put out to pasture" by major news organizations, and I wrote a letter to him to that effect. The next day, to my pleasant surprise, he called me and agreed to do this book.

Too often in our society of sound bites, instant communication, and information overload, we consign some of our most insightful thinkers to near irrelevance. Not only do we not have the time to read their writings, we may not want to be challenged by the provocative things they have to say. Over the past several months, I have gotten to know Eugene McCarthy not only through his writings, of which I had a passing familiarity, but also through interviews, letters, and many hours of conversation. What I have found is a man not only with much to offer present and future generations, but one of the wisest and most insightful politicians in our history. The freshness of his writings, some up to forty years old, is not only the result of great prescience on his part, but also of a wonderful wit and style, becoming of the poet he is. It would be a shame if future generations simply remember him as the one who fought the good fight in 1968; his legacy deserves to be much richer.

This book is a collection of pieces culled from McCarthy's body of work (more than twenty books, many out of print, but most of which are as readable and applicable today as when they were first published), as well as unpublished or limited published articles. I have also included excerpts from interviews I conducted with McCarthy in 2004 touching on the contemporary political scene. The essays appear as they were originally published, with the initial style retained.

In selecting the pieces for inclusion in this book, I looked for those writings that spoke both to our current political state and to the general philosophies underlying American democracy in general. While some of the specific facts mentioned in the original pieces are no longer accurate (and I have used editorial discretion to either omit those facts not germane to the main thrust of the individual articles or have updated facts where possible), the basic premises of McCarthy's writings are still very relevant: that we live in a nation shaped by a strong principle of democracy, requiring involvement by both elected officials and the public; that many of the institutions that allow for the functioning of democracy are in a state of disrepair; that despite this state of affairs, hope prevails; that the two-party system no longer represents the mainstream of American politics; and that America has a unique role in world affairs.

A book is a product of many hands, and I want to acknowledge some of the people that helped make this project a reality: the wonderful team at Fulcrum, including Kay Baron, Jack Lenzo, Jennifer Payne, and Erica Judisch for getting all the materials into electronic format; Faith Marcovecchio, for assisting in the book's organization when I could no longer see the forest for the trees, and being as strong an editor as there is today; Bob and Charlotte Baron, who believed in this project and gave me the support to pursue it; and Stephen Ginsburg and Phil Russell, who first taught me about the significance of Eugene McCarthy and inspired me to always dream big. Special thanks to Eugene McCarthy, who let me interrupt his quiet life, inspired me, and became a friend; John Callahan, for sharing his editorial expertise in addition to preparing a fine introduction; and to my wife, Kristen Foehner, for her support and example of fighting the good fight, and my daughter, Olivia, who I know one day will be inspired by Eugene McCarthy's words and will change the world.

Sam Scinta
Editor
October 2004

3 1833 04819 3111

Introduction

For more than two decades Eugene McCarthy was a politician who was also a writer; now for almost three decades he has been a writer who is also a politician. He was the unlikely, likely hero of the politics of 1968; unlikely because, despite his great gifts, fate placed him in fealty to the ambitions of the senior senator from Minnesota, Hubert Humphrey. That McCarthy chafed at his friend's many tries for national office was evident from his wicked sallies in 1968. "In 1952," he told an audience in Indianapolis, "I nominated Hubert Humphrey for President. In 1956 I nominated him for Vice-President. In 1960 he ran for President. In 1964 I nominated him for Vice-President—that carried. So 1968 was his year to run for President again." Hearing of Humphrey's pledge not to neglect his duties as Vice-President to run for President in '68, McCarthy, one eye on Humphrey, the other on the Constitution, sighed, "How he can neglect his duties as Vice-President if he's been doing what he's supposed to be doing [keeping quiet and healthy] I just don't know."

The smart money had it that with Robert Kennedy in the wings, Eugene McCarthy was a most unlikely challenger to Lyndon Johnson. Doubtless that was why George McGovern apologized to McCarthy for sending Allard Lowenstein his way to plead the case for an insurgency. But a close look at Eugene McCarthy's record up to 1967 reveals a man likely to have challenged the incumbent president's Vietnam position on both moral and pragmatic grounds. Back in 1952, when Theodore Granik of *American Forum of the Air* could not find a sitting senator to debate Senator Joseph McCarthy, he turned to Eugene McCarthy, then a second-term congressman from Minnesota. More remarkable than McCarthy's participation was his refutation of the other McCarthy's charge that the United States had lost 700 million people to Communism since World War II. "Senator, I don't think you can say we have lost them. We never had them ... it is not our policy to have people." Here, in the low-key style that captured the allegiance and affection of millions of Americans in 1968, Eugene McCarthy demolished Joe McCarthy with a trenchant swipe at the senator's condescending, arrogant premises about the United States and the rest of the world. Behind the young congressman's words one hears the Declaration of Independence's call for a "decent respect to the opinions of mankind"—a call savagely ridiculed to almost conspiratorial silence from the American press and media when issued by John Kerry during the 2004 presidential campaign.

The Constitution was and remains Eugene McCarthy's secular scripture. One of ninety-eight senators to vote for the Gulf of Tonkin Resolution in 1964, McCarthy felt responsible for the Senate's failure to reverse the policy and stop the war. Considered then and now, his electoral "challenge to the President's position" seems a matter of vocation. (One thinks of Senator Kerry's creed, uttered in 2004, that faith without works is dead.) Anyone who reads Senator McCarthy's early books—*Frontiers in American Democracy* (1960), *A Liberal Answer to the Conservative Challenge* (1964), *The Limits of Power* (1967)—cannot fail to see a politician uniquely able to recognize "the time when an honorable man simply has to raise the flag."

In 1968 McCarthy was criticized for wanting to curb what his critics, later reacting to President Nixon, came to call the "imperial presidency." Yet for years Senator McCarthy had thought and spoken about the temptations of power. Nominating Adlai Stevenson in 1960, he observed, "this man knows, as all of us do from history, that power often comes to those who seek it. But history does not prove that power is always well used by those who seek it." This is not to say that candidate McCarthy did not understand the uses as well as the abuses of presidential power. During the 1968 campaign, McCarthy alone told the American people that if elected he would retire (or fire) J. Edgar Hoover and General Lewis Hershey for abusing the executive power of the FBI and Selective Service Agency. And his overlooked closing statement in the debate with Robert Kennedy near the end of the California primary in 1968 testifies to how as president he might have mingled leadership and power. "There is something to be said for a President or a Presidential candidate who can somehow anticipate what the country wants, especially when what they want is on the side of good and justice, and to provide not real leadership in the sense of saying, 'You have got to follow me,' but at least to be prepared to move out ahead somewhat so that the people of the country can follow."

After 1968, however, Eugene McCarthy toiled in the political wilderness. One imagines that leaving the Senate was a miscalculation he came to regret. In hindsight there is no question that Hubert Humphrey would have supported his reelection in 1970, little question that McCarthy would have been reelected and remained a force in the Senate and in the Democratic Party for years to come. No longer in the Senate, McCarthy ran for president as an Independent in 1976. He successfully challenged the constitutionality of many state laws that excluded third-party candidates but was largely ignored by the press. In the end, the two parties and the League of Women Voters excluded him from the Carter-Ford debates. Thereafter, like the aardvark of his poems, he chose another, more solitary way, and in succeeding years the writer eclipsed the politician.

That writer is represented in the present volume by selections that cut back and forth over time to reveal Eugene McCarthy's remarkably consistent stance as a political thinker deeply committed to social justice and to the theory and practice of democracy exemplified in the Constitution. Consider his response to the unselfcritical anti-Communism of the 1950s: "Communism's chief weapon against us is the charge—and in some cases the fact—that we have failed in our responsibility as our brothers' keepers." And consider his indictment of the two-party system in 2003: "The crowning failure of the two-party governments is that they have not produced a presidential election process that did not leave the nation dependent in its choice of a president on the 5 votes of politicized Supreme Court Justices and a Florida winner-take-all law, weighted by the votes of Cuban refugees and the votes of refugees from New York state tax laws."

And what contemporary other than Eugene McCarthy would turn the inalienable rights inside out and find inalienable duties? "The three inalienable duties of citizenship have been seriously compromised," he writes, and in these self-indulgent times it is refreshing to find a political figure insisting on the duties, not just the rights, of citizenship. McCarthy's targets are political third rails, which usually escape serious scrutiny by liberals. "First, we have compromised military service with the initiation of the volunteer (mercenary) army; second, we have exempted many of our citizens from responsibility for supporting the government by paying taxes; and third, we have transferred fundamental responsibility for political action from citizens and voluntary associations to the government and governmentally approved political units, the PACs."

McCarthy sees an unrepresentative "volunteer" army as an anesthetic that dulls the pain and awareness of war for most of society. He endorses Jefferson's view that the dangers of a mercenary army to representative self-government create "the necessity of obliging every citizen to be a soldier." Neither is McCarthy willing to exempt any citizen from taxation. For more than fifty years he has fought poverty, stood up for the poor, and supported a progressive tax system, yet he considers "paying taxes, like voting, a basic, if minimal, act of citizenship." Finally, McCarthy observes that the more regulations Congress imposes on the political process, the less open and accessible American politics becomes. Here he faults the press for ignoring and oversimplifying the substance of politics, preferring sound bites and distractions to issues. In its fondness for slogans, the press has reified a two-party system, which in McCarthy's view has played havoc with American government since the 1960s.

At his best Senator McCarthy is a brilliant cartoonist with language. Some of his most trenchant observations come when he takes President George Herbert Walker Bush to task for refusing to take responsibility for his actions or policies. For example, he identifies the elder Bush's predilection for "naked predicates" (sentences lacking the first-person pronoun) as the sign of a missing person. Writing in 1998 McCarthy calls the Gulf War and subsequent Gulf policy "prime examples of the pattern of no-fault presidential leadership [begun under Bush], which President Clinton has continued." And, he notes elsewhere, the process accelerates, as George W. Bush becomes the apotheosis of the "no-fault" president—a man unable to think of a single mistake.

Eugene McCarthy did not progress far enough in his quests for the presidency to warrant that shortest and sweetest of introductions, "Mr. President," but since leaving the Senate he has become an American man of letters. His twenty books mingle genres of history, autobiography, political philosophy, children's literature, and poetry, not to mention satiric commentary on a series of droll, irreverent cartoons in *An American Bestiary*. The present volume ends with a section called "Lyricisms," a reminder that McCarthy's lyrical gift extends to prose. For example, ranking the best and worst cabinet secretaries of the last fifty years, he judged John Connally the worst secretary of the Treasury for "cutting the dollar free and letting it float—or, in a more appropriate Texas image, letting it loose on the world monetary range with no more than a hair brand to identify it." And in "Ares," one of several poems included, McCarthy's craft, wit, and passion as a poet fuse in a dying fall of taut and tender lyricism.

> no computation stands
> and all the programmed lights
> flash
> and burn slowly down to dark
> when one man says
> I will die
> not twice, or three times over
> but my one first life, and last
> lay down for this my space
> my place, my love.

Like a good politician, McCarthy tucks into his work a thinly veiled reference to the redress that is his due: "if someone is speaking sense about current problems and not yet having any significant effect, what he says should be reported." And like a good writer, seeming to have one thing in mind—a "truly good actor's" exit, he voices what could be a wish for, something far more personal: "although the leaving may not have been noticed, the absence that follows is."

But this is no time for valedictions. Unhappy endings concentrate the mind, and the election of 2004 is reason enough for Gene McCarthy to keep his bow at the ready and his shots straight and true for the Republic he loves.

John F. Callahan
December 1, 2004

John F. Callahan is the Morgan S. Odell Professor of Humanities at Lewis and Clark College in Portland, Oregon. He is the editor of *Juneteenth* and the Modern Library Edition of *The Collected Essays of Ralph Ellison*. Callahan is the literary executor of Ralph Ellison's estate.

Courage at Sixty
(*No Fault Politics*, 1998)

Now it is certain.
There is no magic stone,
No secret to be found.
One must go
With the mind's winnowed learning.
No more than the child's handhold
On the willows bending over the lake,
On the sumac roots at the cliff edge.
Ignorance is checked,
Betrayals scratched.
The coat has been hung on the peg,
The cigar laid on the table edge,
The cue chosen and chalked,
The balls set for the final break.
All cards drawn,
All bets called.
The dice, warm as blood in the hand,
Shaken for the last cast.
The glove has been thrown to the ground,
The last choice of weapons made.

A book for one thought.
A poem for one line.
A line for one word.

"Broken things are powerful."
Things about to break are stronger still.
The last shot from the brittle bow is truest.

Editor's Note

When Eugene McCarthy was first elected to national office in 1948, the world was a vastly different place. The United States had just ended almost two decades marked by the greatest economic depression in its history, had triumphed in the Second World War, and was beginning its ascendancy to the pinnacle of world affairs. While optimism reigned domestically, with the dawn of a "baby boom" and mass consumerism and industrialization that would lead to the greatest extended period of economic growth in history, a sense of danger and chaos commenced in the international sphere, marked by the tensions of the Cold War. Despite this tension, it was also a great time of optimism in American politics (a sense sorely lacking today, as we face similar international challenges), the perfect time for a young man from Minnesota to begin a political career and make his mark.

McCarthy the Man

ONE

The Call to Politics
(*The Year of the People*, 1969)

On November 30, 1967, I announced that I would challenge President Lyndon Johnson for the nomination of the Democratic party. This announcement was followed by a rather mixed reaction around the country. The early press reaction was one of surprise, and the political response, generally negative. Most commentators and editors looked upon this challenge as desperate if not altogether hopeless, and columnists and others rushed to explain my motivation. Some said I was acting out of frustration, others, out of anger or enmity; one writer reported that I had run because my daughter Mary had urged me to do so. My explanation is somewhat different.

For nearly twenty years, especially in talking to students, I had emphasized the need for a revived sense of profession and vocation in modern society, not in the traditional or formal way in which these two concepts were accepted in earlier times but in a modern context in which each person comes to an understanding of what his work is all about, what its social implications and consequences are; and on the basis of that understanding accepts those special responsibilities which rest upon all those in a given field of work.

I had suggested several times, over the years, that the list of professions should be greatly extended beyond medicine and law to include almost all work, especially that work which affects society directly, such as certified public accounting, newspaper reporting, investment counseling, and also, in a very special way, politics.

If there were a clear sense of vocation and profession in politics, both the practitioners and the public would have better standards for judging performance. The lack of any standards was clearly evident during the late years of the Truman administration and the early years of the Eisenhower administration when charges of corruption were brought against party officials, officeholders, some of cabinet level, and some presidential aides. In almost every case, those who were called to account explained their actions as having been essentially the same as they would have been in the business or profession had they pursued before taking political office. The men revealed little evidence of understanding that what might be wholly acceptable behavior in a business office was not acceptable on the part of one who held public trust. One of the accused said in his defense that he had not done anything that his mother would not have approved.

1

Comment by Senator Walter Mondale, upon the retirement of Eugene McCarthy from the Senate in 1971:

"[At] the end of this Congress a great American, one of America's greatest ... retires from the Senate, completing 22 years in Congress, in which he established one of the most remarkable parliamentary records in our Nation's history. These have been 22 years in which his name and his leadership were found on virtually every piece of legislation designed to expand the Nation's civil rights and civil liberties, the rights of minorities and the powerless, and the rights of women. In every respect, during these years, he sought to expand the opportunity of the people of this country to obtain the fairest and fullest life."

I had been telling student and professional audiences through the years that acceptance of professional status carries special responsibilities and obligations, including the obligation to take risks. We expect doctors to take chances on being infected as they care for the sick. We expect lawyers to take certain cases—especially those involving crimes—that may bring public judgment against the lawyers themselves. We expect firemen to fight fires and policemen to take risks in the enforcement of the law. And we should also expect politicians, if the issue is important enough, to show a similar sense of profession and to understand the obligation to take political risks when necessary.

When 1968 began, I had been actively involved in politics for twenty-two years. I had been elected five times to the House of Representatives and twice to the United States Senate from the state of Minnesota. Minnesota politics, like its geography and its people, is very open. There was never an established class in our state. Nearly everyone of every nationality came in on essentially equal terms. The various immigrant groups established schools and colleges for the education of their young people. Never for any length of time were there uneducated minorities who could be controlled or manipulated by party leaders, and the spirit of political revolt has always been able to break out as it did in the Farmer-Labor party movement in the twenties and the thirties. In the same way that the state was open to new political ideas and programs, it was also open to new personalities.

My first real participation in politics began almost by accident or default in 1946. As a college student in the Depression, I had not been indifferent to politics or government policies. When I became a teacher of social sciences and economics (both high school and college), I was attentive to current political problems and issues, and took clear positions on social problems and on social legislation. This was especially important in the years immediately following the end of World War II when many students were veterans who had returned to college. American society had changed significantly in the years between 1938 and 1945.

[...]

Government policy to deal with the social changes had lagged behind. I believed that new federal legislation on housing, education, medical care, and civil rights was vitally necessary. Others did too; in fact, 1946 was a year of intensified political activity in Minnesota.

[...]

Democrats had a good year in 1948. Running [for Congress] with Harry Truman, I was elected, and then re-elected for four additional terms.

During my early years in the House of Representatives, halting progress was made in establishing the social programs set out in the Truman campaign. It was particularly slow during the Eisenhower administration, which also was a period of drift within the Democratic party; a period in which there was—especially after the second defeat of Adlai Stevenson—no strong voice to state policy or to provide leadership, although Paul Butler, as national Democratic chairman, tried hard to establish a position for the party and to give it a liberal voice. His efforts were not successful, and gradually the focus of power within the Democratic party shifted to the Congress, and in the Congress eventually to the Senate Majority Leader, Lyndon Johnson.

By 1957, Congressman Lee Metcalf of Montana and I agreed that it had become necessary for the liberal Democrats in the House to state their position on the important issues of the time. House members met in my office or in Congressman Metcalf's periodically for a month. We drafted a liberal program of action which included among other things six vital areas for political action: civil rights, education, health, housing, foreign aid, and atomic policy. Eventually eighty members subscribed to this declaration.

Our basic purpose was to make the House of Representatives meet its constitutional responsibilities and to encourage members of the Democratic party in that body to fulfill their traditional party respon-

Comment by Senator William Proxmire, upon the retirement of Eugene McCarthy from the Senate in 1971:

"I join the other Senators in paying my tribute to a remarkable man who has had a profound, salutary, healthy and wholesome effect on all of us. He has certainly elevated the dialog and discussion here and he has helped all of us to have a better sense of proportion and to not take ourselves too seriously ... "

sibilities, not only of legislating but of providing leadership and a program for the country as well. I have sometimes been accused of being more concerned with the process than with the substance of legislation or of congressional action. I am not disposed to make a defense of myself against these assertions, because the balance between the one and the other is often so delicate that it can be settled only by a subjective judgment. The process is often simply the operation of the institution. Our drafting of the liberal program, which was a proper operation of the institution, was construed in some quarters, of course, as irregular and as a challenge to the Democratic leadership.

In 1952, when Senator Joseph McCarthy of Wisconsin was a particularly strong force in Washington and around the country by virtue of his activities as chairman of the Permanent Subcommittee on Investigations of the Government Operations Committee and for his special campaign against Communists—real or imagined—in the federal government, he was considered to be a politically dangerous opponent. I thought it necessary that someone challenge his position and power, even though I was sure that one confrontation would not stop him. That was why I said "yes" when Theodore Granik, then the moderator and producer of the television program "American Forum of the Air," invited me to debate Senator McCarthy on his program. Granik told me he had asked me to go on the program only after he had been turned down by other members of Congress.

Comment by Senator Ted Kennedy, upon the retirement of Eugene McCarthy from the Senate in 1971:

"I rise today to pay tribute to a man whom I have grown to respect because I feel that he has provided to the whole dialog of American political life a sense of light and reason ... "

"Being in politics is like being a football coach. You have to be smart enough to understand the game ... and dumb enough to think it's important."

I certainly cannot claim that my debate with him was the beginning of his decline. Television commentators at the time described the debate as a draw. Harry MacArthur, a television critic for the Washington *Evening Star*, wrote on July 23, 1952: "The fallacy of Senator McCarthy's invincibility in debate was exploded on Ted Granik's 'American Forum of the Air.' The technique for dealing with him in TV discussion—or maybe any other discussion for that matter—was demonstrated by another and different McCarthy, Representative Gene of Minnesota.

"Senator McCarthy has always been a fearsome opponent. His manner aggravates many people, usually his foe in a debate more than any one else. The result is that he usually reaches the end of one of these broadcast sessions seeming a calm, reasonable and even persecuted man, while his opponent is reduced to incoherent rage.

"Senator McCarthy starts out with the friendly, disarming approach, full of affability and first-name calling. Preliminary debate gets under way and he just happens to have with him something bearing on that first point. From a voluminous briefcase he produces a thick document. It seems to be flowing with seals and ribbons as if notarized several times and is fearfully impressive.

"Representative Gene McCarthy seems to have found the formula, however. There probably was no true victor Sunday night; it is not likely that many McCarthy supporters were won over by any other McCarthy. Representative McCarthy emerged unruffled and unscarred, though. That is tantamount to victory in this league."

As the election of 1958 approached, I began to give thought to running for the Senate, even though the prospects of victory in the election at that time seemed uncertain. The Republican incumbent from Minnesota, Senator Edward Thye, had served two terms as governor and was finishing his second six-year term in the United States Senate. He was popular and respected and had a general liberal identification. I felt that the legislative programs proposed in the campaign of 1948 could be advanced more rapidly, however, and I believed that as a member of the Senate I would be in a better position to speak about these programs and of the nation's need for them. The foreign policy of this country had also become more and more important, and therefore the role of the Senate had become increasingly important.

I had positive views as to what I thought the Senate should be and as to what I would like to accomplish as a Senator. First, I was hopeful that I could advance the passage of delayed domestic legislation through influencing the public as well as by acting in the Senate. Second, as a member of the Senate which has some power over the federal court system, I hoped I could be influential or helpful in establishing a truly national judiciary and thus move the country away from a regional system of justice which existed then and to some extent still exists today. Third, I wanted to do what I could to make the Senate a more effective force in determining foreign policy, as the Constitution intended. The Minnesota voters endorsed my views and sent me to the Senate that fall [...].

Since coming to the Senate, I have been observed by at least one commentator to have been especially active in presidential years. There is truth to this observation. The process of choosing a new President is important not only because much power and influence attends the office, but also because the campaigning puts the issues before the people. The crucial points in the presidential election year are the national party conventions, and the most important action taken at them is the nomination of the candidates, although in some conventions, such as the 1948 Democratic convention in which civil rights was the central point of debate, an issue may become just as important, if not more important, than the candidates.

It is my opinion that members of the Senate particularly should be actively involved in national conventions and, as a general rule, be prepared to incur some risks to their political careers in order to influence the selection of party nominees and platforms. Their responsibility has taken on increased significance in recent years as the importance of foreign policy has come to outweigh the matters handled in the states by governors. Considering this shift, governors continue to be a stronger influence in national conventions than they should be.

When my candidacy was announced [in 1968], there were those within the party who said, 'Let us not have dissent within the party. Let us have unity.' And I said that to split the Democratic party in 1968 is like chopping sawdust.

5

My participation in presidential politics has reflected not only my beliefs, but also the fact that in three Democratic conventions before 1964 I was called upon as a Minnesotan and as one active in our political party to support various efforts and undertakings of Hubert Humphrey.

[...]

In 1960, I was again, by virtue of essentially the same circumstances, made cochairman of the Humphrey for President campaign in the primaries. I participated in the campaign in Wisconsin and in West Virginia.

Senator Humphrey lost the primary election in Wisconsin and also in West Virginia, after which he withdrew from the contest for the nomination. The Minnesota delegation therefore went to the 1960 Democratic convention uninstructed and without a candidate. I was a member of that delegation and uncommitted to any candidate, having done little more after the primaries than attend a Washington, D.C., rally for Adlai Stevenson two weeks before the convention.

Reporter: Senator, with what percentage of the vote in Wisconsin would you be happy?

McCarthy: Well, I have always been satisfied with 51 percent in any campaign I have been in.

At the time of the convention's opening, I had reservations about the candidacy of Senator John Kennedy. I had no positive case against the candidacy, but it was my general opinion that he had not yet proved himself and was less well qualified to be President than either Lyndon Johnson or Adlai Stevenson. I had some reservations about the candidacy of Senator Johnson as well.

I was publicly announced for Senator Johnson at a press conference held by Senator Robert Kerr; however, the announcement was made without my clearance. I did not repudiate it altogether, but said that I thought that Senator Johnson would make a good prime minister—a remark which expressed my reservations about him as President, because a prime minister is much more subject to party limitations than is the President of the United States. I also said I thought that as President, Lyndon Johnson would have the capacity to get as much out of anything as was in it—the Congress, for example—but doubted his ability to move the nation to new and different achievements. I am of the opinion that had Lyndon Johnson come to the presidency through the normal way of first being nominated and then being elected, his leadership would have been strengthened and his presidency different.

During the presidential primaries of 1960, Adlai Stevenson had never publicly said that he was a candidate, nor had he said anything to me in private indicating his intentions. When his candidacy began to come alive—even in a very limited way—I joined in the efforts to advance it, attending a luncheon on July 11 during the convention at which Mrs. Eleanor Roosevelt spoke and a late night rally the same day at which I spoke in support of Stevenson.

On July 12, the Minnesota delegation leaders caucused until six o'clock in the morning on the question of whom to support. Senator Humphrey was undecided, whereas Governor Freeman, who had been endorsed by our delegation for the vice presidency, argued for support of Kennedy on the first ballot. It had already been made public that he would nominate John Kennedy the next day. At that caucus, I announced my support for Stevenson.

On his lessons learned from time in a Benedictine monastery McCarthy noted, "One of the lines in the Benedictine monastery is to keep death daily before your eyes, which never hurts in politics."

[At] about eleven o'clock on the morning of July 13, I was called by Senator A. M. (Mike) Monroney and asked whether I would nominate Governor Stevenson. I was surprised and asked for time to think it over. In about a half hour Adlai Stevenson called and asked me himself. I accepted and went on to prepare notes for the speech which, it was then thought, might have to be given by three o'clock that afternoon.

I was aware, of course, that the chances of a Stevenson nomination were remote and that it could be accomplished only if the Kennedy and Johnson forces deadlocked. But it seemed to me that the Democratic convention should, if Stevenson wished, consider him for nomination even though it might turn out to be no more than a tribute.

I asked the Democrats to accept Adlai Stevenson as a candidate for the third time, and the response in votes turned out to be negligible: he obtained only 79.5 votes out of 1,521; Lyndon Johnson received 409; and John Kennedy won the nomination with 806 votes. But the demonstration following my speech for Stevenson was far more intense and enthusiastic than that given to any other candidate. There were those at the convention who were strongly for the nomination of Adlai Stevenson and they, of course, cheered. And there were those who had been for him in the past and responded to his nomination with cries of approval to make their change of loyalty easier. Finally, there were those who, in whatever category was left, cheered as a kind of testimonial to Adlai Stevenson as a man.

[...]

Extract from radio debate between McCarthy and Senator Joseph McCarthy, 1952:

Joseph McCarthy: Let me say this first: Gene McCarthy, in my opinion, is a high-class legislator.

Eugene McCarthy: And I know you would not under any circumstances misstate the facts.

J. McCarthy: We know we have lost an average of 100 million people a year to communism since the shooting part of World War II ended. Not 100,000, 100 million. Since the shooting part of World War II ended, the total loss has been about 700 million people. I'm sure the Republicans cannot be trusted to continue losing 100 million people a year. Right, Gene?

E. McCarthy: Senator, I don't think you can say we have lost them. We never had them.

Extract from the *Tonight Show*, 1968:

Johnny Carson: Do you feel (well of course you do—and that's kind of a stupid question) that you would make a good president?"

Eugene McCarthy: Yes. I think I would be adequate.

Carson: You would be adequate?

McCarthy: I think I would be adequate, yes. I think I would, yes.

Rumors about my having received an offer of the vice presidency from Lyndon Johnson or from any other candidate at the 1960 convention were without substance. It was obvious that John Kennedy had he not been nominated for the presidency would have been the vice-presidential choice of either Stevenson or Johnson or of any other candidate who might have been nominated.

In the next presidential year, 1964, conservative strength seemed to be growing across the country. In anticipation of what I thought might be a confrontation, I wrote a book in 1963 entitled *A Liberal Answer to the Conservative Challenge*. With the nomination of Senator Barry Goldwater by the Republicans, the need to defend the liberal position from the conservative attack was greatly reduced, however, since his positions generally were so extreme they offered little challenge.

Goldwater's year was also the year in which I was up for re-election to the Senate. On January 8, my campaign committee held a fund-raising dinner in Washington. Scheduled speakers included Adlai Stevenson and Senator Humphrey; President Johnson made a surprise appearance. The President's appearance was not the beginning of a vice-presidential boom, but it fit into a pattern of discussions which had begun to develop. There was never any direct or personal discussion of the office between the President and me, but persons then very close to him in the White House did give encouragement and requested that I maintain an apparent interest in the office. Since I was running for re-election to the Senate, the national publicity was helpful.

Extract from 2004 interview:

Editor: Do you think it was easier in 1968 to stand up and challenge the president? How is the situation in Vietnam similar to the one we are facing today in Iraq?

McCarthy: We [the Senate] had almost twenty years [of involvement by the U.S.] to look at while the Vietnam War went on. This one [the war in Iraq] kind of came on us before we even knew it was there. [The current situation] can't get much worse, but up until now there has been the excuse that we don't know what's going on. Although I think it is pretty evident that it is a desperate kind of war. [Vietnam] reached the point—and I think we're almost at that point now—where you realized that the people running the war didn't know what they were doing. In Vietnam by 1968 you knew that McNamara didn't know what was going on and that Johnson was caught up in thinking, "I'm not going to be the first American president to lose a war." I didn't want to help him maintain his record of not losing a war.

It was my opinion from the beginning that if the President were to make a personal choice freely, he would pick Hubert Humphrey who had been much closer to him for a longer time in the Senate than I had been and with whom he had worked politically.

Before leaving for the convention at Atlantic City, I had my staff check with the White House to make it clear to those with whom we had been speaking that I did not want to embarrass the President at the convention and would be glad to drop out. I was asked not to do so. We set up a limited headquarters, not at a convention hotel but at a motel on the edge of town, principally to keep in touch with the White House and to keep the candidacy alive.

[…]

The day before the vice-presidential nomination was to

Extract from 2004 interview:

Editor: In 1962, Lyndon Johnson approached you and a handful of other senators to discuss the necessity for and implications of civil rights legislation. What were the ramifications of this policy for the Democratic party?

McCarthy: [Johnson] knew we were doomed— the Democrats were—and said so. But he said, "You've got to do it [pass civil rights legislation] anyway. You can't stop it. He wanted action in '63. The Kennedys were going to finesse it. He [Johnson] brought us into his confidence, but he was saying it to other people too. Kind of second-guessing the candidate [President Kennedy]. But he was right.

Editor: So, there was a sense almost of a moral and ethical duty that you owe.

McCarthy: Yes, because you sound kind of self-serving when you say it [civil rights] was an institutional responsibility of the Senate. They [the press] said, well you're just covering your tracks. It's sad: we weren't covering our tracks, we were making them.

be made, President Johnson in a press conference listed some of the qualifications he was looking for in his running mate. It was my opinion that these qualifications fit Senator Humphrey much more closely than they fit me. It was also my opinion that, barring unforeseen developments, Senator Humphrey, with his support from labor, farm, and liberal groups, was strong enough to insist he be given the vice presidency had he been moved to do so.

Since by the evening of that same day, I had heard nothing from the White House, and I was still satisfied that Hubert Humphrey would be chosen, I decided that it was best for me to take action to free myself. Therefore, I prepared a wire for transmission the next morning. It read:

Dear Mr. President: The time for your announcement of your choice of your vice presidential running mate is very close. I have, as you know, during this convention and for several weeks not been indifferent to the choice you must make. The action that I have taken has been to this end and to this purpose: that your choice would be a free one and that those whom you might consult, or who might make recommendations to you, might be well informed. The great majority of the delegates here are, as you know, ready to support your choice. It is my opinion that the qualifications that you have listed, or which you are said to have listed as most desirable in the man who would be vice president with you, would be met most admirably by Senator Humphrey. I wish, therefore, to recommend for your primary consideration, Senator Hubert H. Humphrey.

I instructed a staff man to send it and to call the White House at once to report that he had sent it. The White House spokesman even then urged that if we had not sent the wire, we not do so.

The President called me that afternoon to tell me of his decision, before making any public announcement with reference to Senator Humphrey and before flying him to Washington. He made a point in the telephone conversation to say that he had made the decision before he received my telegram. I think he had—perhaps several days before. Senator Thomas Dodd of Connecticut was asked to fly from Atlantic City to Washington on the same plane as Senator Humphrey. There were some who thought that had I not sent the telegram I might have been on the plane, serving much the same function as Senator Dodd served—to keep alive the illusion that there were other candidates for the vice presidency.

I was asked to nominate Senator Humphrey as Vice President. I did make the nominating speech.

When the presidential year of 1968 arrived, no one who knew my record—theory and practice—should have been surprised by my concern over the campaign, nor by my decision to involve myself in it.

Extract from 2004 interview:

Editor: What would you like to impart to future generations?

McCarthy: I would say that I think the reason things became so disorderly is that Americans don't have a sense of what an institution [like democracy] requires of them. It's all open and loose out there. When thinking in terms of how culture is affected, if you don't have some help from the institutions, it's like every day is a new day. And once these institutions kind of committed themselves to irresponsible action, they have to continue. I must say that I had no boyhood dream of being President of the United States. I wanted to be the first baseman for the New York Yankees. I think that's the kind of dream you ought to have when you are young.

Nominating Speech by
Senator Eugene J. McCarthy for Adlai E. Stevenson,
Democratic National Convention, July 13, 1960

Mr. Chairman, Democratic delegates at this great convention:

We now approach the hour of all-important decision. You are the chosen people out of 172,000,000 Americans, the chosen of the Demoratic party, come here to Los Angeles not only to choose a man to lead this Democratic party in the campaign of this fall and this November, but to choose a man who we hope will lead this country and all of our friends and all of those peoples who look to us for help, who look to us for understanding, who look to us for leadership.

We are here participating in the great test of democratic society. As you know, our way of life is being challenged today. There are those, the enemies of democracy, who say that free men and free women cannot exercise that measure of intellectual responsibility, cannot demonstrate that measure of moral responsibility, which is called for to make the kind of decisions that we free people are called upon to make in this year of 1960, and there are those, I remind you, who are the friends of democracy, who have expressed some doubt and some reservation as to whether or not this ideology, this way of life, these institutions of ours, can survive.

Let me ask you at this time to put aside all of your prejudices, to put aside any kind of unwarranted regional loyalties, to put aside for the time being preferences which are based purely upon questions of personality. Put aside, if you can, early decisions—decisions which were made before all of the candidates were in the race, decisions which were made when the issues were not clear, as they are today.

I say to those of you—candidates and spokesmen for candidates—who say you are confident of the strength that you have at this convention, who say that you are confident and believe in democracy—let this go to a second ballot.

I say let this go to a second ballot, when every delegate who is here will be as free as he can be free to make a decision.

Let us strike off the fetters of instructed delegations. Let Governors say to their people: This is the moment of decision and we want you to make it as free Americans, responsible to your own conscience and to the people of the state that sent you here, and to the people of this country.

This I say is the real test of democracy. Do you have confidence in the people at this convention to make a fair and responsible choice, or do you not have this confidence?

What has happened in this world and what has happened in this United States has been described to you here by great speakers. Each new headline every day that we've been here has been a shock to us; each new headline has been a shock.

These times, men say, are out of joint. They say these are the worst of times without being the best of times—this may be true. But I say to you these external signs, these practical problems which face us are nothing compared to the problems of the mind and of the spirit which face the United States and the free world today.

If the mind is clouded and if the will is confused and uncertain, there can be no sound decision and no sound action.

There's demagoguery abroad in the land at all times, and demagoguery, I say to you, takes many forms. There's that which says, "here is wealth, and here is material comfort." We suffer a little from that in the United States.

There's demagoguery, which promises people power, which is used for improper purposes and ends. And we have seen in this century and in this generation what happens when power is abused.

I say to you there's a subtle kind of demagoguery which erodes the spirit. And this is the demagoguery, which has affected this United States in the last eight years.

What are we told? What have we been told? We've been told that we can be strong without sacrifice. This is what we've been told. We've been told that we can be good without any kind of discipline if we just say we're humble and sincere—this is the nature of goodness. We've been told that we can be wise without reflection. We can be wise without study, we've been told. I say this is the erosion of the spirit which has taken place in this United States in the last eight years. And I say to you that the time has come to raise again the cry of the ancient prophet. What did he say? He said the prophets prophesy falsely and the high priests, he said, ruled by their word, and my people love to have it so. But what will be the end?

I say to you the political prophets have prophesied falsely in these eight years. And the high priests of Government have ruled by that false prophecy. And the people seemed to have loved it so.

But there was one man—there was one man who did not prophesy falsely, let me remind you. There was one man who said: Let's talk sense to the American people.

What did the scoffers say? The scoffers said: Nonsense. They said: Catastrophic nonsense. But we know it was the essential and the basic and the fundamental truth that he spoke to us.

There was a man who talked sense to the American people. There was one man who said: This is a time for self-examination. This is a time for us to take stock, he said. This is a time to decide where we are and where we're going.

This, he said, is a time for virtue. But what virtues did he say we needed? Oh yes, he said we need the heroic virtues—we always do. We need fortitude; we need courage; we need justice. Everyone cheers when you speak out for those virtues.

But what did he say in addition to that? He said we need the unheroic virtues in America. We need the virtue, he said, of patience. There were those who said we've had too much of patience.

We need, he said, the virtue of tolerance. We need the virtue of forebearance. We need the virtues of patience and understanding.

This was what the prophet said. This is what he said to the American people. I ask you, did he prophesy falsely? Did he prophesy falsely?

He said this is a time for greatness. This is a time for greatness for America. He did not say he possessed it. He did not even say he was destined for it. He did say that the heritage of America is one of greatness.

And he described that heritage to us. And he said the promise of America is a promise of greatness. And he said this promise we must fulfill.

This was his call to greatness. This was the call to greatness that was issued in 1952.

He did not seek power for himself in 1952. He did not seek power in 1956.

He does not seek it for himself today.

This man knows—this man knows, as all of us do from history, that power often comes to those who seek it. But history does not prove that power is always well used by those who seek it.

On the contrary, the whole history of democratic politics is to this end, that power is best exercised by those are sought out by the people, by those whom power is given by a free people.

And so I say to you: Democrats here assembled: Do not turn away from this man. Do not reject this man. He has fought gallantly. He has fought courageously. He has fought honorably. In 1952 in the great battle. In 1956 he fought bravely. And between those years and since, he has stood off the guerrilla attacks of his enemies and the sniping attacks of those who should have been his friends. Do not reject this man who, his enemies said, spoke above the heads of the people, but they said it only because they didn't want the people to listen. He spoke to the people. He moved their minds and stirred their hearts, and this was what was objected to. Do not leave this prophet without honor in his own party. Do not reject this man.

I submit to you a man who is not the favorite son of any one state. I submit to you the man who is the favorite son of fifty states.

And not only of fifty states but the favorite son of every country in the world in which he is known—the favorite son in every country in which he is unknown but in which some spark, even though unexpressed, of desire for liberty and freedom still lives.

This favorite son I submit to you: Adlai E. Stevenson of Illinois.

Editor's Note

As a nation founded on the principles of the Enlightenment, including equality, free will, democracy, and freedom from tyranny and oppression, America has served as a beacon to the world for more than 200 years. While many of us can blindly recite portions of the Declaration of Independence or the Constitution, however, we tend to take the basic tenets underlying our democracy for granted. One need only look to declining involvement in the voting process (typically less than 50 percent), to the consistent misapplication of constitutional doctrines by both liberals and conservatives to make their arguments, and to the willingness to suspend basic rights in times of tension in order to appreciate this premise. Today we find our core democratic principles under attack, both from external sources and from our own elected leaders. Like our nation's founders, Eugene McCarthy spent his career looking deeply into the meanings of democracy, providing us with the tools to better understand our political foundations and to encourage us to be better caretakers for this legacy.

Foundations

TWO

Inalienable Duties
(*No Fault Politics*, 1998)

The Declaration of Independence makes clear reference to the "inalienable rights" of all men. Among those rights, it declares, are three of particular political significance: life, liberty, and the pursuit of happiness.

The *duties* of citizenship, essential to securing and sustaining these inalienable rights, are not mentioned directly in the Declaration of Independence or in the Constitution, but their necessity and reality were implicit in the very conception of self-government. What are the fundamental responsibilities, or inalienable duties, of the citizen? They are (1) to defend the country, (2) to pay taxes to meet the costs of government, and (3) to participate in the political actions that are essential to self-government.

I

There was no searching inquiry into defense and into war making at the Constitutional Convention, but providing for the common defense is listed as one of the fundamental purposes of the new government. The inclusion of the right to bear arms in the Bill of Rights was related to the need for national as well as personal self-defense. It was not included to protect the rights of squirrel or people hunters.

As early as 1785, well before he became president, Thomas Jefferson recognized the need for military and naval operations when he wrote to John Jay from Paris: "Our people are decided in the opinion that it is necessary for us to take a share in the occupation of ocean, and their established habits induce them to require that the sea be kept open to them. ... Therefore," he continued, "we should in every instance (even at the cost of war) preserve an equality of right to them in the transportation of commodities, in the right of fishing and in the other uses of the sea."

As president, Jefferson took action against the Barbary pirates. His later experience with the embargo of American goods and his observation of the War of 1812 moved him to an even stronger military position. Although he did not go so far as to support Alexander Hamilton, who wanted a standing army, he came to believe that serious thought must be given to the maintenance of a military establishment, which he thought should be, in a democracy, based upon universal military service or liability for such service. He wrote to James Monroe in 1813: "It is more a

15

subject of joy that we have so few of the desperate characters which compose modern regular armies. But it proves more forcibly the necessity of obliging every citizen to be a soldier. This was the case with Greeks and Romans and must be that of every free state. ... We must train and classify the whole of our male citizens and make military instruction a regular part of collegiate education. We cannot be safe till this is done." The safety he was concerned with related to two threats: outside military action against the United States and the internal danger of a mercenary, nonrepresentive army.

At the outbreak of World War I, the United States had a navy of limited readiness and an army numbering about 200,000 officers and men, which included 67,000 National Guardsmen. A draft registration act was passed on June 3, 1916, and another in 1918. Overall, 24.2 million men registered, of whom 2.2 million were actually inducted.

In 1940 a draft act again was passed as preliminary to full involvement in World War II. In 1951 that act was extended for twenty years, to meet the needs of the Korean War, and it was then allowed to expire during the Nixon administration. This era, 1941–1971, was the only prolonged period during which the United States, in effect, did have a universal military service program. Not all males of eligible age were called up, but all were formally subject to the draft.

Before the act was allowed to die, it had been—first in the Johnson administration and then in the Nixon administration—thoroughly corrupted through the granting of many exemptions, especially to students of almost every kind, in an effort to insulate the war from Americans who might be most likely to criticize it if they or their children were forced into it. Since the Johnson administration believed that the Vietnam War would end quickly, it did not anticipate having to answer for its exemptions. But the war did not end quickly, and the Nixon administration followed a similar policy of exemptions, with the addition of a new device under which a potential draftee could decide within a range of three or four years when he would be subject to the draft.

As the war was winding down in the early 1970s, the draft law expired. No attempt to extend it was made in the Nixon administration, and the drive to establish a large "volunteer" army was initiated. This proposal was supported by militarists, based on their belief that only militarily minded people, either by their nature or by their commitment, would make up the military forces. Consequently, the United States, they believed, would have a ready and uncritical military force.

Antimilitarists in general and anti-Vietnam War activists in particular accepted and supported the volunteer proposal because they thought that their consciences, and the consciences of others in the future, would be eased if they would not have to perform military service.

The volunteer army idea has not worked well. The Department of Defense has not been able to attract enough capable and qualified persons to the armed services. Our armed forces are far from a cross section of the U.S. population; our military is unrepresentative of the nation. Standards of admission have been lowered; financial and other benefits have been increased; cash bonuses for enlisting have been offered.

The volunteer army has been a designation for what is essentially a mercenary army. Alexis de Tocqueville and others have warned that such a military is the most dangerous and undesirable type for a democratic state. This is especially true when a major function of our military is to act as an army of occupation, or as a presence—as ours is in Europe, in Japan, in Korea, and in other parts of the world.

II

The second inalienable duty recognized in the Constitution is the responsibility of citizens to pay taxes. The revolutionary slogan "Taxation without representation is tyranny" is credited to James Otis. Otis did not say, "Taxation with representation is tyranny" or that taxation in itself is tyrannical, or that, in the ideal state, citizens would pay few or no taxes. The Sixteenth Amendment, the so-called income-tax amendment, was the last formal acknowledgment on the part of the people of the United States of their willingness to pay taxes "to pay the debts and provide for the common defense and general welfare of the United States," as stated in Article 1 of the Constitution.

What are the fundamental responsibilities, or inalienable duties, of the citizen? They are (1) to defend the country, (2) to pay taxes to meet the costs of government, and (3) to participate in the political actions that are essential to self-government.

Recent U.S. presidents and presidential candidates seem to have a different attitude toward taxes. Candidate Jimmy Carter said that the federal tax code "was a disgrace to the human race." As candidate, and as president, Ronald Reagan generally opposed taxes, while annual federal deficits run to hundreds of billions and the federal debt is well into its third trillion. Reagan's slogan, in the Otis manner, might well be a declaration in favor of representation without taxation, which, in its consequences, may well be as tyrannous as the colonial taxation without representation.

Opposition to paying taxes is not limited to presidential and other candidates and officeholders. Antitaxation programs are sustained by individuals, by their representatives, by lobbyists, by foundations, by corporations. The drive to eliminate tax paying, to avoid payment, or to be exempted is manifest at all levels of tax paying and directed against nearly every form of taxation, but it is especially evident at the higher and lower levels of income-tax liabilities.

The reasons given for exempting citizens from tax obligations are multiple. Such words as fairness and equity are invoked regularly. Concern is voiced for the poor and for people in low-income brackets. Efficiency in the administration of tax law, simplification of the code, stimulation of business, encouragement of capital formation and savings—all are among the reasons or justifications offered. Lobbyists and various representatives—individual and institutional—are quick to take credit for eliminating high-level income-tax obligations or for reducing them. Politicians generally—Republicans and Democrats, liberals and conservatives—claim credit for reduction or elimination of tax obligations at the lower end of the income scale.

But paying taxes, like voting, is a basic, if minimal, act of citizenship.

[...]

Approximately 50 million of 130 million potential taxpayers (or approximately 38 percent) will pay no taxes (that is, basic income and capital gains taxes to the federal government), thus creating two classes of citizens—one paying basic taxes and the other exempted for varying reasons from fulfilling, even in a minimal way, this obligation of citizenship.

John Wesley is supposed to have said that, even in the church, some small financial contribution should be expected, if not extracted. Certainly the same would seem to be true of support for civil government, even though the rate is very low. Tocqueville reported that in 1831, during his visit to the United States, fifteen of the existing twenty-four states required property ownership, military service, or tax payment as a prerequisite to voting.

III

I have described what has happened to two of the inalienable duties of citizenship—military service and paying taxes. The third is participation in political action and decisions.

Jefferson warned that if the people became indifferent to politics and to government, the magistrates (an early version of the bureaucrats) would take over. Although there were serious restrictions on suffrage in the early decades of our national existence, those who had the right to vote evidently took their responsibility seriously.

Tocqueville was greatly impressed by what he saw or was told, for he wrote in *Democracy in America* in 1831: "To take a hand in the government of society and to talk about it is his [the American citizen's] most important business and, so to say, the only pleasure he knows." He continued, "If an American should be reduced to occupying himself with his own affairs, at that moment, half his existence would be snatched from him; he would feel it as a vast void in his life and would become incredibly unhappy."

In each succeeding election, the percentage of eligible American voters who cast their ballots drops to its lowest level ever. Between 50 percent and 70 percent of qualified American voters regularly decline to vote—the higher number occurring in off election years. [...]

Undoubtedly many voters have been kept from participating by unreasonable registration and residence requirements; by state laws giving special preference to the Republican and the Democratic parties; by laws making it difficult for third- or independent-party candidates to get on the ballot; by machine voting, which makes write-in campaigns practically impossible; and by restrictive party rules.

Some analysts attribute declining and low voter turnouts, in part, to such factors as the high mobility of the American population, disenchantment with the conduct of politics, and the deadening and distracting effect of television.

But are these adequate explanations?

After every campaign, politicians and press deplore low voter turnout. Thus, as each campaign approaches or begins, they encourage political participation and support "get out the vote" drives. At the same time that the drives for voter participation go on, legislative and political actions of various kinds discourage citizens from full participation in politics. Whereas the poll tax has been outlawed as an impediment to participation in political action, in its place, public records and reports of financial contributions, even minimal ones, are now required in many states. Complicated reports are required in many jurisdictions.

But more significant than all of these local and state controls and interferences with basic and fundamental participation in politics is the Federal Election Campaign Act as amended in 1975–76. The law not only sets severe limitations on financial contributions to campaigns but also provides for government financing of political action with operating control centered in the Federal Election Commission.

Not only does the 1975–76 law limit and discourage individual contributions and commitment, but it encourages and strengthens intermediary organizations (the political action committees) to further depersonalize politics and come between citizen and politics and government. Whereas individual contributions to a campaign are effectively limited, the same amount contributed through a PAC is multiplied in power, but only at the sacrifice of the independent judgment of the contributing citizen.

• • •

And so we find ourselves, at the start of a new millennium, an American republic lacking in republican virtues. The three inalienable duties of citizenship have been seriously compromised. First, we have compromised military service with the initiation of the volunteer (mercenary) army; second, we have exempted many of our citizens from responsibility for supporting the government by paying taxes; and third, we have transferred fundamental responsibility for political action from citizens and voluntary associations to the government and governmentally approved political units, the PACs.

The renewal of citizenship—the sort of public happiness the Founders knew, celebrated, and expected—is already twenty-five years overdue.

The Founding of the United States
(*Social Science Record*, 1987)

The founding of the United States included three stages. The first was the Revolution, itself essentially a revolution against government with its purposes stated and justified in the Declaration of Independence. The Declaration was an expression of faith by the men who signed it, [as reflected best in one of its opening phrases:] "that all men are created equal; that they are endowed by their creator with certain unalienable rights; that among these are life, liberty, and the pursuit of happiness ... "

These words were not set down as part of a rhetorical exercise. They were not used merely as a justification for a revolution, or as an inspiration, but rather were intended to persist beyond revolution to become the foundation in belief upon which democratic institutions of government were to be built. The men who wrote and subscribed to the Declaration took what they had done very seriously, for if the Revolution they proposed failed, they were in danger of being shot or hanged. The Revolution "against government" succeeded; the language and thoughts of men such as Thomas Jefferson, Patrick Henry, Thomas Paine, and other advocates of the war were vindicated.

The next stage of the Revolution, following five years of confusion and instability under the Articles of Confederation, began with the convening of the Constitutional Convention in 1787 and the completion of the ratification process in the fall of 1788. This second stage has been called by Professor John Kaminsky of St. John's University (Minnesota) "A Revolution in Favor of Government"; and such it was. The battle of rectification was fought between the anti-Federalists, who clung to the precepts of nongovernment and the antigovernment sentiments of the Revolution—men such as Samuel Adams of Massachusetts and George Mason of Virginia—and the Federalists, whose case was made primarily in the *Federalist Papers* by Alexander Hamilton, James Madison, and John Jay.

The men who participated in the drafting of the Constitution were politicians. They acknowledged the reality of compromise and anticipated that not everything they did would stand the test of history. At the same time, they believed that the principles upon which the new republic was to be founded were valid. They did not look upon what they were undertaking as "The American Experiment," as it is sometimes called, but rather as a test of reason and as historical lessons being tested in a new context.

They did not consider that the intellectual and moral bases for their proposals came from especially gifted or chosen delegates in the convention, but rather that they were drawn from political history and philosophy. They were not "new" political thinkers, although most had some new ideas, but they were students of politics and of history. They brought to the drafting convention the wise experience of ancient political thinkers as well as of those who, by their standards, were modern. Plato and Aristotle were at the convention, as were Montesquieu, Locke, Hobbes, Adam Smith, and Rousseau. Plutarch was there as a special resource both for history and for political theory, as were Thucydides and Tacitus. Contemporary, or nearly contemporary, historical sources also were used. Jay, for example, in the fifth essay of the *Federalist Papers*, quotes from a letter from Queen Anne of England to the Scottish Parliament in which she emphasized the union between England and Scotland as vital to peace. There are, in the Constitution, touches of Machiavelli, although he is not identified. And there is the continuing force of biblical thought.

The third stage of the founding process took but a short time but has had a long, continuing, and stabilizing effect on American life, politics, and government. In 1789, the first Congress, as had been promised by Federalists in their campaign for the ratification of the constitution, proposed as amendments to the Constitution what has come to be known as the Bill of Rights. The congressional proposal was soon adopted by the states and has since been of utmost importance in preserving the personal liberties of the citizens of the United States, for whom it has been a kind of Magna Charta. Jefferson, a Federalist, might well have argued that the rights specified in the amendments were implicit in the revolutionary "inalienable rights." George Mason and Virginia were won over, and Jefferson summarized what had been accomplished in the third stage of the founding by observing that there had "been opposition enough to do good, and not enough to do harm."

Jefferson's Declaration—Good Politics, Good Literature
(*Complexities and Contraries*, 1982)

The creed to which he referred was expressed in these words: "We hold these truths to be self-evident, that all men are created equal, that they are endowed by their creator with certain unalienable rights, that among these are life, liberty and the pursuit of happiness."

The July 4, 1776, declaration followed by only a few weeks the Virginia Declaration of Rights (of June 12, 1776). The document, attributed to George Mason, asserted, "All men are by nature equally free and independent and have certain inherent rights." Mason listed these rights as "the enjoyment of life and liberty, with the means of acquiring and possessing property, and pursuing and obtaining happiness and safety."

There are no notes nor records on why the language of the Jefferson declaration differed from that of Mason. Scholars have reflected and commented on the omission of any reference to property rights in the Jefferson text.

Conservative politicians and commentators have deplored the omission. And a few have held that if the drafters of the declaration had anticipated the income tax, they would have emphasized property rights.

Few persons have noted or commented on the much more interesting question of why the "pursuit of happiness" was included among the unalienable rights.

It is certain that the men who wrote and approved the Declaration of Independence were not careless draftsmen. They were men who, if their revolution failed, were likely to be hanged or shot as traitors, rather than suffering the limited disgrace of losing an election or the harsher treatment of exile to San Clemente.

The declaration was not merely an inspirational piece of propaganda. It was not the product of a task force or of a brain-storming session. It was not drafted after a crash course in the great books. It was intended to be what Chesterton saw it to be: the ideological text upon which a government and a nation would be founded.

Present in the thoughts of the men at the drafting was the wisdom of the past, the record of history. The inclusion of the "pursuit of happiness" as an unalienable right was not an accident. Nor was the word "happiness" included as a catchall, with a vague and undefined and overly comprehensive meaning such as is given to it today.

In 1776, the word was still used in the plural, as it had been used in 1601, for example, by Robert Johnson, who wrote that nature had heaped on England "those delightful happinesses." Thomas Otway, writing in 1678, said, "Ten thousand happinesses wait on you." Colley Cibber in 1739 wrote, "It was therefore one of our greatest happinesses." As late as 1885, Charles Haddon Spurgeon declared, "Heaped up happinesses [in the plural] belong to that man who fears the Lord."

The Declaration of Independence offered as a right only the "pursuit of happiness." This undoubtedly included the right to pursue property as a form of happiness, or as "a happiness."

John Adams, in two separate comments on the American Revolution, identified the different happinesses. One, which he saw as personal, was in the acceptance of the inconveniences of independence, in a changed and more austere way of life. The other was "public happiness," defined as a willingness on the part of the colonists to take public responsibility, to make common decisions and to follow those decisions—a spirit that he said was so strong among the colonists that the Revolution was bound to succeed.

The inclusion of the pursuit of happiness as an unalienable right was a unique act of genius on the part of those, principally Jefferson, who drafted the Declaration of Independence. It distinguishes that document from all other declarations of national or international political purposes.

Theoretical Basis of Democracy
(*The Challenge of Freedom*, 1960)

Democracy accepts that man is rational and morally responsible. It accepts that political life as well as private life is subject to reasoned judgment and to the will of men. On this ground, a democratic society must build institutions through which the judgment and will of its responsible members can be given political form and made manifest in action.

Modern history testifies that the tyranny of the majority feared by so many political thinkers, guarded against by the framers of our Constitution, and darkly foreseen by Plato writing almost 2,500 years ago, has proved less a danger in our century than the tyranny of the few or of the one—of the party or of the dictator.

Perhaps all men may eventually be persuaded to unanimity on all issues, but on the record this is highly unlikely. As long as the differences and diversities of mankind exist, democracy must allow for compromise, for accommodation, and for the recognition of differences.

This raises the first and fundamentally the most difficult problem of democracy: that of reconciling freedom and authority, of striking a balance between personal liberty and the demands of the common good. When one undertakes to inquire into the relationship between the state and human freedom, he must anticipate confusion and conflict. In each historical case there will exist a kind of no man's land in which there will be what in modern military terminology is called a "fluid line." Even though that line is fluid and subject to historical change, it is important that we attempt to draw it with some measure of accuracy or at least to establish the limits of fluidity and variability.

The American attitude toward government has always reflected contradictory attitudes and political positions. The traditional attitude is one of suspicion. The statement ascribed to Jefferson that that government governs best which governs least is widely quoted and accepted almost without question. This attitude of suspicion toward government is rooted in our political history. American political thought from the beginning of our national existence has been strongly influenced by a negative and pessimistic concept of the nature and function of government. The United States was established in a revolt against an arbitrary and despotic government, at a time when the political ideas of Locke, of Rousseau, and of Hobbes were uncritically intermingled and popularly held.

The ideas of Rousseau concerning the social contract and man in a state of nature—the good man—were combined, not without contradiction, with those of Thomas Hobbes who held that man is normally driven by reckless pursuit of self-interest and that government is simply a contractual substitute for a state of affairs in which man would live in continual fear of attack and death. This new political philosophy was given native expression by Thomas Paine, the political philosopher of the American Revolution, who at about the time that the Declaration of

Independence was drawn wrote these words: "Government, like dress, is the badge of lost innocence; the palaces of kings are built on the ruins of the bowers of Paradise. For were the impulses of conscience clear, uniform, and irresistibly obeyed, man would need no other lawgiver ... "

Paine's view of government has, it should be noted, theological elements. The erroneous belief that human nature has been utterly destroyed by sin sustains an unsound philosophical idea. The state, according to this pessimistic theory, arises from evil or from human depravity. The existence of evil and of depravity provides the continuing justification for government—certainly a gloomy philosophical basis for democracy.

[...]

The critical and suspicious attitude toward government has been encouraged by events of recent history. In this century, and more immediately in this generation, the power of government, ruthless, self-justifying—without regard for the rights of persons or of other societies such as the family and religious institutions—has been forcefully demonstrated in Italy under fascism, in Germany under Nazism, and currently in many parts of the world under communism. We have clear evidence and a continuing witness that we must at all times be alert to the danger of the intrusion of the government into areas of culture and into areas in the social and private life of citizens which are beyond the authority of government. Our alertness and vigilance should not, however, lead us to accept unsound theories concerning the origin, nature, purposes, and functions of government. What is called for is re-examination, reflection, clarification, and distinction.

Governments, of course, do have functions and responsibilities which are made necessary by the evident disorder in human nature, the evident presence of evil and of injustice. For the sake of the general good, the government must defend individuals and society from the obvious manifestations of evil and of injustice. The need for government response to such injustice is obvious in at least three areas:

In the area of international justice, when one nation seeks to destroy or seriously interfere with the national independence, with the rights of another nation.

In the area of civil law, when some social class or institution in society violates or threatens to violate the rights of persons or of other classes, groups, or institutions in society.

In the area of criminal law, when individuals openly rebel against the general order by criminal actions.

Government responsibility is recognized in each of these areas. At the international level this is done through the organization of such institutions as the United Nations and the World Court, and the development of international law; in extreme cases, of course, it done by war. Responsibility is manifest at the civil level in the whole body of civil law with court procedures, provisions for settlement and restitution, all of which are a part of the record of every civilization. Similarly in the area of criminal laws, there are procedures and penalties which relate to individual acts committed against the common good.

This negative protective function is not, however, the only justification for government. It is not even the fundamental or primary one. Man needs political institutions. This need is not the consequence of his depravity; neither does it depend on the relative goodness or badness of men at any particular period of history, although these two conditions, general depravity and the level of goodness and badness, will have immediate and practical efforts on government and government actions. Man's need for government remains a positive one.

[...] [A] society of saints would still need positive human law. Grace or the absence of it does not wholly destroy nature or make the essential social or political institutions such as the family and government unnecessary. Aristotle's observation that man is by nature a political animal is sustained by history. One community rises on the ruins of another. As he observed, the state comes into existence originating in the bare needs of life; it continues in existence for the sake of a good life.

Government has a positive and natural function to assist man in the pursuit of perfection and of happiness. Government accomplishes this purpose by promoting the common good.

But what is the common good? The common good—the common *weal*—is difficult to define. It contains many elements, some of which are in competition if not in conflict with others. A further complicating fact is that there is no set limit of government responsibility. The line shifts. Sometimes the common good may require that government authority be asserted in an area previously reserved to individuals or to other social institutions such as the family, the church, the schools, industry, local government, or professional groups; this had happened either because authority thitherto exercised was abused or abandoned or proved inadequate. At other times, the common good may require government to abandon areas which it had previously occupied. Price and wage controls imposed during World War II, for example, were abandoned soon after the end of that war.

If the *common good* cannot be precisely defined, certain of its attributes and its general objectives can be identified. The common good is achieved when conditions are established which assist man in his pursuit of happiness in the temporal order. Two points need to be emphasized: first, that the purpose of the state, of government, is to assist man; second, that the direct function of government is in the temporal order. This does not mean that government is indifferent to the absolute or ultimate end of man which government must take into account; but simply that the competence of government is in the temporal order, and its immediate and direct purpose is this temporal good, this human good, generally referred to as the common good.

This common good includes three principal categories of human goods. First, those material goods—"food, clothing, shelter"—which are necessary to maintain life and necessary as material helps to intellectual, moral, and spiritual growth; second, those intellectual goods—knowledge and culture—which liberate man from ignorance and false fear. And third, moral good, or moral goodness, the mastery of self, the cultivation and possession of those virtues which in the limited order of temporal life are the highest goal. All these things are part of the good life described and sought after by the Greek philosophers.

The essence of totalitarianism is control of the whole man, especially of his higher faculties and gifts. The essence of democracy is to establish conditions under which individual choice and decision, the fullness of personality, can be achieved. The frightening thing about modern totalitarian states has not been so much the economic control which they have imposed, but rather the domination of the intellectual, the moral, and the spiritual life of the people. Modern totalitarian governments have not sought to establish equality among all of their subjects, as is so often said, but rather have taken to themselves the authority for setting the limits and direction of the physical, intellectual, and moral development of persons—thereby subordinating individuals to the purposes of the state and making every aspect of life and society political.

The citizen of a democracy has a general obligation to obey the laws of the country. But absolute obedience has never been demanded. Thomas Jefferson at the very time that the nation was established and its political institutions formed, spoke of the right, if not the duty, of revolution. The defense of the idea of civil disobedience did not end with Thoreau but remains alive today, defended by political, religious, and intellectual leaders in democratic societies in words such those spoken by Dean Francis B. Sayre of the Episcopal Cathedral of Washington, D. C., when he said: "No Christian can grant to the state an absolute right over his conscience."

It is generally accepted that there are two conditions under which obedience to the government may be withheld. First, in the event that the state has extended its authority into fields of life which do not properly belong to it: if, for example, it usurps the authority of the family, of religion, or if it trespasses on areas reserved for individual and personal decision and choice; and second, when the government, acting in its proper sphere, orders actions which are wrong and contrary to right reason, an extreme example of which would be either an unjust war or an unnecessary one.

> Government has a positive and natural function to assist man in the pursuit of perfection and of happiness. Government accomplishes this purpose by promoting the common good.

To demand unquestioning obedience presupposes the existence of an authority which possesses full truth. Human authority, therefore, manifesting itself through governmental agencies, cannot claim such authority and can demand of its subjects only rational obedience—obedience that is founded on the conscientious judgment of the individuals. Through these two reservations, the role and autonomy of nongovernmental institutions are preserved and protected, and the integrity of the human person and his responsibility are given recognition.

Conflict between government and individuals occurs at each level of human goods. Even at the material or economic level—one at which we might expect greater clarity because the problems are more simple than they are at the level of the mind and of the spirit—there is conflict and confusion. The existence of governmental authority stands as a contradiction of the laissez-faire theory which proposed that if everyone sought his own good according to his own judgment of what constituted that good, the whole community would benefit. Governmental authority of both negative and positive force is admittedly exercised and needed at this level.

Government has set limits on individual economic activities. The right of an individual to use his property without regard for its effect on the property rights of others is limited. The right of the community to take private property to serve a public good under eminent domain has long been recognized. The right of government to enjoin labor and industry under certain conditions to produce goods or to perform services is clearly established.

Government has also assumed positive responsibility for the economic and material welfare of the country. The control and management of currency is a constitutionally assigned responsibility of the federal government of the United States. Economic and welfare responsibilities have been made subject to government action.

At the intellectual level, the state has the right to restrain an individual or group in the exercise of freedom of inquiry or of expression if there is any serious interference with the rights of others to pursue and possess truth. Thus the state can, in the interest of common good, suppress error which is subversive of the good of human society in its temporal achievement.

To say that error has no rights is, of course, true. It does not follow, however, that the man who is in error has no rights; neither does it follow that the state should suppress every idea which in the opinion of the rulers of a country is an error, whether the ruler be a monarch or a majority. Whereas the state has the responsibility to assist its citizens to obtain intellectual goods, its power to suppress error is limited to those errors which, if they were propagated, would clearly and directly endanger public health and safety.

In somewhat the same way the state has the right to suppress moral teaching and practices which are contrary to the common good. The United States government has forbidden the Mormon practice of bigamy as destructive of the moral stability of society. The state must not deny moral perfection; on the contrary, it has a positive obligation to encourage morality. Not only is it good for men to be moral, but morality is, as George Washington stated, "an indispensable support of political prosperity."

It is not true, however, that the state has a corresponding right to suppress all immorality. The purpose of the state and of its laws is to secure, as Solovyev has declared, "the practical realization of a definite minimum of good" and "to do away with a certain amount of evil." Thus the law should not attempt to eliminate all evil, but certain extreme forms of evil, and seek to bring about a definite minimal good, to require of all a minimum of virtue.

Man must be left free to develop in virtue. This is indisputable. To reach moral heights, men must have freedom. It is the function of the state to encourage and promote morality, but not to proscribe all immorality—only those extreme forms which interfere with the security of others and the stability of society.

When we come to consider religious and moral teachings beyond what is dictated by natural law, or attainable by natural reason—when we come, for instance, to consider questions of revealed truth, of faith, and of supernatural perfection— the right of the state to determine and to decide and to suppress error no longer prevails. The right of freedom of religion holds the field.

And so the proposition that a religious majority could rightfully suppress a religious minority by political action—a minority which is teaching nothing likely to subvert the temporal common good—is untenable. There is great danger of rendering to God the things that are Caesar's; namely, political authority and political power, just as there is danger in rendering to Caesar the things that are God's, absolute obedience and worship.

The state does not, then, have the right or the responsibility to impose what any majority considers true faith upon all of its subjects. It should encourage and aid, to the extent possible, all its subjects either in their own activities or through the instrumentality of other institutions, to advance in spiritual perfection. This it can do; first, by avoiding unwarranted interference, and second, by positive aid without dictation or discrimination.

The demands of the common good must be met, yet individual freedom protected and individual effort encouraged. The state must fulfill its responsibilities, yet the area of individual freedom and responsibility must be preserved.

Democracy in America: An Overview
(*America Revisited*, 1978)

Tocqueville wrote of two Americas: the one which he saw and which was described to him; and the one which he projected for the future. Much of what he foresaw, or predicted, both good and bad, has occurred. Other things which he expected, both good and bad, have not happened. Many problems, institutions, and ideas remain almost unchanged. The race problem is still with us. We have made little progress either in understanding or in dealing with criminals. Demagoguery is a threat. On the other hand, the tyranny of the majority has not yet become a reality, nor has the movement toward equality, which he thought dangerous and inevitable, reached the critical point. American individualism has not brought about social disintegration, although, as Tocqueville anticipated, more and more matters of controversy are not settled by social practice or precedent or within institutional relationships, but by the courts.

A new judgment of America in the mode of Tocqueville requires recognition of five major institutional changes, no one of which was clearly anticipated when the Constitution was adopted, or even when Tocqueville looked at American democracy and its principles and institutions.

The first such change is in the power of the presidency. Tocqueville recognized that the President necessarily would have great influence on foreign affairs, for "a negotiation cannot be initiated and brought to a fruitful conclusion except by one man." He thought that under some conditions, which did not exist in his time, and which he did not foresee for America, the election of the chief executive could pose dangers to the nation because a change in leadership might interrupt foreign policy, which he saw as needing continuity and stability. But he saw the elections of the President as posing no such danger to the United States in his day. For, he wrote: "American policy toward the world at large is simple; one might almost say that no one needs them, and they do not need anybody. Their independence is never threatened." He quoted with approval parts of George Washington's Farewell Address, which recommended neutrality as a general policy for the United States, with temporary alliances to be used in event of extraordinary emergencies. Tocqueville remarked that Washington and Jefferson had set the direction of American foreign policy. That policy, he said, "consists much more in abstaining than in doing."

This was just as well, apparently, in the judgment of Tocqueville, who believed that a government of the aristocracy was far superior in the conduct of foreign policy to the government of democracy. Democratic governments, he thought, find it "difficult to co-ordinate the details of a great undertaking and to fix on some plan and carry it through with determination in spite of obstacles." For democracy, be believed, "has little capacity for combining measures in secret and waiting patiently for the result." Moreover, he thought that the people of a democracy tended to rely too much on their feelings. This was shown, he said, at the time of the French Revolution, when only Washington's great influence prevented America from going to war with England on the side of France.

The reality of international relations today includes the existing power of the Soviet Union and the growing power of China; the spread of nuclear weapons to smaller countries; the newly found economic and political strength of the raw-material-supplying nations, especially those that produce oil; and extensive American treaty obligations around the world.

The problem is not only one of substance, but also one of form and process. It is quite likely that, if the men who drafted the Constitution had anticipated a time when foreign policy would be so major a part of the government's responsibility, an argument would have been made at the Constitutional Convention for a parliamentary, or quasi-parliamentary system—rather than the prescribed one of the Senate ratification of treaties and confirmation of the Secretary of State and of foreign ambassadors, and the rather vague provision that foreign policy should be made and conducted with the advice and consent of the Senate.

At the time the Constitution was written, treaties involved specific and limited commitments. This is not the case today. Now we have sweeping treaty agreements, executive agreements, and continuing commitments involving great sums of money. The House of Representatives has become more involved in foreign policy as financial support has become a major aspect of that policy.

During the 1960s, in particular, the Senate became more and more isolated from decisions on foreign policy. At the same time, there was growing arrogance on the part of administrations in the conduct of foreign policy. Presidents Lyndon Johnson and Richard Nixon exercised virtual monopoly in that field. Their theoretical statements about presidential power in foreign affairs were accepted uncritically by many Americans until the Vietnam War forced another look at the Constitution. Even after Vietnam, there was a tendency to accept and applaud the private diplomacy of Henry Kissinger, instead of insisting upon genuine participation by the Senate in making foreign policy.

[...]

The second significant institutional change is the rise of the military. The question is not one of whether we need a military establishment, but whether the one we have had to develop in the way it did and whether it should be subject to better direction and control. Is a military establishment of such magnitude compatible with a free, democratic society? Or does it inevitably become a separate force of excessive influence?

Tocqueville did not give much space to the President's role as Commander-in-Chief. He apparently did not think it very important either in the structure of the Constitution or in the context of the early nineteenth century. The President does command the Army, he noted, but "that Army consists of six thousand soldiers; he commands the Navy, but the Navy has only a few ships; he conducts the Union's relations with foreign nations, but the Union has no neighbors. Separated by the ocean from the rest of the world, still too weak to want to rule the sea, it has no enemies and its interests are seldom in contact with those of the other nations of the globe."

Tocqueville did speculate at length, however, upon the possible future military role of the United States, upon the relationship of the military establishment to democratic government and society, and upon democracy and war.

If involvement in a great war were to come for America, he thought it would come at the point where the United States touched Mexico. But Mexico's poverty and backwardness, he believed, would long prevent its having a high place among the nations. In the meantime, the United States was fortunate in its isolation: "How wonderful is the position of the New World," he reflected, "where man has as yet no enemies but himself. To be happy and to be free, it is enough to will it to be so." War with Mexico was to come within twenty years; but it was not to be a great war, and Mexico has remained weak and backward.

Tocqueville predicted that, because of its natural advantages and aptitude for trade, the United States would one day "become the leading naval power on the globe." Americans, he said, "are born to rule the seas, as the Romans were to conquer the world." Americans were great sailors, great shipbuilders, and great traders throughout the nineteenth century; but American dominance of the sea with fighting ships did not come until World War II. The significance of that dominance was reduced almost immediately after that war, by the development of nuclear weapons and by the rise of the Soviet Union as a naval power.

Of more importance than Tocqueville's specific predictions were his theoretical reflections on military power, war, and democracy. Tocqueville thought that the army of a democracy continuously posed the threat of war or of revolution. "For armies," he wrote, "are much more impatient of peace when once they have tasted war. ... I foresee that all the great wartime leaders who may arise in the major democratic nations will find it easier to conquer with the aid of their armies than to make their armies live at peace after conquest. There are two things that will always be very difficult for a democratic nation: to start a war and to end it."

[...]

Tocqueville reflected only indirectly on how the existence of a large military establishment could affect democracy. But he considered quite directly and extensively what war can do to a democracy and how a democracy is likely to respond to war. He pointed out that there are two dangers to democracy arising from war. First, he wrote: "Although war satisfies the Army, it annoys and often drives to desperation that countless crowd of citizens whose petty passions daily require peace for their satisfaction. There is therefore some danger that it may cause, in another form, the very disturbance which it should prevent." This apparently is a reference to internal disorder or even revolution. The record of American participation in wars, before the war in Vietnam, does not sustain Tocqueville's speculation. Most earlier wars were popularly supported. Rather than stirring domestic unrest, they served to ameliorate differences and at least to postpone domestic unrest. The condition of popular support or opposition must depend more on the nature of the war than on any basic theory as to the democratic response to war.

Second, he said: "Any long war always entails great hazards to liberty in a democracy. Not that one need apprehend that after every victory the conquering generals will seize sovereign power by force after the manner of Sulla and Caesar. The danger is of another kind. War does not always give democratic societies over to military government, but it must invariably and immeasurably increase the powers of civil government; it must almost automatically concentrate the direction of all men and the control of all things in the hands of the government. If that does not lead to despotism by sudden violence, it leads men gently in that direction by their habits." The clearest demonstration of this judgment followed World War II, especially with the establishment of the Central Intelligence Agency and the expansion of military intelligence—the one under civilian control, the other under military control. Each accumulated, illegally or extra-legally, information about American citizens. The kind of information-gathering which was tolerated during wartime was carried forward into peacetime, without so much as a nod to legality and without the sensitivity shown in the treatment of dogs that had been used in the Canine Corps.

[...]

Tocqueville offered two solutions to the problem of the restless Army. The first was that the Army should be democratic. This followed naturally, he thought, from democratic theory and experience. He believed that citizens would bring to the Army a taste for order and for discipline. [...] With compulsory military service, he wrote, "the burden is spread equally and without discrimination among all the citizens."

In a pure and fully supported democracy, one can assume that military service would be so respected and so sought after that, if not all men were needed, the soldiers might be chosen by lot. Those chosen might be looked upon, by themselves and by others, as especially favored. Under this condition of democratic dedication, volunteers would not be needed—and would not even be tolerated.

The experience of America in twentieth-century war has been with a mixed system of volunteers and conscripts. It has worked reasonably well, especially since in time of major wars the strength of the military has been drawn from the civilian population. The conscription system has overridden the volunteer system, but generally has done so in an open and nondiscriminatory way. Thus it has met the Tocqueville rule that "a democratic government can do pretty well what it likes, provided that its orders apply to all and at the same moment; it is the inequality of a burden, not its weight, which usually provokes resistance."

The inequality and discrimination of conscription laws and regulations during the Vietnam War did provoke resistance and protest, and in large measure moved the government into experimentation with the all-volunteer army. For practical purposes, this is a mercenary army. It does not reflect, as would a conscript army chosen at random, the civilization which is defended or represented by the army. The dangers that Tocqueville foresaw arising from a large and professionalized standing army must grow as that army becomes less democratic, less reflective of the general populace, and more isolated from society. Recent public suggestions about unionizing the armed forces are not surprising as the army becomes separated from society, from motives of patriotism, and from broad social identification.

[...]

In accepting the volunteer army, Americans have ignored at least three admonitions from Tocqueville. The first is that a volunteer army is likely to be drawn from the poorer and less-educated in the society, while what he called the "elite" avoid military service during peacetime. Second, a volunteer army is run by career officers. Third, the volunteer army "finally becomes a little nation apart, with a lower standard of intelligence and rougher habits than the nation at large. But this little uncivilized nation holds the weapons and it alone knows how to use them."

Tocqueville's second solution to the problem of a restless army was simply to reduce the army's size. "But that is not a remedy which every nation can apply," he observed.

A third point, not noted by Tocqueville, is that political direction bearing on war must always be precise and clear. The military must not be left in doubt; it must not be either tempted or pressured to develop its own political program and purposes. A powerful military institution inevitably expands into a policy vacuum—first in foreign affairs and then, if we look to the experience of recent [history] in Europe and in South America especially, also in domestic affairs.

The Vietnam experience is especially pertinent. In that war military men were called upon to act without clear political direction. In the early years of that war, the declared policy was to stabilize the government of South Vietnam. As military commitment increased in 1965, there was an escalation of policy to include prevention of invasion from the north. By 1966 American military strength in South Vietnam was of such magnitude that a more comprehensive purpose had to be given. The new purpose was to save all of Southeast Asia from communism and, beyond that, from domination by China. By 1967 the security of the United States, its national honor, and the future of the free world were set as the real purposes of the war.

The principal failures in the Vietnam War were not military. Rather, they were failures by American civilian leaders to determine policy, to give direction and to set limits, to take the diplomatic actions necessary to bring the war to an end short of military showdown, and to act responsibly without regard to what such an end might be called—defeat, surrender, stalemate, or victory.

[...]

A third institutional force which creates problems for American democracy is the corporation, a creature of society which exists as a limited person by virtue of socially approved legal action. Because of the concentration of economic power and magnitude of such power, because of the limited definition of "person" which constitutes the corporation, because of the diffusion of responsibility, and because of the escape from responsibility which is almost in the nature of the institution, the corporation has become a foreign force in American society. It is a source which is somewhat unmanageable and antidemocratic.

The historically projected process from noncompetitive feudalism to free, competitive capitalism to socialism is not evident. The process has been closer to a circular movement from feudalism to free, competitive capitalism and then back to a more sophisticated and more highly organized corporate feudalism. The new feudalism is not subject to laws designed for the theoretically free and competitive economy. Rather, it lends itself to negotiated settlements among the feudal powers, or between them and the central government. The central government is now democratically elected, in contrast with the kingly government that marked the controlling or arbitrating force in precapitalist feudalism.

The problem is complicated by the existence in a democratic society of the people's power to vote themselves a share of income or property. There has been a progressive removal of people from the traditional—one might say natural—condition of ownership, in which property can be physically defined as land, buildings, livestock, tools, and machinery. In its place there is a removed and documentary ownership, manifest in shares of stock or contracts or union agreements. This change seems to lead to a diminished sense of the rights of ownership and of the traditional claims to ownership (occupancy, prior inheritance, prior claim, and use). And it leads to another step in which the propertyless—the dispossessed or nonpossessors—move to vote themselves an increased share of what is produced by the whole community, without regard to private or state ownership.

[...]

A fourth problem for democratic society, one observed by Tocqueville in its early stages, is the development of political parties. Beyond that, there has been a move away from representative government and an effort to institutionalize the political process in order to make it more workable as society has become more complex.

A significant retreat from representative government was signaled by the 1913 adoption of the Seventeenth Amendment, which provided for popular election of U.S. senators. Previously, senators were selected by men chosen from smaller population groupings within the respective states. (The system was comparable to the Electoral College process, by which electors chosen in the states meet to elect a President.) Party primaries were developed in the same period. In a variety of ways, they made easier a popular judgment on choice of candidates.

More recently, there have been demands for representation at conventions and in party offices on the basis of quotas numerically representing the racial, sexual, and age components of a party. Following the 1968 Democratic national convention, there was agitation for rule changes to insure more accurate representation of party membership at future conventions. A set of guidelines based on physical standards was adopted. By these standards, convention delegates are encouraged or required to reflect a proper ratio of persons based on age, sex, and race of party members. Yet such standards may leave unrepresented individuals or groups whose ideological position cuts across the lines of age, race, and sex. In principle, the perfect quota system would be one which selects delegates at random from among the total party membership. Those so chosen could then be allowed to make decisions for the party on issues and on candidates. A further extension of absolute, equalitarian democracy would be to have the candidates (assuming there was agreement among them on issues) chosen at random as the representatives of the party position.

[...]

The fifth serious challenge to the working of American democracy is presented by government agencies, popularly labeled the bureaucracies. The complexity of problems, rapidly changing conditions, leaders' desires to avoid political responsibility, and other factors have resulted in the establishment of special bureaus and agencies which combine legislative, judicial, and executive powers.

It is not wise to generalize about agencies or bureaus of government. Depending on the way in which they are organized, or because of their functions or methods, they vary significantly from one to another. In some the dynamism is internal and quite independent of outside control or direction. Others are a reflection of their directors, as was the case with the FBI under J. Edgar Hoover. Some are inevitably taken over by staff experts, and some become projections of their methodology, as in the case of the CIA. Some tend to become separate societies, relatively free of congressional or presidential or judicial control.

The clearest example of such independence is the Central Intelligence Agency. The Agency was designed principally as an intelligence agency for the executive branch of the government. It was anticipated that Congress would have only minimal knowledge of its operations and minimal control over those operations. It was assumed, however, that the Agency would operate within broad guidelines of national and international policy and would be subject to close executive surveillance. The executive branch soon found it convenient to transfer what should have been State Department operations to the Central Intelligence Agency; because if carried out by the CIA, the operations escaped ordinary congressional and public review and could be conducted by internally determined methods of operation. In the case of the CIA, methods which had been accepted and justified in wartime were transferred to cold war situations and even to standard diplomatic relations. Once the principle of secrecy is accepted, and once it is accepted that an agency can determine its own methodology, the agency tends to take on a life of its own— independent even of the executive branch, which theoretically and by statute is supposed to control it. In its freedom, the agency develops and executes policy quite independently. [...]

The ultimate bureaucratizing of democracy was achieved by the 1974 Federal Election Campaign Act, which provided for government financing of presidential campaigns. The conditions for qualifying for such funds were set by law; and a Federal Election Commission, combining legislative, judicial, and executive roles, was set up to administer the law. The combination of roles made the Commission's work a magistrate's proceeding such as Jefferson and other Founding Fathers warned against. The Commission's procedures are like those against which the Declaration of Independence was written in protest.

Bureaucracy in a democracy is near perfection when the political process, through which government officials, policies, and control are to come, is controlled by a bureaucratic creation of the government itself. It is a manifestation of the tyranny of the majority in its purest form—that in which the majority tyrannizes itself.

Intellectuals and Politics
(The Hard Years, 1975)

A superficial reading of the political history of the United States supports the view that American politics is anti-intellectual and that American government is a product of the efforts of "practical" men.

Certainly the founding fathers were practical men. In writing and then defending the Declaration of Independence, they took practical political action—knowing that the consequence of failure was almost certain execution as traitors

American politics is idealistic at the same time, and the reported division between politics and idealism is more fancied than real.

The failure to associate politics with the philosophical and intellectual arena of ideas has sometimes arisen from the very absence of genuine ideological conflict between men of ideas and men of action in American political life. Certainly philosophers, historians, and men of ideas were accepted as associates and advisers of politicians in the earliest days of our history.

G. K. Chesterton, in his book *What I Saw in America*, published in 1922, said that

> America is the only nation in the world that is founded on a creed. That
> creed is set forth with dogmatic and even theological lucidity in the
> Declaration of Independence; perhaps the only piece of practical politics
> that is also theoretical politics and also great literature.

The creed to which he referred was expressed in the Declaration in these words:

> We hold these Truths to be self-evident, that all Men are created equal,
> that they are endowed by their Creator with certain unalienable Rights,
> that among these are Life, Liberty, and the Pursuit of Happiness. ...

These words and these ideas were taken seriously by the men who drafted the Declaration of Independence. They were written by men in danger of being shot or hanged if the Revolution they led turned out to be a failure. The words and the ideas they expressed were taken literally. They were not stated merely as a justification for the Revolution, but were intended to establish a foundation in principle upon which democratic institutions and traditions could be established anywhere in the world. What was incorporated in the early documents was a product of the whole tradition of Western political thought from Plato to the humanist and rationalist philosophers of the eighteenth century.

The fields of study and of intellectual pursuit which bear most directly upon politics today are these three: history, economics, and moral or ethical science.

Politicians throughout history have been somewhat concerned about their place in history and about the movement of history as it has affected their own countries and their own political action. Great military and political leaders of the past sometimes appointed their own historians or even served as historians of their own achievements. They often ordered the construction of their own arches and temples. They patronized artists and poets who in turn were expected to do well by them in the artistic record.

In the nineteenth and early twentieth centuries, the disposition to set one's own country apart from history, to assert its independence and unique character, was very common among Western nations. What passed for history or for political philosophy in too many cases was self-justifying and fictional.

Extremes of nationalism are always something of a threat to historians and to history, since leaders of a strongly nationalistic state, or those who speak for it, are inclined to believe that it is somewhat above or outside history. They tend to think of themselves as the center and focal point of history, to minimize the efforts of the past, and to assume that the patterns they establish will be the model for the indefinite future. The questions of continuity and of relations to the movement of history itself are discounted.

Nearly every politician today who says with some certainty that Columbus discovered America in 1492 is said to have a sense of history. Viewed in a broader context, such observations reflect concern for an understanding of history and a hope that those responsible for government will interpret their own times and will make political decisions within the context and the movement of history.

In the period since the end of World War II, we have come to recognize that the mass of current history and the speed of history make special demands both upon governments and upon people. The mass or the volume of those things which demand our attention is greater than it has ever been. Political responsibility today extends to the whole world. We can no longer set aside whole continents or whole nations or whole races as though they were not a part of contemporary history. We have to accept, and in some measure we must give attention to, all peoples in all places. There is no place in the world today and no person in the world for which we do not have some degree of obligation and responsibility.

But along with the increase in volume, there is a second most significant consideration: the speed of the change and development today is at a rate which is faster than it has ever been before. We are not called on to respond to a timetable or a schedule of our own making—much as we would like to have it that way; rather, we are called upon to respond on the basis of a schedule which the movement of history imposes upon us.

The second intellectual discipline bearing upon politics in a direct way is economics. I do not mean to exclude other social sciences as having no bearing upon government and government decisions, nor would I discount the influence of the natural sciences on our culture. But in a very special and direct way, economic theory has come to play a great role in government economic and fiscal policy.

Some attention was given to economics by government in the period of the Great Depression in the United States. Theories of business cycles were developed. What in rather popular political terms was described merely as Keynesian economics became the limited guide for political economy.

In 1962 President Kennedy requested discretionary power to reduce personal-income-tax rates within limits and thereby stimulate the economy by increasing citizens' take-home pay. In 1963 President Kennedy urged the Congress to cut taxes in order to stimulate economic growth and expansion. This was a new kind of argument for a tax cut. It challenged several accepted ideas in the field of political economy: first, and the principal one, that in times of prosperity budgets should be balanced and federal deficits reduced; second, that federal deficits inevitably resulted in inflation; and third, that government expenditures by their very nature were wasteful and non-economic.

For anyone prepared to challenge those three points, it was almost as important to make a moral case as it was to make an economic one. Economists and others, therefore, had to make it clear that they were not in any absolute or moral sense in favor of unbalanced budgets; that they were not in any absolute or moral sense in favor of inflation—either galloping or creeping; that they did not believe that governmental spending was never wasteful. Each of these propositions, it was argued, had to be judged in the total context of the needs of the country and, therefore, related to questions of war and peace and to the condition of the economy, both domestic and international.

Today, when our economic problems are more serious than in 1963, the importance of economics is obvious. Perhaps less obvious is the need for new interpretations, new theory. We are beyond Keynes. An economist or politician who refused to accept this would be somewhat like a physicist who insisted that only the theories of Newton could be applied.

The third intellectual discipline relevant to politics today is moral or ethical science.

The influence of moralists is most often indirect. Ethics defines the ends and purposes of political power and judges the methods and conditions of the use of political power. But the combination and application is the work of politics.

Moralists, Jacques Maritain said, are unhappy people; so are politicians. Maritain believed that the task of ethics is a humble one. The task of the politician is, in a sense, even more humble than that of the moralist. It is also rather difficult. The fundamental objective of politics is to bring about progressive change in keeping with the demands of social justice. Politics is concerned with ways and means and with prudential judgments as to what should be done, when it should be done, and in what measure and how it should be done. The politician should be a moralist himself; in any case, he must pay attention to the voice of the moralist.

The concern of moralists with the great questions of war and peace has had significant consequences in the last decade. Historians said of the war in Vietnam that it was not justified by history, and economists manifested concern over the effects the war was having on our economy. But the most telling argument was left to moralists and philosophers, who concluded that methods used in the war were morally indefensible and that the violence employed was out of all proportion to any goal that might be won. Their judgment had influence on politicians and also on those who had been called upon to fight the war.

Intellectuals today must deal with serious contradictions. On one hand, in the second half of the twentieth century, people have more freedom than ever before. They are more truly and com-pletely human because they are more free from nature, more free from ignorance, more free from the material limitations of the past, more free of the past itself. On the other hand, there has been a growing separation between reason and life, means and end, society and the individual, reli-gion and morality, action and sensibility, language and thought, men in the community and men in the crowd.

> Ethics defines the ends and purposes of political power and judges the methods and conditions of the use of political power. But the combination and application is the work of politics.

In recent centuries, many intellectual leaders were not as directly and imme-diately involved in the life and problems of their times as they should have been. They were guilty of indifference, detachment, and withdrawal. The gods could climb higher on Olympus and thus avoid the clamor of the world and of the crowd.

In the eighteenth and nineteenth centuries there was a growing rejection of theology and philosophy, and even of history. There was an arrogant assertion that science and technology and new political and economic forms would provide the answers which philosophy and theology and other intellectual disciplines had failed to provide in the past.

The excuse of rejection no longer stands. The world today is not arrogant. It has been brought low. The world today does not suffer from illusion.

There is, of course, still a need for the long view and the search for absolutes, but there is also a great need for the application of that knowledge which we do possess to contemporary life and problems. The dead hand of the past is less of a problem—although we still use it as an excuse—than is the violent hand of the future, which reaches back for us today, imposing most serious demands.

There is little time to escape, and few escape routes are still open. Some may wish to take the advice of Bob Hope, given in a commencement address some years ago, when in mock humor he advised the graduates not to go out and face the world. Or a similar escape suggested by my son when he was very young: when asked what he would have liked to be had he lived in ancient Roman times—an emperor, a soldier, or a martyr—he said that he would have preferred to be a lion.

Full withdrawal or retreat is no longer possible. Intellectual spokesmen and moral leaders are called upon today to prove the relevance of their ideas to life. By necessity of history rather than by choice, those who have long been pilgrims of the absolute are forced now to become pilgrims of the relative as well.

Intellectual and moral leaders today cannot retreat in ignorance and half-truths or go back into their own protected caves. Leonardo da Vinci could speculate on the principles of aerodynamics without giving any thought to the possibility that his knowledge would be used to construct intercontinental ballistic missiles. Rene Descartes could develop new theories of mathematics without anticipating that his conclusions might be incorporated in nuclear bombs. Intellectuals of the past did not have to anticipate what might happen to their ideas when subjected to the power of computers.

Time has caught up with the intellectuals. Their advance positions have been overrun.

The alternative to reasoned direction of life is a return to primitive conditions of ignorance and false fear. If we believe that man is the subject of history rather than simply the object (an object controlled by economics or by some irrational force), if we acknowledge that the period of half-civilization and half-knowledge of the nineteenth century has been shattered, if we accept that we must face the judgment of our nation and of our age, then we need a full and reasoned response from the intellectuals.

We must reaffirm our confidence in reason as the one truly human instrument that we must use for guidance and direction as we continue to live on the edge of disaster. Both the intellectual and the politician must continue to pass reasoned judgment on life and history, for without knowing, there can be no proper doing.

The Book, the Harp, the Sword, and the Plow
(*The Ultimate Tyranny*, 1980)

Albert Schweitzer, speaking of the order of nature, said that if we lose our capacity to foresee and to forestall, we will end up destroying the earth.

In the order of politics, economics, and social organization, failure to foresee and forestall troubles may not destroy civilization, but this failure certainly is destructive of order and socially restrictive. Foreseeing and forestalling require historical judgment and also the understanding and application of ideas. Ideas do have consequences; so does the failure to apply good ideas and judgment in the social order. Knowledge and reason, limited though they may be, are the only defenses of civilization against ignorance and false fear. Together or apart, they give stability and direction to civilization.

In the United States there are at least four major areas in which the application of unsound ideas, or the absence of thoughtful application of principle and of historical judgments, has serious consequences.

The first is the Constitution itself, threatened by an overeagerness to amend it and interpret it in response to immediate pressures, real or imagined, without regard or attention to the principles and historical experience that underlay the drafting of that document. When the Constitution is amended by a three-fourths approval, that three-fourths places itself in a position of being subsequently held to their position by the one-fourth minority.

The second is the careless disregard for one of the major rights protected by the Constitution, freedom of speech. In particular, we tend to manifest willingness to tolerate and even justify limitations of freedom of speech by a monopoly press which does not understand its function, and to grant to a government agency—the Federal Communications Commission—powers to control culture, including the communication of political information and ideas.

The third concerns another constitutionally guaranteed right, freedom of assembly, which Alexis de Tocqueville said was next in importance in a democratic society to the right of individual liberty. This right is interfered with through the limitation of the right to organize for political purposes. The denial of this right was a principal cause of the American Revolution. The principal instruments through which limitations are imposed are state laws, many of which are unconstitutional, and, since 1974, the Federal Election Campaign Act, executed by the Federal Election Commission, which has been given arbitrary and bureaucratic control over the political processes of the nation.

The fourth is the proliferation of government bureaucracies and the danger that comes of delegating them power. As Frankenstein delegated power to the monster, so do we to impersonal, self-motivated institutions operating on a dynamism of their own. Such bureaucracies differ from one another in their sources of power, modes of operation, and political effects. They range from police and intelligence agencies such the FBI and the CIA, to bureaus and commissions and agencies like the Federal Trade Commission, the Environmental Protection Agency, and the Internal Revenue Service, to the newly established Department of Education.

An ancient Irish law held that society could not take from a person his book, his harp, his sword, or his plow in settlement of a debt. His book was the repository of knowledge and the sign of his intellectual, moral, and religious freedom; his harp the instrument of artistic expression; his sword the sign and agent of his political freedom; and the plow his means of livelihood, of economic independence.

Why are we threatening to burn our own books, destroy our harps, break our swords, and let rust the plowshares?

Three Issues for What's Left of the 1990s
(*No Fault Politics*, 1998)

... [S]ome issues simply cry out for attention and for good sense. They ought to be clarified *before* the next century, for we have been kicking them around in American politics for twenty years or more.

These three issues are social and political equality; economic opportunity, specifically the chance to work a job, perhaps even a decent job; and freedom of political expression, specifically the right to protest.

All three issues have been shrouded by cant and nonsense, and all three get at the heart of what the country should be and how it has lost its bearings.

• • •

The first issue is *the new equality*. This is a drive for an equality of result or condition—an equality of conformity. It is not the traditional American desire for equal opportunity allotted to separate individuals.

Alexis de Tocqueville, in *Democracy in America*, wrote of the powerful appeal and danger of the idea of equality in a democratic society. He wrote of its potential for demagoguery.

I would be less concerned about the rise to popularity of the word and the idea if I thought it the result of conscious intention to elicit political support—that is, if those who made the appeal knew that they were being demagogic. I fear, however, that the use of the word is not intentionally demagogic. It seems to approach the automatic "It is good" justification feared by George Orwell.

In his inaugural address in 1980, President Jimmy Carter said, "We have already found a high degree of personal liberty, and we are now struggling to enhance equality of opportunity."

One may well question the president's language. Liberty was a goal of the American Revolution. We have it in this country, not because we "found" it but rather as a result of our having declared it a political and social goal and then having achieved it in some measure. As to the president's second point, that "we are now struggling to enhance equality of opportunity," such language does not clearly describe the concept of equality as it is applied today. Economic, educational, political, and cultural equality—and *not* equality of opportunity, enhanced or otherwise—is the goal in the new application.

Economic equality, in this new conception, is to be achieved primarily through equalizing income. Equalization of wealth—that is, of wealth already accumulated—may come later. Economic equality is conceived not as a base upon which differences may then build, but as an average. One former governor used to ask occasionally if it might be better if people doing unpleasant work were paid more than those whose work is culturally and physically preferable.

Political economists have developed the notion of a negative income tax as the basis for tax reform. Essentially, the idea is this: Everyone should have enough income to pay taxes at the beginning or threshold rate, and if one does not have enough income to reach that level, something should be done to make up for the deficiency. Where the idea came from or how the taxable level of income was chosen as the standard for judgment and adjustments is not clear.

It seems that the tax base is to be accepted as a first principle upon which we are to build. It is an axiom, rather like "I think, therefore I am." One could as well assert that, for the good of the commonwealth, everyone should pay $1,000 in income taxes, and then proceed through measures of redistribution to raise all incomes to the level at which everyone would have to pay $1,000 in taxes.

The idea of a negative income tax is appealing. Professors of political economics can diagram its operation. Ideas that can be diagrammed, especially in economics and in political science, are very popular. It is easier to teach with a diagram or a chart. A diagram conveys an impression of certainty. Thus, the business-cycle theory of economics was popular because the charting of the cycle gave the appearance of scientific order in a confused discipline. Prosperity was followed by recession, and that, in turn, by depression, after which the cycle swung up through recovery back to prosperity. The theory seemed to have the certainty of the seasons or of the phases of the moon—until the economic moon went down in 1929 and did not come up.

The second area in which the new concept of equality is being applied is in politics and government. The principle of "one person, one vote" was formally recognized in a Supreme Court ruling affecting defined political jurisdictions. The court did not in its ruling extend the principle to relationships among jurisdictions. The ruling simply said that within given units of government, each vote should be equal to every other vote. Thus, since the Constitution provides for direct election of the House of Representatives on the basis of population, the rule requires that each congressional district have roughly the same number of people.

The Constitution also provides that each state, no matter what its size, shall have two senators. Thus, the citizen of a small state gets proportionally more of a vote in the Senate than the resident of a large state. The Constitution further provides that the president shall be elected through the electoral college, on a state-by-state basis, thus weighting the votes of smaller states favorably as against those cast in larger states. The drive now is to eliminate that weighting by abolishing the electoral college and instituting direct popular election of the president. No proposal has yet been made to reduce senatorial representation to a strict population base.

The principle of equality is also applied through the Federal Election Campaign Act, which attempts to equalize the nonvoting influence of citizens on candidates for political office. The current law limits the size of contributions to a political candidate in any one campaign to $1,000 per contributor. This limitation is considered a transitional phase to a time when all campaigns will be publicly financed. The argument for the limitation is that the larger the contribution, the greater the influence a contributor has on the officeholder and the more time he gets to spend with the officeholder. Theoretically, with public financing, every taxpayer will have made an equal contribution and will be entitled to as much time with the officeholder as any other taxpayer. What time nontaxpayers will get has not yet been determined by the reformers.

[...]

It does not take much imagination to foresee a time when citizens might go to court, charging that they were discriminated against because their calls were not taken in presidential telethons and transmitted to the president for his attention. A full practical application of this principle would argue for an equal right to speak or otherwise communicate with all officeholders, even removing the personal screening of Jim Lehrer and the commission on debates.

The objective of equalizing communications and influence on officeholders is also sought in efforts to control lobbyists. Proposals generally recommend more thorough regulation of lobbyists, limits on their expenditures, and public disclosure not only of expenditures but also of meetings and communications with officeholders.

It will not be surprising if someone suggests having lobbyists provided at government expense, so as to insulate officeholders from the undue influence of their principles, in somewhat the same way that officeholders are to be insulated from their constituencies. Under this arrangement, anyone who had a case to make to the government would apply for a lobbyist, who would be assigned from a pool in the way that public defenders are assigned by the courts. There could be classes of lobbyists (No. 1, No. 2, and so on) who would be assigned by a commission according to the seriousness or difficulty of the case to be made to the government. This procedure would establish a second level of purity and of detachment. A third and a fourth level might be added in pursuit of that absolute certainty and safety sought by the animal in Franz Kafka's story "The Burrow."

The new concept of equality also is applied in government and government-influenced employment practices, in what has been labeled the "quota system." The rationale of the quota system is that, since not every person can be hired, we should have within each employed group a representation or sampling of the total employable workforce. Selection currently is on the basis of physiological characteristics of age, sex, and race. There are some obvious historical reasons as to why these standards are being tried. There also are some obvious difficulties in their application, especially if one attempts to extend the principle—as will surely be done—to other racial and ethnic groups or to groups defined more in terms of psychological differences than racial and cultural differences—such as manic-depressives or battered husbands.

The drive to realize the new idea of equality has saturated education in recent years. The standardized curriculum, national standards, quota admissions, open admissions, and free college education are all manifestations of this drive. Full application of the principle could lead to compulsory college education, with the level of education so reduced that all who enter do so with the assurance of successful graduation. With no possible abandonment of hope at any point, they could look forward to something like the judgment of the Dodo after the caucus race in *Alice in Wonderland*: "Everyone has won, and all must have prizes."

What are the dangers in this drive to a newly conceived equality?

I see a danger first in the inevitable weakening of those institutions that are expected to give form and direction to society, such as professional and educational institutions, and that have traditionally been treated as having an identity separate from political control.

I also see the new equality significantly affecting the individual American's conception of his place in society. Most people cannot stand either physical or cultural isolation and will seek certainty in a community of people or a culture. The cultural security of Americans traditionally has been found in a society of some tension, but a society in which a balance could be achieved between individual freedom and liberty on the one side and the social good on the other. The alternative now offered, the security of equalization, is depersonalizing. It is a deceptively angelistic conception of man in society. It is one that cannot be sustained. It will in all likelihood move people in search of security, if not identity, to accept greater and greater socialization of their lives.

• • •

The second issue is economic opportunity—the chance to work as well as the chance to enjoy leisure and other benefits of work.

Samuel Gompers, the great leader of the early American labor movement, declared that if one person in America is out of work, we should redistribute existing work so that this person might be employed. Yet, in the course of the last presidential campaign, with 7 million potential workers unemployed and another estimated 7 million underemployed, organized labor ran advertisements advocating the eight-hour day, five days a week of work, and overtime.

A recent Harvard study reports that people in the United States who are employed are working more hours a year than ever before in modern time—on average 160 hours a year more today than in 1969, or the equivalent in hours of a full month of work.

A Brookings Institution report estimates that if the overtime being worked in the United States were distributed, it could give work to approximately 3 million of the unemployed. The average overtime being worked per week is approximately three and a half hours a week, or about 8 percent to 10 percent above the basic legal-hours level. If the current trend continues, the average American will be working sixty hours a week by the year 2020.

Overwork is not just the mark of overachievers, workaholics, and hyperconsumers, according to the Harvard study, but of almost everybody: those in high-income groups, middle- income classes, poorer classes, and the working poor. Two-income families are becoming the norm rather than the exception. Women are entering the workforce and are present in it in unprecedented numbers. Latchkey children have vastly increased in number, and the demand for preschools, kindergartens, and post-school care has increased.

The Japanese, now working an eight-hour-day, six-day week, are considering shortening working time to five days a week, which would leave their workers laboring about 150 fewer hours a year than U.S. workers. Germany, where economic productivity per working person is the highest in the world, has shortened working time to the point where German workers work 300 fewer hours a year than their U.S. counterparts.

In other countries—Australia, the Netherlands, and France, for example—movements to lower average working time below forty hours a week have been successful.

Yet, despite all this evidence that it makes economic and social sense, the shortening of working time is opposed by both management and labor in the United States, by the government, and by most labor economists.

Corporate executives, in a survey conducted by Dr. Juliet Schorr of Harvard, expressed almost unanimous agreement that working hours must be increased even more in American industry if we are to be competitive in the "global market." Their arguments are comparable to those made by business and industry against Henry Ford's $5-a-day-for-eight-hours reform—introduced in 1914.

Ford held that workers not only had to be paid enough so that they could buy what they were producing but also that they had to be given enough time, in the case of the car, to at least drive to and from work. In 1926 Ford went to the five-day week, thus giving workers more time to drive, both during the week and on weekends.

Labor union leaders who denounce state right-to-work laws conversely defend the right of their own members to work overtime.

And the government has shown little interest in the issue, except on the negative side.

[...]

[P]ublic works expenditures make little sense in our current economy. Public works can stimulate our economy where jobs and dollars are scarce. But such spending will not work in an economy already burdened with excessive waste. And waste is the mark of the U.S. economy.

We continue to overproduce and overconsume automobiles that are oversized and overpowered. We have produced and continue to produce unnecessary and obsolete defense materials and services. We carry on a space program without cost control or benefit measurement and carry an obligation to pay interest in the amount of more than $200 billion [currently over $450 billion] a year on the public debt. More pork-barrel spending hardly seems the solution.

Historically, the principal means of dealing with the general fiscal and economic disorders in the country has been unemployment supported by underemployment and overwork. This approach is costly, outmoded, and inhumane. The United States should be providing an example for the industrialized world. Instead it has become an economic and social backwater, standing still or falling behind while newer ideas, or old unused ones, reflecting changes in production and in social institutions, are adopted in other countries like Germany.

Redistributing work is a far more equitable approach to economic stagnation than keeping some employees working full-time and overtime while others are dismissed. The government should reduce the working time of retained employees and spread work among those who would otherwise be dismissed. It should begin by doing this with its own workforce when cutbacks are necessary. It should require contractors and others doing business with the government, especially in military equipment and supplies, to do the same.

When mobilizing for war, we can act with dispatch and reasonable efficiency to make necessary change possible. Yet we resist mobilizing the economy for the purposes of productivity and social justice.

Adjustments to economic reckoning following the borrowing binge of the '80s have left us floundering and confused. But we can manage our economy to benefit people. And that means redistributing work.

Here is a simple principle of social decency and minimal justice: Employ the maximum number of people rather than a minimum of people working maximum hours.

Will this cost? Yes, it will. Some of the overtime pay that already-employed workers would have to give up to employ the unemployed might be returned to them in tax credits or breaks (and offset by more progressive taxation). And some lost income, frankly, would be lost. But what is the social cost of permanent unemployment and a permanent, or an expanded, welfare class?

And what is the social cost if the few who keep their jobs must work continually to keep them? Or if they must use more and more of their income to consume goods that serve (unsatisfactorily) as substitutes for free time with their families and genuine leisure? It's a question of what kind of society we want.

It has been half a century since Congress, with the federal Wages and Hours Act, adopted the forty-hour workweek and fifty-week working year. Add to that all of the progress in technology, automation, computers, and so on, yet the rule accepted by politicians and labor leaders remains the same: Those lucky enough to have a job must work forty hours—plus overtime. It is time to change the rule.

• • •

The third issue that deserves a full airing in the 1990s is civil liberties. The country needs to face new threats to privacy posed by technology, new threats to civil association posed by technology and reform laws, and especially new threats to free speech. In part, this involves the attempt to regulate the Internet in a way that would destroy it. But the threat to free speech today primarily comes from politics and government.

Whereas the threat to free speech and association in the 1950s came from Joe McCarthy and anticommunism (a sort of ism or counter-ism in its own right), the threat in the 1990s has been from political correctness, left and right (sometimes a convergence of the two). The threat today is from a less aggressive but just as pernicious form of political conformity. Today, Americans are even told how to be patriotic.

Several times in the 1990s, the House of Representatives and the Senate have considered a constitutional amendment to outlaw flag burning. The amendment, no doubt, will be back. Forty-nine state legislatures already have taken action indicating their willingness to approve such an amendment when Congress sends it to them. The only thing that has stood in the way has been a few votes in the Senate. And that barricade may now be gone.

The movement to "defend the flag" by prohibiting protest speech follows two Supreme Court rulings (one in 1989 and another in 1990) that protected flag burning as a form of political expression—the one form of speech most clearly intended to be protected by the First Amendment in the Bill of Rights.

Rallying to the flag (as well as to religion) at the expense of what is symbolized is not a new phenomenon. In the 1950s the cross and the flag were used as props in the anticommunist movement.

A "god" float was included in the first Eisenhower inaugural parade. The president-elect composed and read his own prayer for the occasion (Billy Graham was not yet, fully, Billy Graham). In the same period the words "under God" were included in the Pledge of Allegiance to the flag.

Constitutional amendments were proposed in that era to declare the United States to be "a Christian nation." One amendment provided that non-Christians, such as Jews and others, be required to take an oath that was different in form and content, and presumably directed to a different deity, from that to be taken by Christians.

Dennis Chavez, senator from New Mexico at the time, was moved to challenge the abusive use of religion: He spoke on the Senate floor, defending both his Spanish forebears and his religion, declaring, "My ancestors brought the cross to America and you have made a club of it."

George Bush invoked both flag and God in his campaign of 1988. While George was asking the people to "read my lips," his wife reported that she and George knelt each night and prayed out loud—a clear discrimination between people and deity.

But when Bush made an issue of Michael Dukakis's action as governor on a "pledge of allegiance" issue, no rhetorical response comparable to that of Senator

Chavez's was elicited. It should have been challenged, at least, by the simple observation that the persons who seemed most ready to show the flag were automobile dealers (especially those selling Japanese cars); people running roadside stands, who in the South generally also display the Confederate flag; and people who have two or more homes, with the flag usually shown at the country or ocean or lakeside establishment. One seldom sees the flag flying Barbara Fritchie–like out of the windows of apartments on Fifth Avenue in New York, [though this certainly changed post 9/11–ed.] but they are everywhere in evidence in places like Southampton, Cape Cod, and other watering holes.

The flag "defenders" should be reminded that both flags and oaths are and have been respected and treated seriously in Western culture.

The traditional sanction of the oath was the deity. This, in times when taking the name of the Lord in vain was looked upon as a grievous fault.

The taking of an oath, to flag or deity, should be limited to important decisions and commitments and should be a matter of dignity and solemn affirmation. Children should not be conditioned to take an oath casually, nor should it be used as a device to establish order at the beginning of a school day.

It has been the tyrannies, the absolute monarchies, the totalitarian states, and the governments of those civilizations that are uncertain of themselves, and that exist in fear of collapse, that have made oath taking and recognition of signs and symbols a regular, rigid, and universal requirement. For example, in the Nazi period in Germany, each time a citizen met another on the street, he took an oath of allegiance, or declared his allegiance to Hitler and Nazism, with a sign and the words "Heil Hitler."

Respect for oath taking was strongly held by the Founding Fathers. The conservative Alexander Hamilton, for example, opposed the expurgator oath designed to root out the Tories in New York State. The oath, he said, "was to excite the scruples in the honest and conscientious and to hold out a bribe to perjury." "Nothing," he said, "can be more repugnant to the true genius of the common law than such inquisition into the conscience of men."

The members of the current Congress, in the tradition of Joe McCarthy, George Bush, and others, are again exploiting patriotism and loyalty, a matter far more serious than frivolous and unreflective oath taking. It is an action that does more than just erode the First Amendment. It is a frontal attack, running in the face of Tocqueville's assertion, and Jefferson's and George Mason's belief, that freedom of speech and of expression is the first and fundamental condition for establishing and maintaining a free society.

If one were to reach for rhetoric, approaching that used by Dennis Chavez in his defense of a religious symbol, the cross, one would charge that the advocates of this amendment are prepared to take the flag—the symbol of American freedom and specifically freedom of speech—and make a gag of it.

Beyond Thorstein Veblen
(Complexities and Contraries, 1982)

A few weeks ago, I met a young Saudi Arabian. Our talk (this was before the Afghanistan crisis) turned to oil, but not to production levels, prices, or possible invasion of the Middle East by either Russia or the United States in order to secure essential oil supplies. Rather, we spoke of ways and means of reducing the demand for Middle East oil, especially by the United States. The burden, the young man pointed out, is especially heavy for his country, because whenever other countries cut back production for any reason, the burden of making up the shortage falls on Saudi Arabia.

[...]

The young Saudi listed the following reasons why his country wanted to reduce its production and sales: the immediate effects of inflation, unnecessary and inadequately planned urbanization, the inflow of foreigners, corruption, maldistribution of wealth, social unrest. He noted also the long-range disadvantages of rapid and excessive oil production by his country: eventual exhaustion of supplies and unsound investment of oil revenues, with the possibility that such investments might be destroyed by inflation or by expropriation in the country in which they had been made. He preferred, he said, to have oil in the ground in Saudi Arabia rather than bank deposits in Switzerland, corporate stocks and bonds, or even real property like land in Iowa.

[...]

We continue to be the greatest consumers, if not the greatest overconsumers, in the history of the world. [...] Americans are overfed, overtransported, overfueled, overheated, overcooled, and overdefended. Some are overhoused. We are overpackaged and overadvertised, among other things. Conspicuous waste beyond the imagination of Thorstein Veblen has become a mark of American life.

This need not be the mark of our nation. America was not always an overconsuming and wasteful country. Well into the twentieth century, we were a frugal nation. Little fuel was used in agriculture. Horses were a major source of work-power, and they were sustained by the land on which they worked. Workers and their families lived near their work, in contrast with the situation today in which the average distance between home and work in the United States is estimated at fifteen miles.

There was some agricultural exploitation, but reasonable cycles of crop rotation with natural fertilization was the rule. Small-town living, and even city dwelling, did not allow for excessive waste. The six-pack, the throwaway bottle, and the plastic garbage bag had not yet been invented. Restraint during those years was not altogether a manifestation of virtue, although virtue was present. Necessity was a strong force.

Today, the force of necessity is, especially with reference to gasoline and oil, strong. The real test, however, is, one of virtue of the kind that John Adams called forth from the inhabitants of the American colonies in 1776 as a price of political freedom. "We must," said Adams, "change our habits, our prejudices, our palates, our taste in dress, furniture, equipage [it was horses and carriages then, it is automobiles today], architecture." He reassured the colonists that, if they did this, they could "live and be happy."

Editor's Note

Modern political parties are almost as old as the nation itself, with foundations in the political movements of the early nineteenth century. Over the past two centuries, the political parties have evolved to the point that, while they still retain certain independent core values, many of their basic philosophical tenets are common, more distinct shades of gray than black-and-white differences. In a world of "compassionate conservatives" and "fiscally responsible Democrats," the nomenclature for identifying political beliefs is unreliable. Furthermore, because of a breakdown in general civility, party denominations and their correlative titles (i.e., liberal or conservative) are often used as epithets to label (or more often mislabel) one's opponent, with little understanding of the essence of these identifiers. When Eugene McCarthy entered the House of Representatives, he was elected as a Democrat (actually on the Democratic Farmer Labor ticket in Minnesota). Through his career as representative, senator, and presidential candidate, he has been labeled not only a Democrat, but as a liberal as well (in fact, one recent book took him quite wrongly to task for the decline of American liberalism). However, a better label would be "man of conviction," for though McCarthy at times could be identified with a political label through some of his actions, his career was shaped by the ability to follow his inner compass and do what he deemed best and appropriate at the time. His writings on the failures of the two-party system and the essence of political philosophy are essential to understanding not only his career as a truly independent thinker, but also the identity crisis facing our political parties today.

Political Parties

THREE

The Banner Yet Waves
(A Liberal Answer to the Conservative Challenge, 1964)

In the years since the end of World War II, the decline if not the passing of liberalism has been noted and commented on by liberals, conservatives, and neutrals, in the press and on public platforms.

Immediately after the war, the commentaries were, for the most part, by friends of liberalism like Joseph C. Harsch who, in the September 1952 issue of *The Reporter*, suggested that time had run out on the liberals and they were in danger of becoming obsolete. About a year later, in the June 1953 issue of the same magazine, Eric Goldman called upon liberals to rethink their position and to do this "amid the shock of losing the old landmarks and more than a little hand-wringing defeatism."

Conservatism reportedly was rising in the meantime; after the second Eisenhower victory it was said to hold the high ground. Conservatives then asserted quite boldly that they had captured what they called the "American consensus," and were standing firmly astride the "authentic American center."

The warnings, the admonitions, and the suggestions of men like Harsch and Goldman were in order in 1952 and 1953. War, the passage of time, and the changes that had taken place during the war and were taking place in the postwar period called for new thought and new action. But the claims of conservatives as to their gains and positions of positive power were and are subject to serious question.

What liberals have been driven from the field? What kind of liberalism has been displaced?

Liberals come in many varieties. There are pure liberals, self-styled liberals, avowed liberals, and pseudoliberals—to give only the principal labels. There is the liberalism of the 19th century, the liberalism of John Dewey, the liberalism of Reinhold Niebuhr, the liberalism of the New Deal, the liberalism of Adlai Stevenson. There are those called liberals by William Buckley, conservative editor of the *National Review*, who do "not know how to think" in an "enormous area" and who are "inconsistent," "illogical," and "unable to assess evidence." There are the liberals feared by Russell Kirk, who are "rationalists" and lacking in "trust in Providence." Some of these, undoubtedly, have left the field of combat; some have retired, some have been left behind, some were rejected, some defeated—but not all.

The object [of my discussion] is to determine whether there is an authentic American liberalism today and to assess it as a force and power in American politics and life.

Bad Ideas Whose Time Keeps Coming (*Short Takes*)

"I believe in the two-party system." John Adams said that politics controlled by two strong factions, or parties, was the worst situation he could foresee for an effective government under the Constitution.

This task would be much easier if there were an established and clear definition of liberalism. In the absence of that, it might be well to forbid the use of the word "liberalism" as a noun and allow only the use of the adjective "liberal." Under this practice, no one could be simply a *liberal*; he would be a liberal something. Anyone who was called a liberal could demand an answer to the question, "A liberal what?" and insist that the adjective be associated with at least one substantive.

In religion one could not be simply a liberal, but would be a liberal Baptist, a liberal Anglican, a liberal Catholic, or a liberal of some other denomination. In politics he would be a liberal Republican, a liberal Democrat, or a liberal Vegetarian.

Debate without careful and adequate definition of terms may have at least two undesirable results. It may keep people from discussing basic issues because of lack of agreement over definition and it may prevent them from discussing serious practical problems which exist with or without definitions.

The current liberal-conservative debate has in some ways been distracting. It has resulted in name-calling and unwarranted attribution of characteristics. Liberals have been accused of being materialists—conservatives of believing in economic determinism; liberals of lacking faith—conservatives of having no trust in human reason; liberals of perpetuating and sharpening the class struggle—conservatives of advocating unlimited competition, the survival of the fittest as the dynamic of life and progress in society.

To say that liberalism is not what its critics say it is, or, at least, that they cannot prove it to be so, is to contribute little; neither would another definition of conservatism added to the many already offered by both conservatives and liberals be especially useful.

American liberalism is not a particular system of philosophy or of theology. It is not a school of political, economic, or social thought. It is not, as some claim, and as some charge, a "way of life." It is not a "demanding faith," as the Americans for Democratic Action assert, although it does make some demands on its adherents. It is not an "undemanding faith," as it has been described by Professor William Leuchtenburg of Harvard, nor is it without faith or without a "home for faith," as it has been said to be by Dr. Frederick Wilhelmsen of Santa Clara University.

What then is American liberalism?

Is it a purely practical response to current needs or pressures, or does it have a basis in ideas?

American liberalism of the second half of the 20th century is not simply a continuation of the liberalism of the 18th or of the 19th centuries. It retains some of the content, the ideals, and the goals of the New Deal, but these have been changed and adjusted to new conditions.

Threats to Democratic Government and Society
(Short Takes)

Democratic Government and Democratic Society are precarious institutions and must be carefully nurtured, sustained, and defended. American democracy, in major fields of politics, government, economics, and culture is threatened in greater or lesser degree, in {many} ways:

- Nonparticipation in the political process. The clearest indicator of this condition is in the statistics on voter participation in elections, especially those for national office, now hovering around 50 percent.
- Government control of politics, long present in state laws, protecting the established parties, and now also manifest in the Federal Elections Laws administered through the Federal Elections Commission
- Politics controlled and conducted by two strong, protected, and favored political parties or factions (a condition which John Adams foresaw as the worst of all political developments)
- Secret government such as C.I.A. Operations, which are exempted or escape constitutional or popular control
- Exemptions of citizens, in fact or in law, from military service and substituting for citizens' service a mercenary army (which may be called a voluntary army)
- Presidential wars, without popular or constitutional support (Vietnam)
- Excessive use of affirmative action, in the name of equality, which de Tocqueville saw as the basic ingredient of what he described as "they tyranny of the majority"
- Colonies or dependencies, in which different standards and values are accepted or imposed, a condition recognized as dangerous by Charles de Gaulle when he let Algeria go, rather than hold on to it and have it corrupt the democratic society of France. In our case, the place of colonies is taken by dependencies, such as the Philippines, Central and South American countries and migrants.
- Significant numbers of citizens who are exempted from helping pay the basic costs of government (In the United States about 40 percent of potential tax paying citizens pay no income tax.)
- Great disparity of income and wealth, especially when the relationship is frozen in place
- An excessive burden of debt, both private and public
- Inflation
- Persistent unemployment
- A two-tier society (rich and poor, participating and nonparticipating citizens, etc.)
- Government power, or potential power, to significantly affect and limit freedom of speech, to control news, education, cultural development (as in the FCC)
- Lack of respect for traditional rights, for "seniority" in property or jobs, which right de Tocqueville saw as the last defense against chaos and entropy in democratic society

Liberals have not abandoned problems of political economy (as Joseph Harsch suggested they do), for many such problems remain: the economic problems of the aging and of the unemployed, for example. At the same time liberals have in good measure responded in those other areas which Mr. Harsch suggested need attention—education,

The function of liberal Republicans is to shoot the wounded after battle.

for instance, and the defense of liberty in such areas as censorship, loyalty proceedings, security firings, picketing and assembly, and criminal proceedings relative to *habeas corpus*. They have not been unmindful of other things on Joseph Harsch's list: special problems of local or nonfederal corruption, exploitation, and injustice; efficient and fair administration of the law; and proper management of our resources.

The quantitative liberalism of the New Deal has persisted, but the qualitative liberalism asked for by Arthur Schlesinger, Jr. is also being demonstrated.

American liberalism has its roots in the ideas that underlie the Declaration of Independence and the Constitution. The ideas upon which 20th century liberalism is based are those of which G. K. Chesterton wrote after visiting the United States: "America is the only nation in the world that is founded on a creed. That creed is set forth with dogmatic and even theological lucidity in the Declaration of Independence; perhaps the only piece of practical politics that is also theoretical politics and also great literature." The creed, as stated in the Declaration, is this: " ... that all Men are created equal, that they are endowed by their Creator with certain unalienable Rights, that among these are Life, Liberty, and the Pursuit of Happiness—That to secure these Rights, Governments are instituted among Men, deriving their just Powers from the Consent of the Governed. ... "

We should add to this the classic statement of the purposes of government set forth in the Preamble to the Constitution: " ... to form a more perfect union, establish justice, insure domestic tranquility, provide for the common defence, promote the general welfare, and secure the blessings of liberty to ourselves and our posterity. ... " And add also the affirmation of belief in the dignity of man contained in the First Amendment and in other sections of the Bill of Rights.

The basic ideas or concepts are these: self-determination, equality, liberty, and the positive role of government. Of these four basic concepts the only one subject to serious debate is the last—that of the role of government. It is on this point that liberals and conservatives in the United States come closest to ideological or doctrinaire—as well as practical—disagreement. The other ideas are generally accepted by both liberals and conservatives.

We are today in the concluding phase of the controversy over equality. This is not the concluding phase of debate but of controversy, for the debate was settled long ago. The idea of equality as a moral, religious, and philosophical principle was given political substance in the Declaration of Independence. This document requires the acceptance of the idea that each man is by his nature equal in dignity to all other men and that, for this reason, he demands respect. Nothing accidental in individual men takes away this basic dignity: neither race, color, physical stature, nor cultural differences give anyone assured advantages in society or before the law.

The second basic idea is that of liberty. Liberty, too, is recognized and endorsed by both liberals and conservatives. Following this idea—or consistent with it, or arising from it—is the idea of limited government and the protection of areas of free choice and individual decision. In practice it is reflected in the continuing effort to strike a balance or reasonable compromise between individual liberty and the demands of the common good.

This is a historic area of conflict, an area in which lines cannot always be as clearly drawn as in dealing with equality. The liberty of one man may be the restraint of another. In the name of liberty restrictive actions are taken against some. In the name of liberty positive action to insure the exercise of free choice is often taken. In the name of liberty freedom of speech and of worship are claimed. In the name of liberty restrictive ordinances are passed and laws restraining and punishing criminals are justified.

The third basic idea is that of the right to life. This right is unchallenged in American politics, except in those cases when it is forfeited because of criminal actions.

The differences between American liberals and American conservatives are not over acceptance of these basic ideas or dedication to their realization. The differences are rather of application and of attitude.

There are two broad areas of political decision calling for attention and action in the U. S. today. One is the field of human rights, which involves the rights of our own people as well as those of people in other countries; the second is that of economic and social justice.

Basically, what is involved in social justice is production of goods adequate to meet the needs of people, and a system or method of ownership and of participation in production through which a claim to a share in the distribution is established.

> You really have to be careful of politicians who have no further ambitions: they may run for the presidency.

Paul Henri Spaak, the executive secretary of the North Atlantic Treaty Organization, summarized the full significance of these two obligations in addressing the North Atlantic Community Conference in September, 1957, when he said: "There can be no respect of persons if there is no political democracy and there can be no respect of persons without social justice, and only when we have carried this to its maximum, not only in our own countries but also in all places where we have undertaken political responsibilities, shall we find ourselves in a state of quiet conscience and moral peace which will allow us genuinely to take up the challenge of communism."

If the conservatives have a better response to this challenge, now is the time for them to demonstrate it in word and in action. It is not enough to declare for freedom, truth, and justice, or to declare even more vaguely for traditional values and against an inadequately defined "liberalism."

It is certain that the totality of contemporary thought and contemporary problems cannot be fully or adequately separated and classified under the terms "liberalism" and "conservatism." Yet it is under these banners—pale and tattered—that much of the debate in politics, economics, education, and art is being carried on. There is not enough time to change the flags. We must proceed, hoping that clarification and understanding may be reached along the way.

A Place for Liberals to Hide
(New Republic, June 13, 1983)

Liberals have been on the defensive in recent years, under attack from conservatives and other "liberals," for the most part self-defined. The first public challenge to my "liberalism" came in a debate appearance, several years ago, with William Rusher, then an editor of the *National Review*.

Mr. Rusher, the publisher of the magazine *National Review*, is a self-declared conservative. He is also precise about the definition and use of words. In the course of meeting with me, he repeatedly made the point that he and his ideological compatriots are not "neoconservatives," but that they belong rather to the "new right." Since I had made no attempt to categorize Mr. Rusher, I could not quite understand his anxiety about "neoconservatism," and anticipate that possibly he was going to make further distinctions, possibly with respect to "plio-conservatism" or even "mio-conservatism." As it turned out, Mr. Rusher seemed to have some objection to the linguistic impurity of mixing the Greek *neo* with the Latinate *conservative*, but this objection was moderate and almost incidental. The serious basis of his distinction was historical. "Neoconservatives," he said, lacked historical purity. The persons so labeled, either by themselves or by others, were former "liberals," he said, whereas the persons admitted to his group, the "new right," had always been "right," as distinct both from the "old right," which he did not define but implied might sometimes have been wrong, and from the "neoconservatives," who, in their previous incarnation as liberals, had never been "right." I was eager to let the whole matter pass as a quarrel among the various phyla of "conservatives," but then Mr. Rusher insisted on calling me a "liberal."

I objected, going back to an old contention of mine that the word *liberal* should never be used as a noun, only as an adjective. Thus, one may be a liberal Democrat or a liberal Republican, a liberal Catholic or a liberal Presbyterian, but never a pure "liberal." This was a posture I had taken up in the late 1950s, when "liberal," having just achieved status as a noun, was being festooned with derogatory prefixes. J. Edgar Hoover, in those days, was warning against what he called the "pseudo-liberals," William F. Buckley, Jr., was writing about the "illogical-liberals," and others spoke and wrote about the "egghead-liberals," the "crypto-liberals," and so on.

In the days and weeks following my encounter with Mr. Rusher, I began to notice that the word *liberal* was again being subjected to prefix transplant operations. The crucial term in this process first surfaced in the "liberal" press (especially *The Washington Monthly* and the *New Republic*), and then was picked up in the "conservative" press, beginning with an editorial in *The Wall Street Journal* entitled "The Neo-Libs." The *Journal*'s distinction paralleled one made in an earlier article in *The American Spectator*, in January 1982. That article referred to New York City's Mayor Edward Koch as "once a liberal purist." Obviously the author meant to label Koch as "once a pure liberal," in the old style. Strictly speaking, a "liberal purist" would be a purist who was rather loose in questions of purity, and thus would be too lax to practice what *The American Spectator* article referred to as "undiluted liberalism." In this article, Mr. Koch is also called "a liberal with sanity," or, one might say, a "sane liberal," as distinguished from, possibly, an "insane liberal."

Both *The American Spectator* and the *Journal* divided the "neoliberals" into two classes. One is made up of "traditional liberals" who were once what William Rusher would probably call "the old left" (comparable to the "old right" of his world), but have changed some. Yet they do not want to be called the "new left," as Rusher's associates gladly call themselves the "new right," partly because the old "new left," which scarcely exists anymore, used to be so disdainful of "liberals" of any type, but especially "bourgeois liberals." The other division of "neo-liberals," the Koch type, includes persons such as Senator Paul Tsongas of Massachusetts, who called himself a "new liberal" and a "revisionist liberal," and Senator Gary Hart of Colorado, who distinguished himself as a "pragmatic liberal." Both of these wings, I gather, are agreed on one point, namely, that they are different from "unreconstructed liberals."

In the midst of all of these fine tunings, I have concluded that for some time to come, the word *liberal* will be useless as a means of political communication and should be allowed to rest, pending rehabilitation.

What has happened to that good word is roughly comparable to what happened to the goat in history. From humble and useful beginnings, as a source of milk and meat, the goat gradually worked its way up through various orders of religious symbolism to the exalted position of scapegoat, bearing the sins of the tribe into the desert, or over the cliff. From there, the goat began a slow decline, and finally lost even its most ardent supporters, who began to question its powers, allowing it to attend only disreputable revels. The goat finally became the object of derision, eating garbage, used as the image for lewd old men, and blamed for the loss of baseball games.

The word *liberal* has not fallen quite so low. What began as a modest and useful adjective became a noun, the equivalent of deification. It can be saved, possibly even restored to good standing. But until it recovers, those who need a covering term might consider the name of a new group still in the early stages of organization. They are "the neos"—pure, simple, pristine, unmodified, in no historical or ideological context.

The rules of the new order are simple. First, its members must resist any attempt to attach any modifier, whether prefix or suffix, to the key word, *neo*. Second, they must be willing to cast off fixed ideas in politics, economics, and the social field in general every seven years. The seven-year period has been chosen for sound reasons. There is strong biblical support for the number seven. Pagan and Christian civilizations alike have recognized the power of seven. Physiologists say that the chemicals and other physical material of the human body change completely every seven years. Moreover, because seven is a prime number, the "neos" have a running start on survival. As in the case of the seventeen-year locust, the likelihood that natural predators will appear in dangerous numbers is scant. Because of this principle, the "neos" may propose one seven-year term for the president of the United States.

The only organized group that has applied for acceptance into the "neos" is the Pigeon-Kicking Society of America, which has only two members and has one rule of action—that to remain an active member, one must kick a pigeon once every seven years, or submit proof of having made a serious effort to do so.

Alternatives to the Major Parties
(*The Hard Years*, 1975)

Dissatisfaction with the two major parties is widespread in the United States. This dissatisfaction is not regional or sectional. It is not restricted to one economic or cultural group, but is based on frustration and disappointment which have a historical base.

In the case of the Republican party it began in 1964, when many liberal or moderate Republicans, believing that their position was not recognized or represented in the party's choice of Senator Barry Goldwater, refused to support his candidacy. The nomination of Richard Nixon in 1968 did not wholly allay their doubts about their party. [T]he Watergate affair and other scandals of the Nixon administration alienated conservative Republicans, as well as the liberals and the moderates. (It is distressing to hear some people say that the final outcome of Watergate proved that the system works. That is like saying that the crossing of the Atlantic by the *Titanic* was a great success because some people survived. Not all the lifeboats sank—just the ship.)

Many Democrats experienced frustration in 1968, when candidates and proposals of antiwar Democrats were rejected in Chicago and supporters of those candidates and proposals were beaten and abused in the convention hall, in the Conrad Hilton hotel, and on the streets of Chicago.

One of the slogans of the Goldwater campaign of 1964 was, "A choice, not an echo." A cynical observation on the 1968 campaign was, "Not a choice, but two echoes." Reflecting this unhappiness over the lack of choice, many people were involved in efforts to run a third or fourth candidate in 1968.

In 1972 many traditional Democrats were unhappy with the nomination of Senator George McGovern and with the conduct of his campaign. Many other voters were unhappy with both candidates, as was shown by the fact that the voter turnout was the lowest in over twenty years.

Yet there are real obstacles to a third party or independent campaign in the United States. First, party loyalty is still a real force in American politics. The older voters become, the more they have voted for one party, and the greater their commitment to that party is likely to be. Party activists and officials develop even stronger loyalties.

In addition to loyalty and commitment, there is a traditional argument for the two-party system. Throughout most of our history, political action has been centered in two major parties. The working of the two-party system has been a matter of some pride to us. We have been quick to assert that a two-party system makes democracy work, whereas a multiparty system, such as that used in some European countries, is not conducive to good democratic government.

The idea of two-party democracy has been accepted as the mark of political maturity and responsibility, to the point where a challenge to such a system is looked upon as almost heretical. Yet the system certainly shows signs of weakness today.

Party loyalty is declining. More and more persons, when asked to give their party designation, call themselves independents. Many others, who still call themselves either Democrats or Republicans, do not have the kind of loyalty that once marked party membership.

[...]

The theoretical argument for the two-party system is also subject to challenge. A two-party system may be a device that makes immature democracy work, but it is less necessary in a mature democracy; that is, one with more democratic procedures and a better-informed electorate. The two-party system can be defended only if the parties themselves are responsive to the needs of the country and if they give the people a choice on major issues affecting the country.

In fact, a coalition might result in better government. For example, had the choice of a President been thrown into the House of Representatives in 1968, the House might have made as good a choice as that made by the minority of voters who elected Richard Nixon. A formal and identifiable coalition in the House and Senate might work better than the floating coalitions which now mark the Congress.

Theoretical arguments aside, however, the fact is that the two-party tradition is not as strong in the United States as it has been made out to be. It has been challenged regularly through the years. In the election of 1796, for example, there were thirteen candidates for the presidency. Five were Federalists, three Democratic-Republicans, one Anti-Federalist, three Independent Federalists, and one Independent.

Most of the political contests during the early 1800s were among factions within the Democratic-Republican party. But Andrew Jackson and his policies in the 1830s stirred up criticism and brought about party opposition in what became the Whig coalition. This set the stage for the splinter-party movements that followed.

After 1840 there were splinter parties in almost every election. Most are remembered for lost causes such as free silver, greenbacks, and the single tax. But some are credited with developing important policy positions on such things as regulation of the railroads, opposition to monopolies, and establishment of price supports for agriculture.

In addition to their indirect influence, splinter parties have sometimes had more obvious and measurable success.

In 1848 Zachary Taylor, a Whig, won over Lewis Cass, a Democrat, while Martin Van Buren, running on the Free-Soil ticket, drew 10 per cent of the vote. Nine Free-Soilers were elected to the House of Representatives, and two were sent to the Senate. In the House, where neither the Whigs nor the Democrats held a majority, the Free-Soilers held the balance of power in the next Congress.

By 1856 the Free-Soil movement had disintegrated and a new third party— the Republican party—had been born. In that year James Buchanan, a Democrat with roughly 46 per cent of the vote, defeated John C. Fremont, a Republican who received 33 per cent, and also Millard Fillmore, who ran as the American-party (Know-Nothing) candidate and received 21 per cent of the vote.

The main issue of the Republicans was that of keeping slavery out of the territory then being opened for settlement. The Republican party included all-out abolitionists, Free-Soilers, Independent Democrats, Conscience Whigs, Know-Nothings, Barnburners, and Prohibitionists. But more important than the issues was the cultural cohesiveness of the party. The Republican party was then made up principally of "Yankees" in New England and in the northern half of the United States to the west, the population of which at that time consisted largely of those who had moved from the New England states.

In 1860, within ten years after it was founded, the Republican party, with roughly 40 per cent of the popular vote in a four-way contest, won enough electoral votes to make Abraham Lincoln President of the United States. This was quick success for the new party, which went on to dominate the politics of the Midwest until well into the twentieth century.

Other third-party or splinter-party movements were not as successful as the Republican party. Between 1872 and 1936, however, the splinter-party vote was a significant negative influence in presidential elections, particularly in the West. During those years, nearly all the Western and many Midwestern states were delicately balanced between the two major parties. As those states switched from side to side, they generally switched together and helped choose many Presidents.

Third parties have long been successful in electing members of the Congress. A high point of third-party representation was in the 1850s, when the American party (Know-Nothings) in one Congress had forty-three members of the House of Representatives. This was at a time when the total membership of the House was only two hundred and thirty-four. In the late 1890s the Populists, Fusionists, and Silverites together had at least twenty members of the House and seven members of the Senate.

The Republicans are like the lowest form of existence. They don't have much life or vitality at the height of their existence, but they never die.

The high point for third-party representation in the twentieth century was in 1937, when the Congress had sixteen members who were neither Republicans nor Democrats; they were a mixture of Progressives and Farmer-Laborites.

The record of third parties in presidential politics in the twentieth century is one of mixed success. The campaign of Theodore Roosevelt in 1912 was outside the usual context of a third-party movement; that is, it was not a real third-party effort. It was not regional. It was not based upon ideological differences within the Republican party, nor was it carried on as an educational program. It simply sought victory for Theodore Roosevelt. Woodrow Wilson was elected in 1912 with almost 42 per cent of the popular vote. But Teddy Roosevelt received 27 per cent of the vote, which was a higher percentage than the regular Republican candidate received in that year. Roosevelt was credited or blamed for the outcome of that election.

In 1924 Senator Robert M. La Follette, Sr., of Wisconsin ran as an independent candidate for President. Despite a late start and poor financing, he won almost 17 per cent of the popular vote.

Since the end of World War II [and prior to 1992], the only splinter parties to win electoral votes have been based in the South. In 1948 Strom Thurmond's States' Rights (or Dixiecrat) party received 2.4 per cent of the vote and thirty-nine electoral votes. In the same year, Henry Wallace, the candidate of the Progressive party, won about 2.4 per cent of the popular vote but no electoral votes. George Wallace, running in 1968 for the American Independent party, carried five Southern states, drew 13.5 per cent of the national popular vote, and won forty-six electoral votes. Wallace was strong enough to keep both Nixon and Humphrey from winning clear majorities in twenty-five states.

The discontent in the country could well manifest itself in a successful independent or third-party effort in the near future.

The alternative is to surrender the United States indefinitely to the Democrats and Republicans—to let them just take turns running the country. On the record, they have not done very well by the country in recent years.

The two-party system is not a matter of revelation. It was not written on the back of the tablets that Moses brought down from the mountain. It was not even recommended by the very wise, even inspired, men who drafted our Constitution. It does not have an unbroken tradition. So on all counts—revelation and wisdom and Constitution and experience—it is subject to rather serious challenge.

The Rules of Chaos:
Democrats, the Two-Party "System," Perot
(*No Fault Politics*, 1998)

The reform commission that remade the Democratic Party in 1972 was chaired by George McGovern, the eventual party nominee.

Since 1972 the *rules* of the Democratic Party, rather than issues or personalities, have determined who would be the party's nominee for the presidency. But whereas the rule changes for the 1972 and 1976 campaigns were formulated by the national party, the rules and procedures for the elections to follow (in 1980, 1984, 1988, and 1992) showed a progressive increase in the power of state parties, state legislatures, and governors over operations of the national party. There has been a decline especially in the influence of senators, representatives, and what once was the national party.

Candidates for the Democratic Party presidential nomination, following the two Stevenson defeats by Eisenhower, were drawn from the Senate: Kennedy-Johnson in 1960, Johnson-Humphrey in 1964, Humphrey-Muskie in 1968, and McGovern-Eagleton (until Eagleton was replaced by Sargent Shriver) in 1972.

Following the defeat of the McGovern ticket in 1972, state influence became progressively stronger. The committee in charge of rules for the 1976 nominating process and convention included Jimmy Carter. The rules adopted served the Carter presidential effort admirably. They eliminated the winner-take-all primaries, always the contests in which nationally known senators did well. The change assured Carter a share of primary delegates and left him free within the rules to garner delegates from nonprimary states, where state politicians had basic control. Carter won the nomination and picked a senator, Walter Mondale, as the vice presidential candidate, after looking over a list of applications from senators, including Edmund Muskie, Frank Church, Adlai Stevenson III, and others.

Mondale had made an early bid for support as a possible presidential candidate two years earlier, but had abandoned the effort. Again in 1980, Carter, after turning back a challenge from Sen. Edward Kennedy, picked Mondale for the nomination. Mondale picked not a senator but a House member, Geraldine Ferraro, for vice-president.

After that one interlude, the dominance of governors returned. Control or influence of governors and state legislatures, which had been growing following the adoption of the 1976 rules, was further strengthened by the organization in 1984 of the Democratic Leadership Council. The council's declared purpose, as stated by one of its founders, Sen. Sam Nunn of Georgia, was "to do everything we can to move the Democratic Party back into the mainstream of American political life." The council's initial membership of forty-two included eighteen House members, fourteen senators, and ten governors. It was dominated by Southern and Western office holders. Among the governors were Bruce Babbitt of Arizona, Bill Clinton of Arkansas, and Richard Riley of South Carolina.

In 1988 the dominance of governors was restored with the nomination of Gov. Michael Dukakis of Massachusetts. Again there was a nod to the Senate in the choice of Sen. Lloyd Bentsen, also a member of the Leadership Council, as the vice presidential candidate.

By 1992, through the work of the Democratic Leadership Council and others, the power of the state leaders and self-defined moderates was further enhanced, especially by changes in primary dates and laws. States moved to set primary dates early and to advance the dates of caucuses so as to get early attention for both political and financial reasons. Iowa and New Hampshire competed to be the first test.

New Hampshire, several times, has threatened to have its primary ahead of any other state, even if it meant setting the date in the year preceding the election. (New Hampshire in this competition made the mistake of moving its primary date to mid-February rather than having it in mid-March, its traditional date. March is a much better time for decision in New Hampshire. Frost heaves, reflecting thawing, have begun to show on the roads. The sap is rising in the maple trees. The Ides of March and the spring equinox approach.)

More effective and serious in its effect on the nominating process was the establishment, largely with support of the Democratic Leadership Council, of the Super Tuesday primaries, on March 10, 1988. On that day primaries were held in eleven states: Delaware, Florida, Hawaii, Louisiana, Massachusetts, Missouri, Mississippi, Oklahoma, Rhode Island, Tennessee, and Texas.

If a man was drowning twenty feet from shore a Republican would throw him a fifteen-foot rope and say, "Well, I went more than half way."

The early date and the number of primaries on that date, as well as the states in which they were held, gave special advantages to the candidates favored by the Democratic Leadership Council, which in 1992 favored Bill Clinton. Senators who ran in 1992 were pretty much on the outside looking in.

The "bonding" of governors is closer than that of senators. They may even have a slight inferiority complex relative to senators. Carter and Clinton both ran against Washington, including the record of Democratic Congresses.

More important, it is easier for incumbent governors to run and organize: to qualify for matching funds and to campaign without being subject to continuous charges that they are missing votes. It is easier for governors to run against Washington, even against Congresses controlled by their own party, than it is for senators and House members to do so. (Robert Dole tried running as Citizen Dole, after thirty years inside Washington, with virtually no success.)

Well, Bill Clinton was nominated in 1992, and Al Gore, who had as a senator made an unsuccessful bid for the presidential nomination in 1988, was chosen as Clinton's running mate, in a repeat of the 1976 procedure in which Carter, a governor, chose Senator Mondale as his running mate.

And the Democratic Leadership Council has or has had strong representation in the Clinton administration. Both Gore and Clinton were among the forty-two original members, as were Babbitt, subsequently secretary of the interior; Bentsen, later secretary of the Treasury; Riley, secretary of education; Tim Wirth, former senator from Colorado, now in the State Department; and Leon Panetta, former congressman, later White House chief of staff.

And since 1992 additional states have further altered their selection procedures, dates of primaries, and so on. This was, as a rule, done not to open up the political process but rather to give the respective states real or imagined advantages over other states in the process of selecting the presidential candidate. Arizona challenged New Hampshire with proposals for an earlier primary, as did Louisiana.

$$\bullet \quad \bullet \quad \bullet$$

What has been the net effect of these two influences—the Democratic Leadership Council and state and local politicians—upon the Democratic Party? They are almost obvious. By embracing a vaguely Republican form of moderate-ism the party has been able, at least in the short run, to co-opt the Republican national ticket (aided, it must be said, by aging and inarticulate ticket leaders who themselves were quite vague). But the sacrifice the party has made has been the loss of its soul.

The party can no longer articulate what principles it stands for; it cannot hold together congressional coalitions because it no longer has the principles with which to do this; it can no longer inspire the young; it can no longer lead the people toward ends that require selfishness and sacrifice. To co-opt or outmaneuver is different than to lead.

The Democratic Party no longer stands for work, social justice, an enlightened foreign policy. It is the party of lesser tax cuts, of lesser balanced budgets, of big government, but smaller, more efficient big government.

The Democratic Party is no longer a progressive party. And the nation needs a progressive party, just as it needs a conservative party.

It is fine to be in touch with "the mainstream" of the American people, but it is the special mission of the Democratic Party to be in touch with the people who are *not* a part of the bond markets, not members of PACs, not even members of labor unions—the millions of Americans who are frozen out of the politics and the economy of the nation. In some cases, they *are* the mainstream, or the silent majority.

A Democratic Party that can win but forgets the disenfranchised people of the country is a hollow party that wins hollow victories.

The impact of state legislators and governors has been to make the party more parochial and more narrow in vision. State government is largely administrative, and Bill Clinton, as governor of the United States, approaches the presidency as a series of administrative tasks and compromises.

State politicians also are more likely to be dominated by special interests—lobbyists, unions, special pleaders, local fixers, and the large corporations. Clinton brought to the White House the Little Rock mentality on fund-raising and presidential access to special interests.

What he did not bring was knowledge of Congress and the executive branch, which a governor does not get through his basically subservient dealings with the federal bureaucracy. The president, of course, now has that experience. But this is expensive on-the-job training, and the people who staffed the Clinton White House in the first term were also largely inexperienced in federal government. They too got experience, but *they* have now left the White House. Moreover, the Clinton staff has all along been largely based on the gubernatorial model—political and administrative personnel, but few Washington veterans who could be called wise men or long-range thinkers.

In the Clinton presidency, the dominance of governors and of so-called centrists in the Democratic Party is now firmly established. But this has made the party less clearly defined and less Democratic, while it has made the first popular Democratic presidency since Roosevelt and Truman more confused and less Democratic.

ELEANOR ROOSEVELT

On college campuses these days, I am often asked who my heroes are, or role models, or persons I respect. I am not sure about heroes, but Franklin Roosevelt was certainly the decisive political figure of my generation. And, as I have said, people with whom I served in Congress, like Sam Rayburn and Wayne Morse, Paul Douglas and Phil Hart, were people I respected.

Some of my teachers at St. John's University had a great impact on me, as did the life and legend of Thomas More and his book *Utopia*.

But there are two people who, it seems to me, personalize what the Democratic Party ought to be and once was. One is Eleanor Roosevelt; the other is Adlai Stevenson.

Eleanor Roosevelt entered the marketplace of action and controversy unwillingly. She never left it. She was also a commentator. Yet she always saw her accepted role as not to judge the world but to improve it. Mrs. Roosevelt had the qualities of tolerance and forgiveness, for she knew the capacity of men for confusion and misunderstanding. She never allowed her interest in humanity to distract her from interest in individual men and women.

Although she believed that the movement of history was toward a better life, she never allowed hopes or dreams of a better future to interfere with dedicated action and attention to the present. *Tomorrow Is Now* was the title of her last book.

Eleanor Roosevelt was a realist, ready to accept compromise, but only when principle was recognized and given the greater weight on the scales. She was prepared—when she could not be sure—to make mistakes in public policy on the side of trust rather than on the side of mistrust and suspicion, to err on the side of liberality and hope rather than on the side of narrow self-concern and fear. She was blessed, as were all who knew her, in that as she grew in age, she also grew in spiritual strength and wisdom.

In the 1950s, when truth was being driven from the field, when doubt was expanded, when suspicion and accusation held the high ground, when younger persons fled in fear, Eleanor Roosevelt stood firm.

One writer described her as "fine, precise, hand-worked like ivory." And like a figure carved in ivory, she became more beautiful with age. Eleanor Roosevelt reached that high state of serenity in which she moved and spoke and acted freely, without fear and without concern for the judgment of biographers or any judgment of the world.

ADLAI STEVENSON

When Adlai Stevenson died, we lost the purest politician of our time.

Stevenson's approach to politics was marked by three principal characteristics:

A decent respect for the opinions of mankind in world affairs

A willingness to accept the judgment of the majority in domestic politics and in general elections

The unselfish surrender of his own personal reputation and image for the good of the common effort if, in his judgment, that surrender would advance the cause of justice and order and civility.

Adlai Stevenson did not grow in honor and in reputation through the organizations he served, but rather they grew by virtue of his service.

He demonstrated early in his career, and throughout his public life, the highest degree of political humility in his indifference to what historians and biographers might say about him.

Stevenson was not ahead of his time or outside of his time, as some of his critics said. He was a true contemporary, passing judgment on his own day, expressing that judgment in words that proved his deep concern for the integrity of the language, and finally committing himself to the consequences of his judgment.

I would feel better about the future of the Democratic Party if I felt it was drawing its inspiration from the life and work of Adlai Stevenson, rather than from the playbook of Dick Morris.

In the words of Chaucer, Adlai Stevenson was a worthy knight who from the time he first rode forth "loved chivalry, truth and honor, generosity and courtesy."

THE TWO-PARTY SYSTEM: FORMULA FOR DISASTER

John Adams, as previously cited, in a commentary on the politics that might follow the adoption of the Constitution of the United States, stated his opinion that the worst possible development would be politics controlled by two strong factions.

We now have the very condition that Adams warned against. Today free and effective participation in the process of choosing a government, especially the president of the United States, is limited and controlled by two parties: the Republicans and the Democrats. Not only is effective participation in the political process denied to new parties and independent candidates, but recent restrictive laws and practices have had the effect of suppressing limited movements of protest or division within the two major parties.

The moves to control politics in the interest of the Republican and Democratic parties did not begin until early in this century. When the Republican Party was born in 1854 as a party of protest against the extension of slavery into territories, it combined various dissident Whigs, Free-Soilers, Anti-Slavery Democrats, and fringe groups, including Know-Nothings and Barnburners. In this century, following the success of Teddy Roosevelt and his Bull Moose Party in the 1912 campaign (in which Teddy ran ahead of the official Republican nominee), Republican Party initiatives were undertaken to restrict third-party activities.

In some states, laws were passed to limit the effectiveness of movements such as those of Populists, Progressives, and various socialistic, possibly communist, parties. The limited successes of Henry Wallace and of George Wallace in more recent elections resulted in the imposition of additional state restraints on any political action outside the two established parties.

Prior to the passage of the amendments to the Federal Election Campaign Act in 1975—amendments that, for the first time in our history, gave federal preferential status to the two established parties—laws protecting, advancing, and securing the two parties were largely actions of state legislatures, sustained by state, and occasionally federal, courts. The one exception was a federal law passed in the 1950s that outlawed the Communist Party in the United States, a law subsequently declared unconstitutional by the U.S. Supreme Court.

Republicans and Democrats usually found common ground in supporting legislation to give either or both protected status. The "two-party system" came to be accepted, not only as a condition to effective government in the United States but also as an article of public faith, accepted by politicians, professors, and the press.

Gerald Ford stated his faith, saying, "I believe in the two-party system." Marshall Field, a prominent newspaper publisher, expressed the faith of the press in a 1976 statement, declaring, "This is a two-party country," much as an editor of *Pravda* might have declared of the former Soviet Union: This is a one-party country. One might just as well say: This is a two-religion country. Freedom of religion would mean that the citizens could choose one established church or the other.

As a result of these laws, media support and propagation, and popular belief, third-party or new-party or independent candidacies have had little success in the United States in this century. The ultimate barrier to significant independent or third-party success is the generally prevailing rule of practice of the winner-take-all state electoral votes. Only Strom Thurmond and George Wallace, using the race issue as the basis of their campaigns, have won electoral votes as independent candidates. Ross Perot, although he received almost 20 percent of the popular vote in the 1992 presidential election, got no votes in the electoral college. He did come close to winning one electoral vote in the state of Maine, which allocates electoral votes on the basis of congressional districts combined with statewide results.

The state-imposed limitations on any independent or non-Democratic or non-Republican presidential candidate have been challenged with very little success in the past two decades. Any successes came largely as a result of court actions. Court decisions usually occur after the election is over and the damage has been done, as in the case involving Dr. Benjamin Spock and the People's Party. A court held that Spock had been wrongfully excluded from the presidential ballot in Hawaii.

In 1976 I ran as an independent candidate, principally to establish a basis for a second Supreme Court challenge to the constitutionality of the 1975–76 amendment to the federal election law, and also to challenge the exclusionary and discriminatory state laws and practice.

Our effort had little effect upon the federal law, but as a result of the campaign, election laws in eighteen states were altered or struck down by both state and federal courts. Three cases reached the Supreme Court. When we abandoned our ballot placement effort, my name was on the ballot in only thirty states. However, when John Anderson ran as an independent candidate for president in 1980, building on our '76 effort, he was able to get on the ballot in about thirty-five states.

[...]

THE PEROT PHENOMENON

Through 1997, the ongoing Perot campaign might have become a "movement." If it has, it runs quietly, either deep or shallow. Some pundits say it is dormant but will revive as the 2000 campaign comes on, and that when it does, it will be directed against President Clinton, Al Gore, and their administration, as in 1996. Others say it will be directed against Republicans. Most pundits say the Perot campaigns hurt George Bush and Bob Dole more than they hurt Clinton. Perhaps so.

Totem animals are the Democrats' donkey and the Republicans' elephant. The Perot movement, if it has become one and is searching for an animal symbol, might best choose the aardvark. The aardvark, according to naturalists, did not evolve from any other animal or previous state of being, and it is not evolving into something different. It is both genus and species. It is like the pig in some respects, like the anteater in others, although the aardvark eats only termites because it has no gizzard. It is somewhat like a rabbit and like a kangaroo. It is like a donkey, like an elephant, etc. But no animal is like the aardvark unless it is an aardvark.

As was the Perot movement of 1992, the aardvark is a kind of existential experience, not continuing anything from the past or moving or changing to become something different in the future.

Perot supporters or, better, followers in 1992 numbered about 20 million people. They were not a single-issue group, nor were they fanatics or "kooks" (with the usual exceptions). Their conventions and meetings had the look of Amway or Tupperware conventions. Overall they appeared to be better balanced than people one sees at Republican and Democratic conventions. Many of them are from a recently identified sociological group, the exurbanites: people living beyond the suburbs and beyond coherent legal and political structures. Perotistas apparently live beyond the reach of public transportation, water systems, and sewage, having their own wells and their own septic tanks (the ultimate symbol of independence) and served by volunteer fire departments and county policy.

What they have in common is the belief that the country is not being well governed by the Republican and Democratic politics. They are willing to cast votes that can, at most, communicate disaffection and the desire for some small measure of nobility in politics.

Given recent history, Perot has had easy pickings for his critical observations, and it appears that the second Clinton administration will not leave him without targets.

The Perot campaigns have shown that on occasion a person of wealth is willing to spend a good part of his fortune (in the spirit of which Jefferson wrote the Declaration pledge of "lives, fortunes, and sacred honor") for the common good. Perot's willingness to put his fortune on the line has been a positive thing. The campaigns also have shown how ridiculous the campaign laws of the country are. Most important, the two Perot drives have given vent to voter frustration and reinvolved millions of citizens who had given up on politics.

The Perot movement may encourage citizens not only to examine the substance of government but also to examine the election laws and procedures, so that effective political challenges can be made not only by outsiders of great wealth but also by ordinary citizens and citizens' groups. That is what the rights to free speech and assembly in the Bill of Rights are really all about-the right to take part, especially for the dispossessed.

As Perot would say, "It's as simple as that."

• • •

State and federal election laws are not the only obstacles independent and third-party candidates face. Of a different origin, but just as serious as exclusion from the ballot, is the exclusion from coverage by the media, especially from television. The media's position against third or outside-party candidates has been shown also in dealing with candidates of the two major parties if they show signs of weakness.

Shortly before the election of November 1964, President Johnson announced that he was going to give a major address. In fact, it was not much of an address, and the television networks gave some thought to covering it simply as a news story. When Johnson learned this, he let it be known that he was unhappy. He wanted the speech broadcast live. The networks carried the speech live. Sen. Barry Goldwater and the Republicans asked for equal time, but their request was turned down by the courts, including the Supreme Court.

Twelve years later, in 1976, shortly before the election of that year, President Ford announced a news conference. Most broadcasters treated the Ford appearance as an unimportant event. None carried it live. News polls at the time indicated that Carter was likely to win. The media were not eager to give time to a candidate who was likely to lose. This was called the "nearness doctrine" by one network spokesman who thought defeat was near for Ford. Better nearness than fairness.

In the 1992 campaign, the Republican Party's nominating process rendered ineffective the David Duke effort to be included among that party's candidates, but Pat Buchanan was admitted, after proposals to exclude him by legal action were abandoned.

In 1992 the Democratic Party excluded from party notice all but five candidates. Only the chosen five were included in party-sponsored debates, and the exclusion was honored by the television networks, including Public Broadcasting. The combined thrust of the legal and other actions taken by the two major parties—and supported by the Federal Communications Commission, and the media, generally, and especially those elements of it that profit from having television and radio licenses—is that there shall be only two parties, and also that within those two parties, dissent shall be discouraged.

Candidates planning to become involved, as either independent or third-party candidates, or even as modest dissenters in either of the two established parties, would do well to look to the record of the two parties' officials, of the Federal Elections Commission, of the Federal Communications Commission, of the courts, and of the media.

[…]

RETURN TO CHICAGO

The choice of Chicago as the site of the 1996 Democratic Party convention was a surprising one, unless the president and leaders of the party, for reasons as not yet evident, felt the need for the kind of protective security that only an experienced Chicago police force and the Illinois National Guard could provide.

In the past half century, the Democratic Party has faced two important moral-political challenges. The first was that of civil rights, the focus of the 1948 convention, in Philadelphia. At that time, the party acknowledged its responsibility to take political action following the example of the Supreme Court in 1944, first because of the importance of the matter, but also because the Democratic Party, especially in its southern components, had, with some aid from Republicans, exploited racial differences and divisions.

For the Democrats to raise civil rights was high risk. The choice promised to be divisive, if not disastrous. But the party took the moral high road.

The results were divisive but not disastrous. The convention approved a civil rights plank. The Dixiecrats walked out and ran their own candidate. Truman was nominated and then elected in the November election of 1948.

In 1968 the Democratic Party faced a comparable political and moral challenge: the Vietnam War.

The issue was not as deeply divisive as the civil rights issue of 1948, nor did it promise to be disastrous to the party if the antiwar position carried the day. The heart of the conflict in Chicago was over whether the party would ratify a war to which the country had been committed in its enlarged state by the Johnson administration; this, despite what seemed to be a pledge to avoid such a commitment made by candidate Johnson in the 1964 campaign for the presidency. Johnson had promised not to expand the war.

The Johnson administration was firmly set on having the party accept, and thus share, guilt for the war. In the most controlled, violent, and undemocratic convention in the history of the country, the prowar position was endorsed.

Those of us who opposed the war expected that delegates we had won, or deserved to have won by every reasonable standard, would be accepted; that a reasonable debate would be conducted; and that a plank reflecting the differences existing among the delegates would be accepted. It was not to be so.

The unit rule, under which a majority of a state delegation or a state party was allowed to control the entire delegation, was supposed to be abolished in 1968. It was not. Those in control of the convention put off that change until 1972. Delegates who had been chosen two to four years before the convention, long before the Vietnam War had even become an issue, were seated and did the administration's bidding. Their credentials were challenged but without success.

The administration and the party officials controlling the convention did not limit their defenses and offenses to party rules and procedures. The approaches to the convention hall were protected by coils of barbed wire. The Chicago police were present in great numbers. The police were joined by the state National Guard, courtesy of then Gov. Otto Kerner. They were equipped with guns and a "crowd container," consisting of a frame of barbed wire mounted on the front of a jeep or other military vehicle.

We learned after the convention that there had been a third line of offense: the U.S. Army Reserves. They had been put on partial alert to move into action if the Chicago police and the Illinois National Guard proved inadequate.

The surveillance and control preparations went beyond these more or less open demonstrations of force.

When I moved into my suite of rooms in the Hilton Hotel, the Secret Service, which proved itself wholly loyal to its code of professionalism and honor, told me that I had their word that my rooms were not bugged and that we could speak freely within those confines, but they warned that they could not say the same for the telephones, which they said were tapped. They warned us not to say anything on the telephones that we wished to keep private.

In later congressional hearings, it was acknowledged that army intelligence, indeed, had tapped our phone lines.

The saddest and most incredible occurrence of the convention was that of the evening of August 28, following the vote nominating Hubert Humphrey. One would have expected that with the pro-administration position sustained and their candidate nominated, the Johnson forces would have been somewhat satisfied. Not so. Beatings of students and others among my supporters took place on the sidewalks and streets outside the Hilton Hotel and in Grant Park, across Michigan Avenue. Dr. William Davidson and my brother Austin, also a surgeon, set up an emergency hospital on the fifteenth floor of Hilton Hotel.

This was not the last act of violence perpetrated by the police. We spent Thursday cleaning up our campaign headquarters and preparing to leave on Friday. Sometime between 3 and 4 A.M., as nearly as we could mark, the police, aided by hotel employees, raided our rooms and working space on the fifteenth floor. Some fifteen or twenty police officers burst out of the elevators into the fifteenth-floor lobby. They proceeded to round up people in the lobby and then to open bedroom doors, get people out of bed, force them to join others in the lobby, and then to conduct all of them downstairs into the main lobby, where, ringed by police, they were forced to sit on the floor like prisoners of war.

One girl, near hysteria, told me that she had been playing bridge, and holding a 21-point hand, when the police broke up the game.

When, having learned of the raid, I reached the lobby, I asked who was in charge. No one stepped forward. I directed the captives to rise and return to their rooms on the fifteenth floor. The police left the hotel.

My last warning from the Secret Service was that as soon as I left Chicago, planned for Friday, the Daley police intended to arrest anyone found in the city having any identification with my campaign. I delayed my departure to Saturday after advising—actually warning—all supporters to leave Chicago or at least to find some space, such as the airport, which was beyond Mayor Daley's jurisdiction. As our chartered American Airlines plane flew out of Midway Airport, the pilot came on the public address system and said, "We are now leaving Prague."

Years later, I was sent an album put together by someone who had been at the convention, showing, on opposite pages, scenes from Prague and from Chicago, 1968. The differences were marginal: military uniforms rather than those of police, tanks instead of crowd containers, gun smoke instead of tear gas.

Apparently, these events were supposed to be wiped from memory, or from consideration, by the Democrats returning to the Chicago scene in 1996, and sealed or supplemented by having the current mayor of Chicago, a son of the Richard Daley of 1968, and Tom Hayden, a protester in Chicago (but not a campaign worker), plant a tree.

If the Democrats were seeking a former convention site that would remind the party of past acts of political courage and credit, they should have gone to Philadelphia and recalled the work of that convention, rather than to Chicago, the scene of the quasi-fascist convention of 1968.

The Two-Party System
(*Minnesota Law and Politics*, April/May 2004)

In 1780, John Adams, anticipating what kind of politics might develop in the new American republic, warned of the dangers of "two party" politics. "There is," he said, "nothing I dread so much as a division of the republic into two great parties, each arranged under its leader and converting issues in opposition to each other. This, in my humble apprehension, is to be dreaded as the greatest political issue."

This year (2003), in the midst of much criticism of the two main parties, Professor Lisa Ditsch of the University of Minnesota has written a book entitled, *The Tyranny of the Two-Party System*. Her attack on the two-party system is frontal. She challenges the labeling of the Republican and Democratic parties as parties, and also their claims of having governed the country successfully.

The two-party system, she points out, has become more than a thing. She challenges its status as something we can invoke casually and dare not challenge. It is in fact, she says, "no more than a name for a feature of our reality," when, in fact, "It forms the very fields to which it only refers," and thereby escapes critical examination and review and becomes a covering word for a complex of "alleged" facts regarding the inevitability of third-party failure (and the wastefulness and futility of third-party votes) and about the superior accountability and stability of two-party democracies.

In the roughly sixty years since the end of World War II, the two-party democracies have not proved to be more stable and more effective than established multiple-party democracies. The two dominant U.S. parties, Democratic and Republican, have survived because of protective Federal and state laws and Constitutional fixed terms. Only two presidents of the last eight elected have served the eight years allowed under the Constitution.

The record of the governments produced by two party politics has been less than inspiring. Both parties gave continuing and irresponsible support to the anti-Communism of the nineteen fifties, competing with each other to establish which could be more extreme. Both gave continuing support to the Vietnam War—first through Truman in aiding the French; then through Eisenhower in sending advisors; then through Kennedy in sending special troops to protect the advisors; then through Johnson in sending over five hundred thousand combat troops; then through Nixon who extended the War into Cambodia. Both parties took turns under the two-party system in controlling the government in the years following World War II, during which time the United States went from being the most trusted and appreciated nation in the world to being the target of terrorists and the object of hatred on every continent except Australia, New Zealand, and North America.

Both of the protected parties share responsibility for failure in unsuccessful wars in Cuba, Vietnam, and Cambodia, and for lesser wars, incursions, and engagements in South America, the Middle East, South Eastern Asia, and Africa. And the domestic record of the governments produced by two-party politics is not much better. It includes such things as the savings and loan scandal, the stock market and corporate financial scandals, and a national debt that is out of control and eroding the future financial stability of our nation.

Both parties supported provisions in the Federal Election Reform Act of nineteen seventy-five, which opened the way to making corporate PACs a major source of campaign funds, and corporations the dominant force in the creation of public policy.

Of more serious consequence, in the long run, is their opening the way, and aiding the growth of military power over non-military power in both domestic and foreign affairs. DeTocqueville, in his book on American democracy written 175 years ago, warned that in a democracy a military establishment too large to meet current military needs would become "a little nation apart." He predicted that it would have its own political, cultural, economic, educational, and other institutions, comparable to and competing with similar institutions in civil society.

In his farewell address in 1960, retiring President Eisenhower warned us that the changes DeTocqueville had warned of had already occurred. "In the counsels of government" he said, "we must guard against the acquisition of unwarranted influence, whether sought or unsought by the military-industrial complex. We must never let the weight of this combination endanger our liberties or democratic processes."

The military establishment did not fade away after WWII, as it did after WWI. It expanded its operations in both the military and non-military affairs of the country. The Secretary of Defense at various times assured us that we were prepared to fight three kinds of war—nuclear, conventional, and guerrilla—and "fight two wars like that in Vietnam and still have butter." Military missions to foreign countries became quasi-diplomatic. Schools supported by the military duplicated civilian schools. Military grants for research and study became more common. A structure for the handling of educational programs developed within the military establishment. Medical and hospital services developed. New G.I. insurance programs were introduced. The Corps of Army Engineers took new duties. The retail service of the PX grew until at one point, only Sears & Roebuck alone among retail establishments was larger.

Despite this record, the two-party system is still invoked as the keystone of U.S. politics. Newspaper editors, like Marshall Field, defend it with editorial certainty, declaring that the United States is a "two-party country," as the editor of *Pravda* might have declared that the Russia of times past was a one-party country. Gerald Ford, when President of the country, said that he believed in the two-party system when he signed the 1975 Federal Election Campaign Act, which he said he thought was unconstitutional, giving the "two-party system" standing above the Constitution.

In 1975–76, the League of Women voters gave up its vow of non-partisanship in order to give exclusive TV coverage to Republican and Democratic Presidential candidates, and thereby risk its non-political virginity, by affirming its belief in the "two-party system." Seven out of eight Supreme Court Justices made their

Extract from 2004 interview:

McCarthy: In my judgment it doesn't make much difference what you do while trying to reform politics as long as the two-party system is there, standing above and apart from the Constitution. One of the claims they make for the two-party system is that it works, and yet it hasn't worked in the last fifty years. We had the two-party system and they allowed Joe McCarthy to run. Both the Republicans and Democrats supported him. They tried to outdo each other and then the two-party system started the Vietnam War. Both sides took turns. The two-party system, in part, went into Cambodia. The two-party system allowed the economy to get into the shape it's in. Both parties are responsible and we've actually lost four or five wars in the last fifty years between the two-party system, one party or the other. Even the current war in progress [in Iraq]: again, both parties are for it.

declaration of belief in the "two-party system," as in a kind of Thomas More act of faith, justification for their approval of the 1975–76 Federal Election amendments presented to them in the *Buckley vs. Valeo* legal case. The Court by its action established the first federal two-party system, thus demonstrating the operation of Parkinson's Law that institutions that are failing naturally seek to prolong their lives and make up for failure and weaknesses by seeking legislative props.

More and more military men and women appear in corporate offices. The former army chief of staff appears as Secretary of State and a former corporate officer and congressman as Secretary of Defense. Language and title changes are not over-looked. World War II was fought under the direction of the War Department. To the surprise of many, both in the military and out of it, the department emerged in the Appropriation Bill of 1947 as the Department of Defense. Why the name of the department was changed, and by whom, was never explained. We now declare, not "war" but "national defense," either in Grenada or Iraq. We conduct incursions rather than invasions.

The independence of the military from civil control was further advanced when the two party government allowed the draft law to expire during the Nixon administration, and a voluntary-mercenary system for gathering military personnel to come into play. The danger DeTocqueville foresaw in a large standing army was that as the military became less democratic, it could become less reflective of the general population, more isolated from it, and more ready for war. He predicted that the military would be drawn from the poorer and less educated in society and that what he called "the elite" would avoid military service. With the War Department now called the Defense Department, a military officer seeking funds need only ask for money to be used for defense (of which there can never be enough) and not have to mention or respond to questions about war, real or potential.

There is no limit to what a country might spend on defense. Like the animal in Kafka's "Burrow," if we listen we can always hear a scratching sound.

The military establishment has not left anything to chance. In 1965 the army contracted with Douglas Aircraft for a study called "Pax Americana" to determine what might be necessary to impose an American peace on the world.

Then the drive for standardization and unification that came with the secretariat of Robert McNamara was accepted despite the fact that he had, as president of Ford Motors, failed in his

> Lobbyists really are men of revolutionary background—they are careful to see that no one who is taxed is unrepresented.

attempt to make the Edsel the "everyman's car" of America. As Secretary of Defense he had tried unsuccessfully to get the three branches of the armed services to adopt the TFX fighter air plane, and to have the Marine Band absorbed into the Army band complex. He failed in a final effort at unification, which may still be waiting in the files or on a computer somewhere, namely to have a single religion for everyone in the armed services, thus eliminating the need for separate ministers, priests, and rabbis. It was projected that persons leaving military service could go back to their pre-military religions, or take their military religions with them, along with their fatigues.

There is little evidence that the two-party system has dealt very successfully with either the Israel-Palestinian conflict or the Iraq war.

The crowning failure of the two party governments is that they have not produced a presidential election process that did not leave the nation dependent in its choice of a president on the 5 votes of politicized Supreme Court Justices and a Florida winner-take-all law, weighted by the votes of Cuban refugees and the votes of refugees from New York state tax laws.

Editor's Note

Among the many unique facets of American democracy, two stand particularly tall: the idea of a peaceful transfer of power among and between candidates and parties at a regular interval, and the separation of our government into independent, and yet co-dependent, branches. Having served in the legislative branch for over twenty years and having run for president several times, Eugene McCarthy brings a unique perspective to understanding our political institutions and the electoral process that fills such institutions. Like so much in American societies, both of these facets have changed dramatically in the past fifty years: the barriers contemplated by the founders between the institutions have become less apparent (including a politicized judiciary and legislative activity undertaken by the executive branch) and campaigning now increasingly acts as a drain on time actually spent governing and is controlled to a large extent by the media and large donors. McCarthy's writings on these topics urge us to reexamine not only the role of these institutions and processes, but how they might better serve American democracy and society.

FOUR

The President, Congress, and Elections

Standards and Guides for Picking Presidential Candidates
(Adapted from New Republic, February 22, 1988)

Until 1960, the presidential selection process was reasonably structured, if not standardized. Party rules were generally consistent from one election to another and seldom changed. Radio and the written word were the principal means for communicating political ideas and the views of the candidates.

Two changes occurred in the 1960 campaign that altered the politics of future campaigns. John Kennedy's victories in primaries established the base upon which he secured the nomination, and his acknowledged success over Richard Nixon in the televised debate of that year established television as a major instrument and force in presidential politics. In subsequent campaigns, primaries have taken on new importance and have proliferated. More money is spent on television than on any other means of political communication.

In consequence, the selection of presidential candidates and the election of a president have come to be based, or at least strongly influenced by, considerations other than basic qualifications for the office. Primaries enable candidates to circumvent or overcome party controls. Television emphasizes the importance of criteria such as a candidate's appearance and projection of personality. Makeup persons become as important as speech writers, while the presidential selection process moves closer to a state of entropy: disorder, randomness, and chaos.

Since there is little evidence that the procedures are likely to become more orderly or rational before the next presidential election, it is important that individual voters simplify the process for themselves, establishing standards that may reduce the limits of chaos. Here are some suggestions that may be helpful. Persons in the following categories should be automatically, or categorically, rejected.

1. Governors or former governors, unless they have had experience with the federal government, either before or after their governorships. Governors in the presidency are overconfident. They are inclined to believe that they can balance the federal budget if they have balanced a state budget; that they can handle the Pentagon because they have sent out the National Guard to suppress student protest or control a strike; that they understand federal bureaucracies, such as the Internal Revenue Service, because they have reorganized a state highway department.

2. Vice presidents or former vice presidents. First, because they are too often put

on the ticket for political reasons, rather than for their potential to be president. Second, because of the validity of the observation made by Senator Paul Laxalt while he was still a candidate for the Republican presidential nomination, that the office is likely to weaken and confuse character. Both government and politics would be well served if the vice presidency were eliminated, a proposition that was given serious thought in 1803.

3. Ministers, sons and daughters of clergymen, and even persons who let themselves be called "leading lay persons." Religious judgment and commitment is fundamentally different from that of the political-secular order. The medieval distinction between the First Estate (religious) and the Second and Third Estates (both secular and civil) was a useful one, anticipating Oswald Spengler's observation that in any society the basic struggle is between only two estates, the religious and the civil.

4. Generals and admirals, for obvious reasons: the differences in authority, command, and the use of power in the military from that exercised in civil democratic order.

5. Heads of major corporations, "CEOs," as they are generally identified, whose experience of power and its uses is essentially feudal rather than democratic. This is especially true of former heads of major automobile companies.

An early checkpoint for judging candidates is their announcement of candidacy.

1. A voter should be highly skeptical of any candidate who makes his or her announcement in February. If a candidate does, it is fair to assume that the decision was made in that month, or that the candidate is unaware of the danger of making decisions in February, a time that throughout history has been considered a bad time for decisions. Ancient civilizations reserved that month for worship of the dead and the gods of the underworld.

2. Be wary of announcements that include a spouse and children, having them present on the platform or mountainside, or, in the worst case, with the family dog.

3. Caution is advised if a candidate claims to represent a generation or special demographic/sociological group, such as the "war generation" or the "baby boomers." A candidate might claim a right to govern on the basis of having been conceived during the great blackout of New York City, approximately a generation ago.

4. Question a candidate if he or she publicizes medical reports (unless the candidate is suffering from a physical or psychological disorder that might immediately or seriously affect service in the presidential office). Jimmy Carter's statement in 1976 that he was allergic to beer, cheese, and mold, and that he sometimes suffered from hemorrhoids, was a case of unnecessary if not indecent exposure, as was Walter Mondale's revelation that same year that he had a hernia.

5. A candidate is suspect if it is stated that he or she has wanted the presidency very much and from an early age—say, twelve or eighteen years. Anyone under fifty is suspect, especially since one should be "willing" to be president, rather than "want" it.

Voters should also look for more subtle signs of demagoguery, which may be part of a candidate's past or may emerge during the presidential campaign. There are at least five such signs that are worthy of attention.

1. Does the candidate reserve the first seats in the second-class section of an airplane, thus being in position to greet and be seen by the tourist or second-class passengers on boarding but also to slip through the curtain to work the first-class section and even be invited by airline personnel to move up?
2. Does the candidate now—or has he in a past campaign—call himself, for example, William (Bill) or Robert (Bob) or Patrick/Patricia (Pat)? Or does the candidate, known previously as John III or IV, drop the III or IV for the campaign, thus in effect repudiating father, grandfather, and possibly great grandfather?
3. Is the candidate so heavily into physical fitness (e.g., jogging) that he reports his time for the mile or two-mile run, or for longer distances? In the presidential campaign, does the candidate walk or bicycle across a state? These actions are marginally acceptable in campaigns for governor, but not for the presidency or even the Senate.
4. Does the candidate cry easily and often in public? What brings on the crying? Does the candidate cry out of the inner corner of the eye, the outer, or straight down the center of the lower lid, as Bette Davis did? Or do the eyes just well up? These distinctions should be observed.
5. Does the candidate take credit for—or has he or she been credited with strength of character because of—a primitive experience, without protesting such attribution? Jimmy Carter was given a high mark by *Newsweek* in 1976 because he had used an outdoor toilet, and Senator Muskie had his character formed and strengthened early in life because he was bathed in a washtub. I have had both of these experiences without realizing what they have done for my character.

There is a final set of candidates' attributes, claims, and experiences that deserves some weighing by prospective voters, and it involves more subtle physical, psychological, and political distinctions.

The first, and possibly most important, is represented by the generally approving statement "He (or she) knows the numbers," a reputation carried by Robert McNamara and David Stockman. Second, offered as a credit as well, is the statement that "He (or she) makes no small mistakes," also an achievement attributed to Robert McNamara. The danger in both of the above statements is that potential critics, so taken by the numbers known, fail to consider the significance of what is being numbered, or are so intent on watching for small mistakes that the big mistakes are likely to go unchallenged and unnoticed until too late. Third is that a candidate should not have survived on artificially supplied oxygen for long periods of time, either in outer space or in a submarine, or possibly as a mountain climber or a scuba diver. Fourth is speed reading. President Carter reportedly took it up while he was president and reported at one point that his retention rate had improved by 50 percent. He did not report the base from which the improvement had taken place or what was not retained. As a rule, what can be read quickly should not be of much concern to a president, and what should be of concern should not be speed read, considering the possibility of limited retention. Fifth is that a presidential candidate should be checked to determine whether he or she knows the difference in the techniques used to drive cattle and hogs. A cattle drive is started very slowly, best accompanied by gentle singing (e.g., "Get along, little dogies"). But once the herd is started, the pace is slowly and subtly increased; as they approach the stockyard or corral, the cattle are all but stampeded and given no time for thought. This was the favorite, near-exclusive technique used by President Johnson, and it was especially evident in his handling of the Vietnam War.

Generally recognized as more intelligent than cows, hogs must be panicked into motion. They must be yelled at in Latin (*"Sui, sui"*). Once hogs are started, they must be allowed to slow down gradually so that they arrive at the desired point at a slow walk, and are moved to think they knew where they were going all the time. As a rule, the House of Representatives should be subjected to the cattle technique, and the Senate to the hog-driving method.

If all of this is too much, the potential voter can follow the more cynical rules for political participation and (1) pay no attention to what a candidate is or has been; (2) pay no attention to what a candidate says he or she will do if it is something that cannot be done (e.g., "making the mountain come to Mohammed"); (3) pay no attention to what a candidate says he or she will not do, if it is something that he or she couldn't do in any case, as when King Canute said, "I will not turn back the tide"; (4) pay little attention to what the candidates say they will do, if they could do it, unless the matter is of great importance; and (5) look especially to what a candidate says he or she will not do if it is something he or she could do (and might do), and is something the voter considers important. Application of this rule would have warranted a vote for Richard Nixon in 1968, if one believed that recognition of China was of paramount importance, and a vote for Ronald Reagan in 1980, if one believed that reductions in nuclear arms, together with a partial nuclear disarmament of Europe, was the pressing issue of the eighties.

And if the voter is in despair, or near it, he or she might follow the advice of the man in the gold breastplate under the old stone cross, as reported by William Butler Yeats:

Stay at home and drink your beer
And let your neighbor vote.

How Not to Make a President (Or an Administration)
(No Fault Politics, 1998)

Suggestions for reforming the election process are mostly doomed to failure, since basically what is called for is responsible decision making on the part of the electorate, sustained and assisted by a creditable press.

Both are getting harder to hope for.

Meanwhile, we are inundated every four years with proposals to reform American politics. In 1997 the postelection guilt of 1996 caused politicians of all stripes to promise campaign reform and the press to promise to somehow make itself grow up in time for the campaign of 2000.

Some procedural changes may be necessary as a matter of self-defense against more ambitious reforms. Other minor changes might do some minimal good, clearing the way to responsible decision making. There are at least five such changes that would be useful and easily achieved. They could be effected without seriously interfering with freedom of speech or assembly—the two basic constitutional rights that bear on political choice in the United States.

The office of vice president should be abolished. Provisions for replacing a president in an orderly, rational, and prompt way could be applied, similar to the procedures outlined in the constitutional amendment on presidential disability. They worked well enough when Gerald Ford was chosen to replace Spiro Agnew, following Agnew's resignation.

There are at least three good reasons for abolishing the office of vice president. First, having a vice president on the ticket clutters the election campaign, offering the voters an apparent choice when in fact only the presidential

Words and Phrases That Should Be Banned from the White House (Short Takes)

1. The bottom line
2. Competitiveness as in "managed"
3. A business government (as in Savings and Loans)
4. The work ethic (Usually used with the adjective "Protestant." Catholics have one too, and it's just as bad.)
5. In the national interest.
6. Free trade (the American Revolution was a protectionist movement. Jefferson urged the people of the United States to "buy American" even if it cost them more to do so.)
7. Protectionism and the Smoot-Hawley Tariff of 1930—for the same reason given in number 6.
8. Reform: and almost anything beginning with "re," according to an old new deal Congressman, who in advice to post–World War II congresspersons advised against votes for re-organization, re-codifications, resolutions reforms, and Republicans.
9. The peace increment. We have been waiting for it since 1945.
10. Conventional war and conventional weapons; neither exists.

candidate will—while he lives—be in a position to direct and significantly affect policy. And in principle a ticket made up of two unbalanced persons might well appear to constitute a balanced ticket.

Second, the existence of the office of the vice president puts people in line for the presidency who would not necessarily be the best choice to run for that office. Recent examples include Richard Nixon, who probably could not have made it to a presidential candidacy had he not been vice president under Dwight Eisenhower. The vice presidency can appear to dignify a fool; it can make a nonpresidential person *seem* almost presidential. This certainly applies to Spiro Agnew, who had no national political reputation and no known qualifications for the presidency when chosen to be Nixon's running mate.

Third, the office can waste the abilities of a good politician for four or eight years—years during which he or she could serve more effectively in some other office. Examples include Lyndon Johnson and Hubert Humphrey, whose talents went unused when they served as vice president. Holding the office may also seriously impair the officeholder's chances of being elected president, even though it may help to get him nominated. It is commonly held that both Humphrey and Walter Mondale were hurt as presidential candidates by their vice presidential services.

If it is too much trouble to abolish the office, we at least ought not to fill it: Leave the post empty and use the offices in the Old Executive Office Building to house the many presidential commissions that are forever being formed to study problems Congress and the president could not or would not solve.

The Federal Election Campaign Act and its amendments of 1975–76 should be repealed. This would open up the political process as it was open before that legislation was passed. A politics that brought to the country such presidents as Franklin Roosevelt, Harry Truman, Dwight Eisenhower, and John Kennedy—in contrast to Jimmy Carter, Ronald Reagan, George Bush, and Bill Clinton—cannot be judged to have been all bad.

Televised political advertisements should be abolished. Or, if that is not possible, severely regulated so as to minimize the conditioning effects of current ads. (For example, candidates would have to speak for themselves, a la Ross Perot.)

The country has long accepted the idea of a de facto ban on televised advertising of liquor and cigarettes, presumably protecting U.S. citizens from physical corruption. Similar bans should be applied to the other end of the spectrum of human needs and wants—namely, politics and religion. Television could continue to carry ads for deodorants, detergents, pain relief, and automobiles.

The equal time and fairness doctrines should be rigorously applied to televised reporting of political campaigns, even though the presentation of such news might be severely limited as a result. The spoken word (primarily radio) and the written word remain the best means of political reportage. For it was in the period approximately from 1930 to 1960—after the advent of radio and before the coming of television—that the best communication of political ideas took place.

Finally, televised debates should be eliminated unless used as a device to attract the attention of voters during primaries—a compromise justification. But they are best wholly banned in the showdown campaign between major candidates. Presidents, unlike senators, do not have to be great debaters. Once elected, they will not be debating anyone.

Most candidates admit that the people who most influence them are their spouses (and second, their vice presidents). If a debate is to have significant bearing on the presidency, perhaps it should be held between the presidential candidate and his or her spouse, or between the presidential and vice presidential candidates of the same party. A Dole-versus-Kemp debate would have been more interesting than the Dole-Clinton debates were. And Al Gore, whom we now know to be an aggressive debater, might have forced President Clinton to actually talk about something real, rather than just emoting.

With the course cleared by these changes, there would be time to look to the positive and substantive basis upon which presidents should be chosen—job creation, debt reduction, foreign policy, and global economics—and to the actual means of selection and election of presidential candidates. Those means are now utterly chaotic and unrepresentative, and the way to fix them is not more primaries, a national primary, more caucuses, or campaign reform, all of which will lead to the further triumph of corporate money and special-interest domination of the process. The cure is a more *representative* process.

JUDGING THE CABINET

In a parliamentary system, like that in England, voters usually know before an election who the principal members of the next cabinet will be. In the United States voters can only speculate, with the help of columnists, who have not been very accurate in their predictions on who will be appointed by the newly elected presidents.

Occasionally, a candidate will hint at prospective appointments. In a recent campaign, only one likely candidate, Robert Dole, named a possible appointee. He said that he would give Colin Powell "almost any job he wanted."

Twenty years before, Gerald Ford proclaimed a similar confidence in Henry Kissinger. Ford said that, if elected, he would make Kissinger secretary of state—Henry and God willing.

Both the Dole and the Ford pledges were looked upon as signs of political weakness, and perhaps they were. But a pre-election announcement as to major cabinet appointees would also be good government.

Immediately after the election, the timidity, secrecy, and hesitation that marked the former candidate disappear. Presidents-elect begin to talk about the important choices they are prepared to make, and soon they begin to leak prospective cabinet officers through friendly (or willing) members of the press. It is as though election had given them the special grace of office, not unlike the gift of infallibility that follows from a papal election.

[...]

In judging the choices future presidents make, it is useful to recall the qualifications, characters, and performances of cabinet members in past administrations.

I would rate George Marshall as the best secretary of state in recent decades. Marshall was experienced in war and in peace; he was pragmatic. He saw foreign policy as an extension of national character and interests. He was a historian. The worst secretary of state was John Dean Rusk, although pushed hard by John Foster Dulles. Dulles laid down the ideological lines for the Cold War "confrontation": "massive retaliation," "the immorality of neutralism," and so on. He also arranged covenants, executive agreements, and treaties to sustain these moral judgments. Rusk, succeeding Dulles after a brief interlude, accepted the ideological dicta and took action to support them. He was to Dulles what Oliver Cromwell was to John Calvin.

The general conclusion is that the secretary of state should not be an ideologue. The appointee should not be from a family with strong traditions in the religious ministry, nor be a geopolitical thinker, nor be schooled in the balance-of-power theory of the Austro-Hungarian empire. And, preferably, he or she should not have been "with" a foundation or, as they say, "of" an institution, like Brookings. He also should not be a former campaign manager, fund-raiser, or corporate lawyer.

The best secretary of the Treasury in the past fifty years probably was Henry Morgenthau of the Roosevelt administration. He was skilled in politics and in finance, informed of world affairs. Among recent secretaries, three deserve praise: Henry Fowler, his successor, Joseph Barr, of the Johnson administration, and George Shultz of the Nixon administration. All three understood that the U.S. dollar was a force for stability and economic growth at home and a force for order in world affairs. The worst recent Treasury secretary was John Connally, who in a short term achieved a significant failure by cutting the dollar free and letting it float—or, in a more appropriate Texas image, letting it loose on the world monetary range with no more than a hair brand to identify it.

The best attorney general of modern times was Francis Biddle, who held that office under Roosevelt and under Truman, with William Rogers of the Eisenhower administration as a runner-up. Both Biddle and Rogers kept the office above politics. Both understood that the attorney general was the top law officer in the land. Both probably would have resigned if it had been suggested to them that a special prosecutor be appointed to handle matters under their jurisdiction. The worst attorney general of our times was John Mitchell, for politicizing the Justice Department even to the point of involving it in campaign politics. The attorney general should not be the campaign manager of the president who appoints him. Preferably this person should not be from the president's own political party. Nor, for that matter, from the president's family.

[...]

Louis Johnson, secretary of defense under Truman, was the last secretary to stand against the growth of the military-industrial complex. Melvin Laird, secretary of defense under Nixon, was a militarist, but he directed and controlled the expansion. Laird's political experience was a good preparation. His record supports the argument that the secretary of defense should be drawn from Congress.

The worst secretary of defense must be Robert McNamara. He brought to the office the arrogance of the automobile industry, which previously had been represented by Charlie Wilson of General Motors. One sure conclusion is that the secretary of defense should not be a former automobile executive. A football coach might do or possibly two—one for defense and one for offense.

The postmaster general is no longer a member of the cabinet. But without question, the best postmaster general was James Farley of the Roosevelt administration. He ran the post office, and also the Democratic Party. He kept politics in the post office, where it could do little harm. He recognized that politics is like pigeons: If it is concentrated in one building or in one department, you should not scatter it to others.

The worst postmaster general was Arthur E. Summerfield of the Eisenhower administration. He let politics get out of the post office and let the service deteriorate. Then he took up pornography and censorship (he was against the former and for the latter). *Lady Chatterley's Lover* was banned from the mails under Summerfield, as was Aristophanes' *Lysistrata*. The ban on the second item was lifted when Summerfield learned that the play had been written more than 2,000 years before he moved to ban it.

The best secretary of labor was Frances Perkins. The poorest was Martin Durkin of the Eisenhower administration. Durkin had been a union member. Perkins was a graduate of Mount Holyoke. The lesson is obvious.

The best secretary of agriculture was Charlie Brannan, who delighted in arguing with Agriculture Committee members. The worst was Ezra Taft Benson, an elder of the Mormon Church. A good rule for picking a secretary of agriculture is to get someone from the opposite party to take the job, someone who will not introduce religion into the department, and someone who knows that ethnic jokes, which may be accepted quite without prejudice by farm audiences, are not generally acceptable. If hard pressed, the president might look to Minnesota, which in recent years has become the mother of secretaries of agriculture.

Harold Ickes of the Roosevelt cabinet was a model secretary of the interior. He not only was a conservationist but also was a capable defender of his policies, able to draw criticism away from the president, and unquestionably politically helpful. Ickes was credited with typing Thomas Dewey, Roosevelt's opponent in the 1944 presidential election, as "the little man on the wedding cake." He once defended the government policy of killing young pigs to reduce the supply of pork during the Depression by saying that he had "never known a pig that died of old age." The worst secretary of the interior was Douglas McKay of the Eisenhower administration, appointed for no discernible reason other than that he had been governor of Oregon, a state with many trees. Before becoming secretary, he had owned and operated a Chevrolet dealership.

The best secretary of health, education, and welfare (HEW), now the Departments of Education and of Health and Human Services, was Wilbur Cohen, a nonpolitical career person. Cohen knew the programs and knew how to administer them. He never complained of the burdens of the office or suggested that they were beyond his powers. He left the proposing of new programs to the elected politicians. The worst HEW secretary possibly was John Gardner, who resigned from the office in protest over "priorities" and other things. Gardner was miscast; he misunderstood the office. Gardner would have been a good person to preach the Crusades or proclaim the westward movement in the United States, but he was not the person to be put in charge of the march to Jerusalem or of a wagon train passing through Indian territory. The guiding rule in picking a secretary of health and human services is that his or her motto should be "Sufficient unto the day are the problems already assigned to this department."

Appointing a secretary of commerce is one official act in which no president should fail. The secretary of commerce should be a nice person, decent, contented, full of pleasantries, with no further political ambitions—ideally with no ambitions of any kind. He or she should be able to report encouraging or discouraging business reports with equal assurance and optimism. The best secretary of commerce in recent administrations was Luther Hodges of the Kennedy administration. Luther wore a fresh flower in his coat lapel each day.

[...]

The U.N. ambassadorship should be an important post but is generally treated as a door prize. Clinton awarded it to a professor in 1992, and Madeleine Albright did a good job. But the person appointed to this position should have some national standing and some standing with Congress as a sign of respect for the United Nations. Dwight Eisenhower sent Henry Cabot Lodge to the U.N. John Kennedy sent Adlai Stevenson. Gerald Ford sent William Scranton. All had been contenders for national office. All did well at the U.N. Richard Nixon sent George Bush, at that time a defeated congressman, while Bush sent a former CIA man (and retired general), and Ronald Reagan sent Jeane Kirkpatrick, another professor, whom he admired for her articles in *Commentary* magazine.

[...]

It would be good for the nation if each candidate for the presidency were compelled to announce his three or four top cabinet choices during the presidential campaign. The country ought not to be surprised or generally unenlightened about who, along with the president, is running the government.

For the most part—with the exception of Ford, who made some good appointments—all of our presidents since Truman have downgraded the cabinet and turned the cabinet secretaries into personal assistants to the president. This practice has made for a mediocre as well as undistinguished executive branch, sometimes an incompetent one.

The president is not a plant manager; he is more akin to a CEO. He cannot run the federal government by himself or out of the White House.

When the country elects a president, it elects an executive branch. It would be well to act as if this is what we are doing when we hold national elections. The person a president is likely to appoint as attorney general or secretary of state matters far more to the good of the republic than does the candidate's party platform on school prayer or abortion.

We are a government of people as well as laws. Yet our national campaigns give virtually no attention to the people who will make up a candidate's future presidency.

Often the candidate himself does not know. He is focused on election, not government (like Clinton in 1992). We ought to make him think about his government and then tell us what he thinks.

AN ANTIREFORM REFORM

The Constitutional Convention in 1787, after prolonged debate and after having considered procedures for choosing a president—election by the national legislature or by state representatives or directly by the people—finally, by a vote of nine states to two, approved the principle of electing the president by a body created specifically for that purpose, namely, the electoral college.

In the first presidential election some electors were appointed by state legislatures. A few other states, including Pennsylvania, Maryland, and Virginia, provided for popular election of the electors.

By 1796, the first election after George Washington's two terms, electors were chosen by the people in six states and by legislatures in ten states. By that time, within eight years of the adoption of the Constitution, partisanship had reached the point that, in every one of the sixteen states then a part of the union, electors were picked as men pledged to one candidate or the other: John Adams or Thomas Jefferson. The electoral college as conceived by the Founding Fathers—a body of responsible, trusted persons—was already effectively discarded. (And it had hardly been tested.)

As partisan politics has become more dominant in the republic, the independent role of the electoral college has been all but forgotten, and electors have come to vote automatically for the party candidate to whom they are committed. Because of the development of partisan politics, and for other reasons, the original conception of how the electoral college was intended to work has been confused and neglected. A popular opinion has developed that the electoral college is either a bad idea or one that is unworkable. It is neither. The trouble is that it has not been used as it was intended.

The original conception was that electors would be chosen for one task only—a very important one in the new republic: the selection of a president of the United States. As electors they were to be agents of the people of their states. It was anticipated that the electors would be wise and responsible, but more that they would be free of immediate involvement with politics and legislative matters because they were not themselves members of Congress or of state legislatures.

The electoral college, as it was called, was designed to deny both Congress and the voters total, direct power over an election. Whereas the Founding Fathers were familiar with political factions—division being the mark of every political society—they hoped and believed that these divisive and power-seeking organizations would have a limited influence in the choice of the president.

Ironically, the electoral college in its more or less original form would be more useful and more rational today than ever. It would involve popular sovereignty over the nomination process—quite absent now—but with the popular wisdom, and reactions, molded and refined by those elected by the people to choose a president.

A revised electoral college certainly beats what we have now.

Our political parties—as armies of political organization and as platforms of principle—are dead. Our presidential candidates are therefore now picked by those who have great wealth; the media, those whose profession is the packaging and mass marketing of politicians; and a very small number of primary voters in a few states. It is not a democratic method of selecting presidents but a manipulation and perversion of democracy, and it is not reflective democracy because the process is not representative in any way.

How to get back to the electoral college?

The states could, by individual and separate actions, restore the electoral process to what it was intended to be. But they are as unlikely to do so as they were to extend the vote to women or to people between the ages of eighteen and twenty-one before constitutional amendments accomplished those purposes. Maine is the only state that has moved, even modestly, to conform to the constitutional intent.

The Maine system—by which one electoral vote goes to the winner of the popular vote in each congressional district and two electoral votes go to the winner of the statewide popular vote—is clearly better than the winner-take-all rule applied in the other forty-nine states in the current operation of the electoral college.

But even better than the Maine district system would be one dividing the states into presidential electoral districts, each smaller than a congressional district, which now includes about 450,000 people.

If each presidential elector represented, say, a district of 100,000 people, a candidate for the electoral college could campaign effectively without spending great sums of money. One person with a few volunteers in the course of a presidential campaign could reach all voters in his 100,000-person constituency. If the country were divided into some 2,000 such districts, 2,000 presidential electors would be chosen. Obviously, if a majority of those chosen were Democrats, a

Democratic president would be chosen; if a majority were Republicans, a Republican would be president. If neither party had a majority, the third- or fourth-party electors would hold the balance of power, and their votes would have to be solicited by other parties.

This procedure is no different from the one followed within U.S. political parties at their conventions (or on the way to conventions). In Great Britain it is used in choosing the prime minister, under the parliamentary system.

A president chosen through this process would clearly be a constitutional president, and he or she would be chosen by electors who represented a majority—if not of the voters, almost certainly of the citizens.

We should follow the advice of John Holcombe, who in the early years of [the last] century argued that "in no reactionary spirit, therefore, but with views thoroughly progressive," we should "return for relief to the wisdom of the fathers by making effective their admirable device—the electoral college."

In so speaking, he sustained the judgment of James Madison, not only as expressed in the Constitution but also as late as 1823, when he wrote, "One advantage of electors is that, although generally the mere mouths of their constituents, they may be intentionally left sometimes to their own judgment, guided by further information that may be acquired for them; and finally, what is of material importance, they will be able, when ascertaining which may not be till a late hour, that the first choice of their constituents is utterly hopeless, to substitute in the electoral college the name known to be their second choice."

The need for purifying and perfecting the process of the selection of the president is most important today, because of the complexity and weight of the demands of the presidential office and because voter knowledge of the qualifications of the presidential candidates is obscured or distorted by spin doctors and media hype. It is better to improve the representative process, as conceived by Madison, than to propose that it should be done away with.

The electoral college has not worked because, mostly, it has not been tried—its function as a means to perfect the representative process was abandoned or forgotten.

The problem is not a defect in the conception of this unique constitutional institution but rather the intrusion of partisanship and faction between the people and the executive branch of government. It is the electoral college that should stand between the two.

The No Fault Presidency: Who, Me?
(*No Fault Politics*, 1998)

Harry Truman was noted for saying of his presidency, "The buck stops here," a phrase that has nothing to do with dollars, but is one drawn from poker and referring to the marker designating the next player to deal the cards.

President Eisenhower accepted responsibility for the U-2 flight over Russia during his administration. John Kennedy did the same for the failed Cuban invasion. Both Eisenhower and Kennedy could have justifiably given excuses.

Subsequent presidents have been less ready to accept and acknowledge blame for either foreign or domestic policy failures.

As U.S. involvement in Vietnam deepened, President Johnson invoked the Tonkin Gulf Resolution as a protective defense and noted that he was carrying on a policy in Vietnam accepted and advanced by the three presidents who had preceded him in office. President Nixon, in turn, noted that he was carrying forward, even in Cambodia, what four of his predecessors had sustained. He labeled the Vietnam War a "Democrat war."

President Carter attributed domestic failures during his administration to the "malaise" that he said had settled on the nation. He occasionally gave examples of those stricken with malaise: Members of the medical profession, he said, were fine as individual doctors but were suspect as members of medical associations.

President Reagan took credit for military success in Grenada but passed over the deaths of marines in Lebanon as a kind of biblical event.

This progressive rejection of presidential responsibility came full term and possibly reached institutional status in the [first] Bush administration. President Bush blamed the budget deficit on the Democratic Congress. He might have gone further, in Carter style, and blamed it on the American electorate, since that electorate chose a Democratic Congress in both 1990 and 1992, despite the president's appeal for the election of Republicans. But Bush settled on Congress. It was Congress, he said, that controlled the federal budget. The president, according to Bush, was a sort of regent, basically unable to do much about federal spending and fiscal priorities. Harry Truman would have been astounded at such an abdication.

Bush took no responsibility for the savings and loan debacle or for related difficulties in the deregulated banking industry or in the Department of Housing and Urban Development.

Bush did not even take responsibility for his choice of a running mate. Other presidents and presidential candidates had been held responsible for their vice presidents and running mates. And none had even attempted to dodge responsibility. Franklin Roosevelt had rejected two vice presidents, John Nance Garner and Henry Wallace, as running mates. Dwight Eisenhower answered for Richard Nixon in 1952. George McGovern was held responsible for his choice and subsequent rejection of Sen. Thomas Eagleton (a good man who, incredible as it might seem today, was driven from the ticket in 1972 because he had been treated for depression). Nixon, belatedly, had to take the blame for his choice of Spiro Agnew. And Walter Mondale suffered for his choice of Geraldine Ferraro. George Bush treated Dan Quayle as a kind of accident or an act of nature—something found on the doorstep one morning. Bush may have wanted to dump Quayle in 1992, but finding no one who would do it for him or make the decision for him, he failed to take responsibility for removing Quayle from the ticket.

Bush's distancing of himself from responsibility was not limited to domestic and official actions.

Whereas Lee Atwater, manager of the Bush campaign, apologized a few months before his death for some of the things he had done to help defeat Michael Dukakis in the 1988 campaign, especially the racial exploitation of the Willie Horton ad, there was no comparable expression of regret from George Bush, the beneficiary of Atwater's work.

The most glaring demonstration of denial of presidential responsibility by Bush occurred on April 7, 1992, following the successes of the Gulf War, when the president, in a church in Houston, publicly absolved himself—and, by extension, the United States—of any responsibility for the condition of various Iraqi rebel and refugee groups.

We had, he acknowledged, encouraged them to revolt against Saddam Hussein, but the United States had not, he asserted, promised those who responded to that encouragement any support in arms or otherwise.

Moreover, the president noted, bringing legal support to his abdication, any assistance would have been an intervention in the internal affairs of another nation, an action not allowed by the United Nations. This was an assertion almost breathtaking in its hypocrisy and intellectual dishonesty. Had the United Nations been in existence as World War II was about to begin and had Adolf Hitler (Bush had called Saddam "Hitler") promised to give up conquered territory, to suspend production of weapons of mass destruction, and to make reparations or the promise of them, he might have been allowed to go on—as long as he executed only German Jews.

[...]

A further question of responsibility was raised regarding earlier tacit and under-the-table support for Saddam Hussein. The United States certainly tilted toward Iraq in its war with Iran. And the United States under Bush may well have initially given Saddam reason to believe that his disputes over oil and borders with Kuwait were of little concern to the United States. Moreover, our friendly relations with Saddam had continued long after it was suspected, if not known with certainty, that he had used chemical weapons against the Kurds.

Yet, Bush acknowledged no responsibility or fault. The explanation of U.S. policy toward Iraq was left to a career foreign service officer, April Glaspie, who served as ambassador to Iraq. The ambassador's explanation of the apparent contradictions between policy and action was as follows: She said that the United

States had made the mistake of not realizing how "dumb" Saddam was in believing that we meant what we said. When we indicated our indifference to what he might do about Kuwait, he should have realized that we did not really mean it.

Glaspie did not report at what level in the State Department the mistake (of not realizing how dumb Saddam was) was made. Nor did she explain whether the mistake occurred because our officials were too "dumb" to realize how dumb Saddam was or because the general level of intelligence in the administration was so high that no one in the department could comprehend dumbness of the level at which it evidently exists in Saddam Hussein.

In any event this was the level of explanation or justification by the Bush presidency for a de facto alliance with a man against whom the United States was to soon wage war and whom the president called as evil as Hitler. Bush created an intellectual and moral void out of which emerged the "no-fault presidency": If things went wrong, no one was responsible and no one was to blame. If things went well, everyone was responsible and it was to the credit of the president.

It may be that President Bush's disposition to avoid responsibility was nurtured by his experience in the political offices that he had held prior to his election to the presidency, mostly unelected. Moreover, even his record in electoral politics,

---

Extract from 2004 interview:

Editor: You talk quite a bit in your writings about the responsibility of a senator. Could you elaborate in terms of getting involved in the 1968 election?

McCarthy: The Senate has a primary responsibility for foreign policy. That means they have a primary responsibility for war, which is the ultimate foreign policy act. To say we're not going to do anything about war but we'll do something about the migratory bird laws as a part of the senator's responsibility is really not to fill or meet your obligations. I thought the Senate had primary responsibility to do something about war. It wasn't up to young people marching, it wasn't even up to the House of Representatives. It was the Senate's primary responsibility to hold the president in check. And if the whole Senate won't do it, you're still responsible as a single senator. The fact that the Senate wouldn't act didn't excuse an individual senator from doing something. I don't know if [name of another senator] thought about it that way or if they were making excuses. [My opposition to the Johnson administration] wasn't a personal act of political courage, it was an obligation of a senator.

Editor: How do you think the Senate today is measuring up to that standard?

McCarthy: [The current situation] is a little more difficult, a little more complicated. The consequences of stopping the Vietnam War, and what would happen, I thought were indicated; the side effects were not really important. With this thing [the Iraq war], it's a little bit different. There was more of a reason from the facts of the situation in '68 to do what I did than there is for senators to do something now. They're still caught in the trap between the president and opposition to them.

prior to seeking the presidency and vice presidency, was one of fundamental com-
promise. Bush first ran and was elected to the House of Representatives as a liberal
Republican. He subsequently ran for the Senate twice, unsuccessfully, as a
Goldwater and then as an Agnew conservative.

Bush then became ambassador to the United Nations. He was appointed to
the post by Richard Nixon, who wanted to downgrade the job. For Bush, who had
just narrowly lost his second Senate race and had nowhere to go in elective politics, it was a political lifesaver and a huge step up from former congressman. Bush
was most grateful.

His next job was as chairman of the Republican Party, where he replaced
Robert Dole. Again, Bush was appointed by Nixon. Bush's job was to defend the
integrity and honor of Nixon during Watergate. Chairmanship of the Republican
Party (one can say the same of the chairmanship of the Democratic Party) is not
recommended for character building.

Bush was also liaison to China—not even ambassador but the president's personal liaison and Henry Kissinger's. In this post Bush reportedly played a great
deal of tennis and perhaps arranged for Kissinger's visits.

The other office held by Bush before he sought the presidency and vice presidency in 1980 may have profoundly affected his attitude toward personal
responsibility and his sensitivity to truth: He became head of the Central
Intelligence Agency.

Bush's last post before he became president was the vice presidency, where he
served eight years. Bush accepted the vice presidential nomination after having
vigorously denounced Ronald Reagan's economic views as "voodoo economics." He
then became a most enthusiastic and dedicated convert to Reaganism and
Reaganomics.

It is hard to imagine any politician who had followed this career path emerg-
ing as a decisive and responsible national leader.

Peggy Noonan, in her book about the Reagan administration, *What I Saw at
the Revolution*, makes several observations that may help explain the Bush detachment or flight from responsibility.

According to Noonan, a speechwriter for Bush, her early offerings were rejected,
principally because the pronoun "I" was used too often. According to Noonan, candidate Bush hated to say *I*. If she wrote an *I* in a speech for him, he would drop the
phrase or construction containing the pronoun or drop an entire sentence rather than
say the *I* word. Eventually, she accommodated her texts to the candidate's desire.
Instead of writing, "I moved to Texas," she would write, "moved to Texas." Instead
of "We joined the Republican Party," she wrote, "joined the Republican Party."

Noonan speculated as to whether when he took the oath of office Bush would say
"solemnly swear," not "I solemnly swear," and "preserve and protect," not "I will preserve and protect," in keeping with his favoring naked predicates, rather than complete
sentences with both subject and predicates. Noonan suggests that Bush's disposition to

avoid the use of the pronoun *I* had its beginnings in Bush's childhood. His supposedly stern mother admonished him, when he was a boy, not to use the *I* word.

Noonan later was accepted into the speechwriters' group and took, or was given, credit for adding the "thousand points of light" and "read my lips" lines to the standard Bush campaign speech. So even the phrases for which George Bush is remembered are the work of someone else. Bush said them, but Peggy Noonan was responsible.

GEORGE BUSH'S WAR

The labeling of the original U.S. military action in the Persian Gulf as "Desert Storm" followed a little-noted precedent by which the Pentagon named its wars in advance. The Grenada invasion was officially known in military circles, or pentagonals, as "Urgent Fury" and the Panama action as "Just Cause." Neither of these titles took hold as historical markers, possibly because the action in each case was relatively short-lived and both interventions were of limited objective.

Neither did Desert Storm or the sustaining action, "Rolling Thunder," make much impact. Neither will make it into the history books as major chapters in military history, great or not so great—like the Battle of Britain or the Battle of the Bulge or the Vietnam War.

The Gulf War has become a sort of nonwar—almost immediately forgotten except for the U.S. soldiers injured or disabled there. Indeed, the only "heroes" of the war were Gen. "Stormin' Norman" Schwarzkopf, Gen. Colin Powell, and President Bush. Two soon went into civilian life, and one was soundly beaten in a national election.

A whole (or a half) presidency later, nagging and basic questions remain: Why did the United States fight the Gulf War? What did we hope to accomplish? What do we think we did accomplish? And have we stabilized the region? Neither the press nor Congress has seemed very curious.

President Clinton's parenthetical bombing in northern Iraq in the summer of 1996—during the presidential season—seemed to be in keeping with what is now the established U.S. stance in the gulf: When things heat up, do something. Since George Bush, we have taken actions without aims or even clear military strategy. A president, by these lights, must "show strength" and "not go wobbly," but long-term diplomatic goals are optional.

The purpose of the Gulf War as first stated—namely, to protect access to Saudi Arabian oil supplies—was wholly defensible. The United States had a clear right and obligation to intervene in our own interest, but also in consequence of obligations accepted under NATO and under our treaties with Japan.

The justification for our intervention was comparable to that underscoring our intervention in Korea: principally, to assure nations dependent on us in the Far East of the seriousness of our commitment and of our integrity.

But as the magnitude of our military movement grew, so did the magnitude and number of reasons given for our being engaged, just as purposes magnified and multiplied and the commitment of arms and men had increased in Vietnam.

There are many questions that President Bush should have been asked and that he should have answered as conditions for advancing and extending the Gulf War. Most of them remain unanswered today:

- Was the liberation of Kuwait contemplated?
- Was the deposing of Saddam Hussein considered?
- Was the destruction of Iraq's potential to produce nuclear weapons and its real capability to produce chemical and germ warfare a primary objective? Or was the war to protect American pride?
- Why was the advice of military experts or those reputed to be experts, for example, retired Admiral William J. Crowe, Jr., ignored?
- Why were the military forces of the Arab nations aligned against Iraq, most of them armed with U.S.-made weapons, not asked or urged or required to assume major military responsibilities in the war? These aligned Arab nations had a combined population of approximately 100 million people versus an Iraqi population of about 12 million. Egypt, alone, had an army strong enough to have fought the Israeli forces to a draw in 1973. The Saudis and the smaller oil-producing countries had advanced U.S. equipment. And the Syrians, one of what were called "the coalition allies" had arms enough for continuing military action in Lebanon.
- President Bush spoke of "the new world order." What was, what is, the new world order to be established?
- How was this world order to be maintained?
- What were the plans for meeting the costs of the war, since it appeared early that Saudi, Japanese, and German contributions would fall far short of what we might have expected them to contribute? Did our government know this would be the case from the start?
- Immediately after the war, why did President Bush not take the initiative in setting up a general conference on the problems of the Middle East, or indicate a willingness to follow the initiatives of others, especially since the changes in Russia and the accompanying possibility of constructive participation by the Russians greatly increased the chances of success in efforts to establish peace and order in the area?
- Why were efforts not being made to make the Middle East a nuclear-free area as part of a more comprehensive nuclear nonproliferation and nuclear disarmament effort?
- With chemical and germ warfare a possibility (even, it appears, a reality) in the Middle East, why was there no significant effort or disposition in evidence on the part of the United States to move toward banning such weapons, including our own neutron bombs?

- Can anyone explain U.S. support of Saddam Hussein during the Iran-Iraq war?
- After we "won" the war, why did the president not propose a world conference or U.N. action to re-examine the 1923 mapping, principally by the British, in the Middle East?
- Why were the Israelis not permitted to "take out" Iraqi nuclear installations, thus establishing a basis for respect and appreciation among the Arab nations threatened by Iraq's nuclear arms?
- Is it true, as some have said, that the strength of Iraq's army was never what the president represented it to be and that the sending of 500,000 military personnel with supplies, weapons, and other material to the Middle East was primarily an exercise in logistics and a test of acceptance by Congress and by the people of the United States of presidential power?

These questions still matter today, not only so that we may clearly see where we have been and how some of the peoples of the Middle East might see recent history but also because it might help U.S. policymakers to clarify our aims and objectives in the future. [...]

Before you fight other nations or attempt to bring them together, it helps to know what you are trying to accomplish.

The Gulf War and subsequent gulf policy are prime examples of the pattern of no-fault presidential leadership, which President Clinton has continued.

President Bush acted as if he had inherited a military and political posture whose purpose had never been made quite clear to him. Such posturing is exactly what did happen to President Clinton, but it did not move him to attempt to understand the war, its aims, or its consequences. He merely assumed the rhetorical pose—"I will do something"—and continued the posturing.

THE BUSH PRESIDENCY:
REPRESENTATION WITHOUT TAXATION

War or no war, the Bush presidency was marked by some of the silliest personal behavior of a president in this century, beginning with a post-election pre-swearing-in photo of the president-elect and his wife, Barbara, in a large bed, surrounded by dogs and grandchildren. This was followed by sports scenes: tennis, golf, baseball, and even horseshoes, plus almost daily excessive and intensive jogging. (One reporter who jogged with or near the president said that near the end of the first two miles, there came a period lasting about 200 yards when the president spoke clearly and in complete sentences.)

There was a succession of baseball-type caps, and the president, in a golf cart between holes, pausing to give short press conferences on war, taxes, and unrelated matters. The president would then move on with his standard phrase of dismissal: "Gotta run now."

Silliness extended beyond personal and incidental behavior. It was demonstrated most clearly with the president's persistence in appropriating stock and macho political phrases, sometimes spoken by President Reagan and sometimes borrowed from Clint Eastwood movies: "Go ahead, make my day," "There you go again," etc. This became the basis of taxation or fiscal policy. "Read my lips" became the moral basis, such as it was, of the Bush presidency.

In the course of the history of our country, revolts against taxes have been a standard bill of fare, although the general and continuous thrust has been against particular taxes, not taxes in general. The patriots of Boston, anticipating the Revolution, opened the antitax action by dumping tea into the harbor in protest against what they declared to be a discriminatory tax on their favorite drink (next to rum). James Otis took up the cause, not by denouncing taxes, even particular ones, but by his bold declaration that "taxation without representation is tyranny." The implication of the Otis thesis was that taxation *with* representation was defensible.

This thesis was challenged soon after the adoption of the Constitution and the election of George Washington as president. Washington, with whom George Bush claimed some connection in a campaign slogan, "From George to George," never indicated orally or in writing or by lip movements or even by hand signs whether he was for taxes in general or in particular.

But he put down a tax rebellion during his presidency, and so the matter rested, more or less, until the imposition of the income tax and the various tax rebellions of the twentieth century. (There were minor protests along the way.)

For most of the past fifty years of this century, the continuing position of the Republicans has been to assert that "Democrat" taxes discouraged business expansion and stifled the free enterprise system. The Democrats, in turn, have asserted that taxes favored the rich, were unfair, and fell as a heavy and inequitable burden on those least able to pay, who, if relieved of their tax burden, would purchase more goods and thus stimulate the entire economy. Neither party seriously challenged the actual right and necessity of government to impose and to collect taxes.

George McGovern in his 1972 campaign proposed using taxes or the tax system as a direct, if not automatic, means of moving income closer to equality among the American people. Under this proposal, the government would collect taxes and then distribute collected revenue to all eligible persons, in the amount of $1,000 per person—to those who had paid at least $1,000 and to those who had not paid that much, or to those who had not paid *any* income taxes. The $1,000 was to fall like the biblical rain on the just and on the unjust alike and on the taxpayers and the nontaxpayers.

The proposal was not well received by the electorate. This was not surprising since it violated one of Machiavelli's fundamental rules, which is that in taking something from the people, the prince should take from everyone in one act and then return it slowly and selectively. McGovern proposed the opposite.

Jimmy Carter, as a candidate, asserted that the U.S. Tax Code was a "disgrace to the human race," a declaration not wholly endorsed by Democratic members of

Congress or former members, who through the years had labored hard on the code. (I myself spent twenty-two years on the tax-writing committees of the House and Senate.) As president, Carter proposed a variation on the McGovern proposition. It was also a variation on the rebate programs being offered by the automobile companies at that time. The rebates proposed by Carter were to be smaller than those proposed by McGovern and spread out in monthly distributions.

As a former peanut processor, President Carter was prepared to think small. But his rebate proposal was not accepted. Instead, as his fiscal policy, he opted for what in his campaign he had called the "cruelest tax": inflation. The inflation rate rose from approximately 7 percent a year at the beginning of the Carter presidency to 13 percent by the end of it.

Carter, because of his declaration not against taxes but against the tax code, was a precursor to President Reagan. The Gipper was the first American president to oppose taxes per se. Reagan's position on taxes was comparable to the Carter position on the war in Vietnam. Carter was for it, he said, but against the way it was conducted. Reagan was not against the way the tax code was written, as Carter was; he was against the code itself. An appropriate slogan for Reagan tax policy was a variation on the James Otis declaration—in effect that "taxation even with representation is tyranny."

Reagan proceeded, with a supporting Congress, to cut taxes, substituting federal deficits and borrowed money—what had previously been called fiscal irresponsibility—for taxation. Reagan thus made future tax collections by the federal government a most popular investment for Japanese, Germans, and other foreign investors.

The political secret of the Reagan policy was laying the burden of accumulating debt not on the next generation of taxpayers—who, anticipating it, might reject it—but on the succession of generations succeeding them. The *children* of the next generation are not in a position to do much about what will happen to them as a consequence of current policy.

President Bush in his no-new-tax policy carried tax policy to a neo-revolutionary postmodernist stage. Bush went beyond Otis and beyond the advanced variation on Otis—Ronald Reagan—to the ultimate formulation of tax policy in a postmodern democracy: simply, representation without taxation.

The House of Representatives, under Newt Gingrich, proposed and passed legislation along these lines—the line-item veto and the balanced-budget agreement. The danger is that in the interim, before this idyllic state of zero taxation is reached, simple-minded or logical or patriotically motivated taxpayers may accept that Bush and Gingrich are right—that all new taxes are bad and that most old ones should go.

More and more Americans may come to accept the declared wisdom of the antitax politicians: that the people's money is best used if kept from the government and used according to the determination of the people who earn it, or gain control of it, through investment or inheritance.

Logically, then, we should all on our own stop paying taxes, thus serving the common good and bringing on immediately the happy state of a democracy without obligation and representation without taxation.

[...]

FULL EMPLOYMENT FOR EX-PRESIDENTS

What to do with surviving ex-presidents, or what they should do or be allowed to do, has become a matter of some national concern.

Of the four surviving presidents and former President Nixon, who is only recently departed and still very much in the news, the popular judgment is that former President Carter had made the most useful contributions as well as the most healthy adjustment with his work in Habitat for Humanity. Indeed, this is an outstanding organization designed to encourage volunteer nongovernmental efforts to provide housing for the poor. In lending his reputation and his person to Habitat, in supervising elections in various countries of the world, and in acting as a diplomatic middleman, Carter *has* made a mark. His more recent efforts—some call them intrusions—into peacemaking in Bosnia, on the other hand, have had mixed results.

Before his death, Nixon, according to some, was rehabilitating himself and his reputation. He did this principally by making foreign policy recommendations, as events and time gave him openings. (Recent revelations from the finally public Nixon tapes, as to what might be called his Oval Office temperament, have set the rehabilitation campaign back a bit.)

President Ford plays golf, often with Hollywood types, and sits on several boards. He has made little claim to continuing a public role of any significance.

President Reagan, after one lucrative commerical trip to Japan, settled for making occasional ceremonial appearances at Republican Party affairs, riding horses, and cutting wood. He then became ill with Alzheimer's disease and withdrew from public life. Some pundits have said he has "done a lot" for the disease, just as he did for colon cancer, just by contracting it and then guarding his privacy and dignity.

Perhaps. But one still feels we may know too much about our leaders without much real benefit from the knowledge. Reagan's predecessors had not "done much" for their physical disorders or disabilities. President Eisenhower, although he had ileitis and also a heart attack during his administration, was not said to have done a lot for either. John Kennedy did not make public reports on the state of his health. He did publicly relate the use of a rocking chair to his bad back, an action that may have done something for rocking chairs.

Lyndon Johnson, although he publicly displayed the scar left over after his gallbladder operation, was not credited with having done a lot for gallbladders or their removal. Nixon played down his phlebitis, and Carter, who in his physical report noted that he had occasional problems with hemorrhoids, let it go at that. And as president, George Bush did not make a case for fellow sufferers of thyroid deficiencies.

But presidential retirement is apparently no day at the beach, even with good health.

It is, we are told, hard to adapt to driving again. And supermarkets are a bit of a mystery. And there is the weighty issue of one's "continuing role," if any.

Bush does seem inclined to accept the postpresidential role carved out by Ford: virtual retirement. Nor has Bush fit easily into the elder statesman mode of Carter or Nixon. After five years at it, he seems rather lost and forlorn.

What Bush might consider, possibly setting a precedent for future ex-presidents, is taking up some of the unfinished business of his presidency:

1. He could broker the sale of arms to Saudi Arabia.
2. He could lobby for the sale of more tanks to Kuwait.
3. He could take up the private sale of pollution rights.
4. He could take up the sale of radio licenses and commercial television channels, as proposed by ex-Sen. Bob Dole (they could be limited partners) and use the proceeds to pay for various cut-back or underfunded programs such as Head Start and welfare. The program might be extended to include the offering, under competitive bidding conditions, of all existing radio and television licenses when they come up for renewal. Those proceeds could balance the budget—an old Republican goal.

Most networks have carried programs or news stories about the bargains cattlemen are getting in leasing public lands for cattle grazing. The right to graze on the public mind and will, now given free to television and radio licensees, is much more valuable than the right to graze on western grass and sagebrush.

The former president might have another try at selling cars in Japan, roughly comparable to selling coal in Newcastle.

And he might also handle the sale of the five ex-presidents' autographed group photograph, which was sold to raise funds for their individual libraries.

Congress—It Used to Work
(*No Fault Politics*, 1998)

[...] Between the time they are elected and the date of their swearing-in, new members of Congress live precariously—in a condition not very different from that of newly hatched green turtles on the shores of Tortuga as they make their run for the safety of the sea. The young turtles are beset by attackers from the air, by land animals, and even by fish waiting for them in the shallow waters offshore.

Waiting for new members of Congress is a variety of predators: various committees of their own parties, numerous foundations, think tanks, "public interest" groups, and special interests. Some of these are concerned about policy, some about procedures. Some are concerned about morals and deep ethical concerns. Lobbyists lurk in the shadows or hover in the air.

The press, especially the columnists, gives advice—solicited or unsolicited.

The John F. Kennedy School of Harvard—somewhat in the way of Mohammad inviting the mountain—hosts and instructs new members, telling new congressmen how to be congressmen.

The Brookings Institution stands ready, not so much to advise as to pronounce. Note that Brookings is an institution, not an institute, like the Carnegie. Members of Brookings do not say that they are with or from the organization but of it, just as members of separate choirs of angels do not say they are with or from the cherubim but of it.

The Heritage Foundation will be waiting for conservatives in need of help. Common Cause will be present, insisting that it is, possibly, the only pure, uncontaminated public interest lobby. The Americans for Democratic Action, which originated in order to protect liberals from communist influence and now includes as one of its purposes protecting little liberals from toys that are dangerous, physically or psychologically, is still around. (The ADA is strong on maintaining attendance records of members of Congress.)

Newly elected members, of whatever class, will be asked by one or more of these organizations or people to support reorganizations or reforms of various kinds. They will be told that it is essential to their success to have a dedicated, hardworking staff; that it is vital that they know the rules of procedure of the body to which they have been elected; that they should maintain a near-perfect, if not perfect, attendance record; that national politics is very complicated, or that it is simple, if one only follows the principles of the organization applying the pressure.

Some of these counselors will condemn the seniority system.

Party spokesmen will emphasize the importance of party loyalty. Democratic Party spokesmen undoubtedly will quote remarks long attributed to Speaker Sam Rayburn that "those who go along get along." Others will praise "the middle way," the vital center, and the art of compromise. A few will explain how important it is to have good relationships with the press.

Most of this advice is questionable. Some of it is very bad. Every two years, I offer a set of ten countercommandments, which, if observed by members of Congress, will save them much time and save them from making many mistakes.

1. Do not have a perfect or near-perfect attendance record.

2. Watch ADA on this. If a new member has an attendance record that is better than 80 percent, there is reason to believe that he or she has been wasting time. A member who has been in office for several terms should work his attendance record down to 65 percent to 75 percent.

Note that this will not be well understood by the press.

3. Do not worry too much about rules of procedure or spend too much time trying to learn them. The Senate rules are simple enough to learn, but they are seldom honored in practice. House rules are too complicated. Use the parliamentarian. (My own rule in the House of Representatives was not to trust a member who quoted the Bible, chapter and verse; the Internal Revenue Code, section and subsection; or the Rules of the House.)

4. Beware of a staff that is too efficient. My old administrative assistant, Jerome Eller, advised that a member of Congress should never trust a staffer who regularly got to the office before the member did. Or who stayed later.

5. Don't worry too much about understanding the issues or being a "policy wonk." Remember that politics is much like professional football. Those who are most successful are, as the dean of my college said, smart enough to understand the game but not smart enough to lose interest.

6. Don't knock seniority. You may have it sooner than you anticipate.

7. And remember what Gilbert Chesteron said: that it makes no sense to have the oldest son of a king succeed his father, but it saves a lot of trouble. (Alexis de Tocqueville held that in a democracy, seniority is a last defense against anarchy.)

8. Unless the issue is of overwhelming importance, don't be the only one or one of a few who are right. It is difficult to say to one's colleagues in Congress, "I am sorry I was right. Please forgive me." They won't. It is easier to say, "I was wrong." Forgiveness is almost immediate.

9. Remember that the worst accidents occur in or near the middle of the road. Bipartisanship and balance are usually stressed by the League of Women Voters. Be wary of all three.

10. Do not respond to the appeal of "party loyalty." This can be the last defense of rascals.

11. Abide by the advice given to young members of Congress forty years ago by a leftover New Dealer: "Vote against anything introduced that begins with the syllable *re*." Reorganizations, recodifications, reform, and especially resolutions. The puritans really do slay St. George and feed the dragon.

Perhaps most important: the advice of Ed Leahy, noted reporter for the *Chicago Daily News*—"Never trust the press."

A Good and Becoming Exit
(Required Reading, 1988)

A truly good actor, it is said, is marked by his or her exits. At best they should be made such that, although the leaving may not have been noticed, the absence that follows is.

When Harold Macmillan died last month, the former prime minister of the United Kingdom took to his grave a singular distinction. He was the last prominent Western head of government to resign over a matter of principle. Though other factors (such as his ill health, Tory party divisions, and the Profumo scandal) had dimmed his will to govern, his failure to secure British membership in the Common Market rankled most. He had not lost a vote in the House of Commons; he had not lost his seat in a general election; yet he felt he could not in conscience continue to lead Great Britain. His subsequent career, though obscure, was wholly useful. Most recently Macmillan, as Lord Stockton, was an admonisher against current Thatcher policies, which he felt were demeaning to Tory tradition and, worse, likely to lead to the defeat of the party in the next election.

[...]

In the United States, [until the Clinton administration] sexual conduct seems to have little bearing on politics, or on political resignation. Financial dealings of

---

Bad Ideas Whose Time Keeps Coming
(Short Takes)

"What we need is a practical person." Of which Gilbert Chesterton said:
Unfortunately there are always one or two available, who come in and take over, when what is needed is a thoughtful, reflective, informed person.

"He makes no small mistakes." Usually accompanied by a "steel trap mind" or a "computer type mind" and "he knows the numbers." A questionable qualification, attributed to Robert McNamara, as it leads one to watch for small mistakes, while larger ones go unnoticed until it is too late to do much, if anything, about them.

"He has never met a payroll." Usually offered in criticism of an officeholder or a candidate for office, especially for the presidency. In fact, no one has ever met a payroll like that of the federal government, and if this standard was applied absolutely about 99 percent of the U.S. citizens would be disqualified from office.

"I am for workfare not welfare." A phrase used most by recent presidents, with some variation, including Presidents Nixon, Carter, Reagan, and Clinton. It may be effective in a campaign, but in application after victory, seems to have little effect on the reduction of poverty.

"An efficient bureaucracy is the greatest threat to liberty."

questionable legality and morality are more often causes for resignation, and are sometimes followed by court proceedings and prison sentences. The usual defense is that the person accused believes he or she deserves the blame, but should not be held responsible. Businessmen, when under similar pressure to resign, more commonly say that they are responsible but not to blame. In both politics and business, the underlying assumption seems to be that unless one is both responsible and deserving of blame, somehow one is not guilty.

Officers of government below elected and cabinet rank have less occasion to depart than their superiors, if only because their responsibilities are lesser. When finally motivated to act, public officials who leave an administration whose position they can no longer support usually go quietly. They have been known to obscure their real reasons for leaving with explanations about health, family problems, or the need to earn money for educating their children. In the fifties and sixties, the fact that their corporate pensions would be in jeopardy used to be mentioned frequently. Nowadays, either private pension rules are more favorable to those who undertake government service, or else the fashion in excuses has changed—wanting to have more time with one's children tends to be today's popular reason.

Some stay on in service and, to all appearances, continue to support a policy of which they later say they did not approve. As time runs on, more of the persons who seemed to support the Vietnam War, and who stood against those who opposed the war, are saying that they really were against the war—or at least did not believe in it. Robert McNamara and Walter Mondale are prominent examples.

Others stay on and try to present their views from within, hoping that they can be more effective than if they left the citadel of power and joined, or attempted to lead, those outside the walls. George Ball evidently accepted this role in the Johnson administration and functioned as the devil's advocate on Vietnam. There is a prejudice against the devil's advocate, since he is cast as one resenting the bad side of a good cause.

Others may stay on and disagree publicly, at least as long as allowed to do so. When General Douglas MacArthur, in command of our military effort in Korea, chose this course, President Truman responded by dismissing MacArthur. Watergate Special Prosecutor Archibald Cox met a similar fate in the Nixon administration.

Officials of high reputation may leave quietly and be silent forever. In unusual circumstances, silence itself can be construed as protest. Sir Thomas More, who left his position as chancellor of England when he could no longer support Henry VIII, went silently. But as playwright Robert Bolt reports it in *A Man for All Seasons*, Thomas Cromwell, Henry's chief secretary, complained that "this silence is bellowing up and down Europe." More was beheaded.

Other officials may leave in violent protest. There is no good American example: One must turn to Samson for a clear illustration. A political prisoner blinded by the Philistines for sport, Samson, as the Scriptures say, " ... took hold of the two middle pillars upon which the house stood, and on which it was borne up. And he bowed himself with all his might, and the house fell on the lords, and upon the people that were therein." It also fell on Samson.

There is another way out; namely, to leave with a frank statement of reasons for leaving. This is the way that is least used in American politics. There are strong cultural and historical reasons for this. First, although it is perhaps time to establish one, there is no tradition of resignation for purpose in American politics, as there is in England, other European democracies, the Commonwealth, and Israel. Second, the structure of parliamentary government leaves little room for a dissident in a functioning government, whereas in our system the concept of cabinet members, in their relationship to a president, makes it easier to accept the immunity of agency.

There are also strong forces in American politics that run against dissent and against resignation. Loyalty to party is one such force. Thus, Governor Nelson Rockefeller received little party support for the Republican nomination in 1968 because he had refused to support the party's nominee, Senator Barry Goldwater, in 1964. However, most of the candidates for the Democratic party's presidential nomination in 1968—even, or especially, those who opposed the war in Vietnam— were quick to say that they would support the party's nominee no matter who he might be or what his war platform would be.

Besides party loyalty, another inhibiting force is the implication, usually propagated by the administration in power, that anyone who leaves is a quitter. A term from cattlehandling, applied in politics by Lyndon Johnson, saying that a departing official has "cut and run," might depict the attitude of most presidents to their subordinates, whether on or off the ranch.

In each case the person or persons involved must consider how to act with dignity and integrity, as related to the office that they hold or the seriousness of their disagreement. Bernard Kalb offered a useful example when he resigned as press officer at the State Department, rather than continue as spokesman for an administration that advocated "disinformation."

Some officials may stay on and murmur against presidents and policies in the gates and porticoes, at dinners and at cocktail parties, and offer high-level leaks to columnists and editors. This is the most reprehensible, though most frequent, response.

[...] A person in public office is never wholly free to keep private his views on vital public matters. That person must accept those times when the public good overrides personal considerations, and when loyalty to party, to an office, or even to a president should be set aside.

A time when resignations with explanations are both right and necessary for the public good comes infrequently. But when it does come, the statesman should sit up and be heard.

On the Road
(*Complexities and Contraries*, 1982)

No other country in the world winnows out its would-be Presidents the way we do in the United States. There is a little of the Roman arena about it, a serious, grueling matter that also aims to provide a full measure of entertainment for the spectators.

Every four years, as sure as ritual, aspirants for the Presidency willingly submit themselves to the campaign trail, accepting its bumpiness, its humiliations, its diet, and its disappointments. The way is long, yet candidates spring up by the dozens. My heart goes out to them, for in the wise words of television correspondent Herb Kaplow, "No two campaigns are different." I know, and I remember it well.

It is not the stuff of history that grinds a candidate down. It is not the search for a broad and winning campaign strategy. It is not the unfounded attacks on your position, the cream pies with your name on them. Those one can handle, like the heat in the kitchen.

The abrasive part of any campaign is made up of small things—people and events that seem to count for little. But as the old hillbilly song has it: "It's the little things you do that count. Little things, my dear, but how they mount."

Take drivers, for example. Campaign chairmen and press secretaries are important, of course, but the humbling truth is that they are expendable and easily replaced. Not so with drivers. A reliable, steady automobile driver is integral to a comfortable and terror-free campaign, and every candidate should carry such a person with him from state to state. It is a question of self-defense, for if a candidate arrives driverless in a new city, he will be given over, like a prisoner to the Inquisitor, to the local drivers. These are picked for fidelity and service to the party and not for skill behind the wheel. The worst of all—the driver who haunts my campaign nightmares—is the kind with a pulse in his foot. He has a personal interior metronome that causes him to speed up and slow down for no reason apparent to others. The statesman in the back seat, intent on scribbling immortal rhetoric on the back of an envelope, has every chance of arriving at the next event whey-faced with nausea. There are, of course, no heroics to be demonstrated or votes to be gotten from an announcement that the candidate is carsick.

Much has been written about the Secret Service and the personal security it provides. This is a real and welcome umbrella, no mistake about it. Yet, the usefulness of these quiet, somber men does not stop there. They are excellent advance men and a valuable source of excuses for not going where one doesn't want to go anyway. Further, they are usually fine drivers. In three campaigns during which I had Secret Service escorts, I found only one with the dread pulse in his foot. The director of the unit burdened with me promised that this agent would be watched carefully.

There are dangers on the campaign trail against which the Secret Service can do little. These are the dangers that the candidate, out of zeal to be a good sport, inflicts upon himself. There comes a time in any campaign when softball is in season, and it is a must for candidates. I regard softball as the ultimate perversion of baseball—especially slow-pitch, Jimmy and Billy Carter's favorite, which I think is far more dangerous than hardball. (This is certainly true if one counts sprained ankles and thumbs.) Yet, if I may say so, it is the importunities of photographers—who always want something visually arresting—that put the candidate in harm's way on the softball diamond.

The same goes for skiing, as George Romney found in New Hampshire. I learned only after making the commitment to play in an old-timers' hockey game in New Hampshire that "old-timers" was a term deceptively defined. Players merely had to be too old for the juvenile league and could not have played for the Boston Bruins. That left an appalling amount of room for talented players. I felt blessed to survive three turns on the ice and get my picture in *Time* magazine. My breathing returned to normal about two o'clock the next morning. Despite the risk, I could discern no difference in the outcome of the New Hampshire primary.

Another rule for thinking candidates is to stay away from horses. Even well-known horses are not to be trusted, especially in Fourth of July parades. A candidate on a sidling, skittish horse gives the voters second thoughts about the hand holding reigns of power. Unknown horses are not to be trusted under any circumstances.

A resolute candidate who is willing to risk being labeled a bad sport can avoid participant sports and their attendant risks. However, one must eat, and the dangers imposed on candidates by that fact may be the most fearsome of all. After all, President Harding died of food poisoning, or so they say. In the name of hospitality, candidates are threatened by good food and bad food, by food offered early in the day or late, by too much food and by too little food. It has sometimes seemed to me that the hot dish, usually a variation on macaroni and ground meat or, on Fridays, tuna fish and noodles, has become the sacramental offering—not to mention the burnt offering—of political campaigns. [...]

One must also sleep. When Walter Mondale announced that he was giving up his Presidential campaign in 1974 (a year in which one could not, in fact, run for the Presidency), he gave as one of his reasons his experiences in sleeping in motels.

Sleeping in motels can be an adventure, but it is scarcely traumatic enough to warrant dropping out of a campaign. The question for the candidate is what kind of bed arrangement he will find in his room: one double bed, two single beds, one double and one single, or two doubles. Alone in rooms with multiple beds, one may sleep restlessly, expecting to find the other bed occupied by morning. But sleeping restlessly in a Holiday Inn is far better than accepting the invitation of a campaign worker to stay at home with him. Such workers, while well intentioned and loyal, sometimes consider mattresses to be as permanent and unchangeable as the principles of the Democratic party. Almost eternal, that is to say. And even with new mattresses gratefully received, the candidate runs the risk of predawn discussions with the campaign worker about, say, the practicality of mutually assured nuclear deterrence.

A marginal risk, and one that must be accepted, is the rite of shaking hands at factory gates. It should be done while the workers are heading into the factory; the politician who stands at the gate at the end of the day will find himself, like a flaming sword, in the way of a tired worker who wants to go home, or—chancier still—between a thirsty man and his pub. The risk of plant-gate campaigning comes not from the unconvinced—people who aren't going to vote for you sidle quickly by. The danger is posed by your supporters, who will wring, squeeze, and pump your hand with slight regard to metacarpal alignment. At the end of the 1968 campaign, my doctor told me that I had a bad case of tennis elbow. Odd, I thought, since I had not picked up a racket once during the whole campaign. Then I remembered the arm-wrestling at those factory gates.

One learns on the long campaign trail that there are places where a politician may not be welcome. Beauty parlors, where tangle-haired voters shrink from your grasp, are an example. Drugstore campaigning also has its limitations. Customers there are often buying things for highly personal reasons. When sorting through corn plasters, denture adhesives, or trusses, they may not value the interruption of a politician asking, "How are your corns today?"

At the end of the trail, there is the problem faced by most political hopefuls: how to deal with defeat. After a fourth-place finish in Wisconsin in 1972, Ed Muskie said, "Winning isn't everything, but losing isn't anything." Dick Tuck, best known as a political prankster, faced his defeat in a California election by saying, "The people have spoken, the bastards." It matters most, I suppose, whether the defeat is intermediate or ultimate. Along the way, a candidate can tell his supporters, after a loss, say, in Indiana, "It's on to Michigan!" After a loss in Nebraska, one can try, "We will now hit the Oregon Trail." A loss in the East can bring forth Horace Greeley's "Go West, young [or old] man." Sallies like these will bring cheers from supporters, sometimes heartfelt, sometimes hollow. The candidate may also be tempted to drag out excuses or explanations, as if there were a difference between them: "We ran out of time." "The third candidate made the difference." "The weather was bad on election day." "The press coverage was inadequate."

Then there is the inevitable morning-after press conference with the ineluctable questions: "Are you ready to throw your support to another candidate?" "Do you look upon yourself as a spoiler from now on?" Reporters forget the answers almost immediately, but, from generation to generation, they do not forget the questions.

Vision of defeat: the abandoned campaign headquarters, with posters looking like broken kites; pamphlets and pictures strewn on the floor; crushed straw hats, plastic cups, the debris of American politics. In the room where the candidate and his top advisers waited out the results, morning dawns on the remains of the night's cocktail party, set up to celebrate the joy of victory but used to ease the pain of loss.

The most memorable morning-after for me was in the Cornhusker Hotel in Lincoln, Nebraska. I had lost the Nebraska primary of 1968, a defeat I had thought almost certain after two campaign stops. One was at a university and the other in the heart of the land of *O Pioneers!* My references to Willa Cather stirred no response.

Next to the hotel was the headquarters of a fundamentalist religious group. On the roof of their building was a red neon sign that night and day intermittently asserted JESUS BLED FOR YOU. From the building, again throughout the night and the day, hymns were not exactly broadcast but rather allowed to leak out.

The sun does not seem to rise over the prairies of Nebraska. The land sinks, and the sun is waiting. The flat light of the morning, of that particular morning, showed in the suite the remains of the previous night's indulgence. In the bowl that had held crisp crevettes on ice, only a few limp shrimp remained floating in the apologetic water. Scattered around the room, like specimens in an abandoned laboratory, were half-empty glasses of Scotch and bourbon. They stood among plates smeared with the remains of cocktail sauce.

Defeat in politics, even relative failure, is not easy to accept. Dismissing the troops, as both Napoleon and Robert E. Lee learned, is not easy. Soldiers do not want to take their horses and mules and go back to the spring plowing.

It is better to win.

Bring Back Polo: How to Kill October
(*Complexities and Contraries*, 1982)

The Federal Election Campaign Act of 1974, as amended after the Supreme Court found it defective on at least two major constitutional points, has properly been characterized as an incumbent insurance law. It is an insurance policy for the incumbent parties (the Democrats and Republicans) and for House members and Senators in office at the time the bill was passed.

The election is also a rich man's license to hunt in the field of politics. It limits campaign contributions generally to $1,000 per contributor, per candidate, per campaign; but it allows a wealthy candidate running for Congress to spend his own and his family's money without limit.

[...]

To restore order in both civil and military affairs two things are necessary: First, polo must be made, again, the exclusive game of the rich and of the wellborn. This should not be so difficult since although the game has declined, it has not been vulgarized. Second, the cavalry must be brought back as the branch of the military reserved principally for the noble and wellborn.

Action on the cavalry is secondary. The key is polo.

The early history of polo is unclear, both as to how the game was played and when it was invented. But there is no uncertainty about the fact that it was a game played only by kings and princes, and by those in the higher order of the nobility, including horsed warriors, who in the beginning of mounted warfare were drawn from the upper classes.

When polo was brought to England from India in 1876, and then to the United States a few years later, it was a game exclusively for the better classes. Polo playing fields were located in the areas in which the rich lived: Evanston, Illinois; Old Westbury and East Aurora, New York; Westport, Connecticut; Grosse Pointe, Michigan; Delray Beach, Florida; Harbor Hills, Ohio; Santa Barbara, California. Later, they were in areas near old cavalry sites or communities of the new rich like Phoenix, Arizona, and Austin, Texas. The list of players with handicaps, as late as 1949, was made up almost exclusively of Anglo-Saxon names like Abbot, Campbell, Evans, Pedley, and Guest. There was an occasional McCarthy, one Milton Untermeyer, a Darryl Zanuck, and a William Ylvisaker.

The decline of polo resulted from many forces. It never fully recovered from the Depression, and it was set back when the cavalry was abandoned in World War II. The automobile culture also had an adverse effect on polo. The new rich moved in on the game. Things fell apart.

The time has come to bring back the game, in pure and defined form. It must be restricted to the rich and to the wellborn. It must have a schedule that respects the seasons. It must be played only in the late summer and the fall. This time bridging the two seasons has become a time of restlessness and discontent for the

116

young rich, especially the males. There are things to be done in the winter: skiing, for example, and cruising in southern waters. Spring follows with golf, outdoor tennis, and early fly fishing. In the summer, there is the challenge of keeping cool, of Maine, of climbing mountains, of sailing in northern waters.

But what of the fall? "How do you kill October?" one rich young man was recently heard to ask sadly of another. With nothing challenging to do in the fall, and with politics the only thing going, the young rich have in greater and greater numbers been running for office. Even the old rich, beyond their polo-playing days (men like Averell Harriman), have dismounted and run for office.

The answer is polo. The restoration of the game would take care of the general need of the rich for action in the fall. It would also keep them out of politics.

Editor's Note

America is not only a nation of principles, it is a nation of institutions that help define and carry out these principles. In addition to examining the core political institutions that dominate American life in previous sections of this book, Eugene McCarthy has also written extensively on the subsidiary institutions that shape our lives, namely the military, the media, and corporations. While these three institutions have contributed many positive aspects to our nation, they have also at times wielded their influence in abusive ways, in a sense overreaching their position in society. Today, as we are faced with a press that oftentimes no longer strives for objectivity or skeptical inquiry, a federal government that often shapes policy to the will of corporate interests, and a military that shapes foreign policy, McCarthy's critical writings on these institutions serve as a call to action against such abuse.

FIVE

The Military, the Press, and Corporations

A Warning about the Military Establishment
(*The Hard Years*, 1975)

The military-industrial-academic establishment in America has become a kind of republic within the Republic. The military influence, as President Eisenhower warned in his Farewell Address, "is felt in every city, every State house, every office of the Federal government." Since he spoke, the situation has become more serious, more dangerous. [...] With military bases and missions in many nations of the world, with intelligence operations that include eavesdropping ships and spy satellites, and with sales of several billion dollars' worth of arms around the world, the Defense Department has become perhaps the strongest independent power in world affairs.

Defense Department actions are to a large extent beyond the effective control of the Congress. There is no conspiracy. Rather, the influence of the military in American life is something that happened to us almost without critical judgment and with little evaluation of the process.

The Pentagon spends much of its budget in direct procurement here at home. As the military budget has climbed, the Pentagon has had greater influence upon our foreign policy, upon our domestic policy, and upon the educational institutions of the United States. If it had a significant influence on only one of these, we would have cause for concern; as it has considerable influence on all three, we need to be triply concerned.

Increasing militarization of our foreign policy has been evident in our readiness to respond in military terms to problems around the world which may or may not be susceptible to military solutions. We sponsored an invasion of Cuba in 1961. We intervened, in violation of treaty commitments, by sending troops to the Dominican Republic in 1965. We sent over five hundred thousand troops to Vietnam, sponsored a mercenary army and heavy bombing in Laos, and also intervened in Cambodia.

The tendency to seek military solutions was encouraged by the many contingency plans of the Pentagon and the CIA. When a plan is developed and looks reasonably good, there is always a temptation to try it. This may have been what happened with the Bay of Pigs plan for the invasion of Cuba; it looked so good on paper that somebody said, "Maybe we should give it a try." Or perhaps someone said, "Those fellows over at the CIA and the Pentagon have spent so much time working on this plan, it would be a shame not to use it."

There was also a rumor that the Bay of Pigs plan was prepared in digest form for the Eisenhower administration, which always worked from summaries, and then was speed-read by the Kennedy administration. Under those circumstances it was bound to come up somewhat short, as in fact it did.

Often a plan is largely contingent on an effort by Communists to take over a government somewhere. In the 1965 Dominican Republic crisis, the United States ambassador in that country wired Washington about the trouble, stressing the fact that some Communists were involved in the revolt. A contingency plan was ready. So President Johnson decided that we had to save the country from the Communists and sent in the Marines.

Most serious of all was our involvement in Vietnam. The history of how and why we came to have more than a half-million American troops bogged down in Vietnam is long and complex. Yet if there was one crucial decision that set the course more than any other, it was the decision to commit American troops and try to impose a military solution in a country where the problems are chiefly political and social. The Johnson administration claimed that the real war was "the other war"; it held that the civilian-pacification program—or whatever it happened to be called at the moment—was of greatest importance to the outcome of the struggle in Vietnam. But even the pacification program eventually was turned over to the military.

The tendency to look at political problems in military terms was largely responsible for getting us into Vietnam. It was also responsible for much of our difficulty in getting out. Several incidents showed the confusion of roles between the military and the political. In April 1967 the military commander in Vietnam, General William C. Westmoreland, spoke to a joint session of the House and Senate. At that time I questioned on two grounds the appropriateness of having him speak to the Congress. First, it made Congress a captive audience for the presentation of a position on Vietnam which was well known, but which was at the same time highly controversial. Second, it meant using a field commander on active duty to make a case which was political as well as military.

Later in 1967 General Westmoreland returned to the United States and appeared on television with the United States Ambassador to South Vietnam, Ellsworth Bunker, in an attempt to justify the effort in Vietnam. This use of a military commander in what was essentially a public-relations capacity was contrary to the tradition of subordination of military to civilian authority, and of military judgment to political judgment, on which this nation was founded.

Early in 1968 the Joint Chiefs of Staff advised President Johnson that the American outpost at Khe Sanh, then besieged by the North Vietnamese, "could and should be defended." The first part of that assurance was a military judgment; the second may have been partly a military judgment, but the context in which it was given was largely political. We ought not to concede a political role to the Joint Chiefs so easily.

As a member of the Senate Foreign Relations Committee, I saw growing evidence of subservience of the State Department and the Johnson administration to determinations and judgments by the military. This observation was sustained by what happened in Vietnam.

It was also sustained by the decision to build an antiballistic-missile system, which Robert McNamara and other experts had admitted would add little or nothing to the nation's security.

It was sustained by what happened on arms sales to developing nations. The Johnson administration at times seemed to lobby harder for its arms-sales program than for civil rights or aid to education. The Foreign Relations Committee tried to place limits on American arms distribution around the world in 1966 and 1967. Despite administration opposition, we set limits on weapons sales to Africa and Latin America. In opposing these restrictions, the administration claimed that they would seriously hamper our foreign policy in those countries, which, of course, was precisely what we were trying to do.

Administration officials claimed that limits on arms distribution would seriously interfere with military strength in Greece. The Greek colonels, however, seemed more interested in overthrowing their own government than in making a contribution to the North Atlantic Treaty Organization (NATO). The administration said that it needed arms for Iran because of the unsettled situation in the Middle East, and added, "If we do not sell planes to Iran, they will probably go to the Russians for military equipment." We did sell the planes to Iran, and a short time later the Iranians went to the Russians for additional military equipment anyway.

Arms sales were continued and expanded during the Nixon administration. The United States continued to arm the military dictatorships of Greece and other nations. When India warred with Pakistan in 1971, both sides used arms supplied by the United States. The same thing had happened during their 1965 war. Sales to governments in Latin America increased; this encouraged military coups and border disputes and distracted governments from the economic development needed by their people.
[...]
Much of our representation overseas is military. [...] We consider very seriously whether we ought to have diplomatic representation in certain countries, and the Senate examines quite thoroughly the qualifications of ambassadors who are sent abroad. Yet the military-aid groups, which are sometimes more important, are sent without any kind of formal congressional examination. Without publicity or even public awareness in the United States, these officers carry on missions which have strong political overtones.

The Special Forces, too, are not subject to normal congressional or public supervision. We used to know when the Marines landed and also when they came home. With the Special Forces, we do not know when they go in; we know little about what they do while they are there; and we are never sure about whether they have come home. [...]

In addition to its influence in the international arena, there is serious involvement of the military establishment in domestic affairs of the United States. It is not necessary to accept the old argument that war production stimulates the economy. What is much more significant today is the particular interest developed in certain industries and certain areas of the country with reference to military contracts and other military spending. [...]

What are the effects on our economy of this enormous economic power? Sudden surges within the military sector have certainly contributed to inflation. We still suffer from the inflationary spiral started by deficit spending for the Vietnam war. But this is only one part of the military impact on our economy.

[...] Military technology has become very sophisticated, and its workers are often better paid than workers engaged in other production. Professional workers and skilled blue-collar workers make up a large part of the military employment. Thus military work not only draws away many workers from civilian activities, it also takes a proportionately large number of highly qualified workers.

Entire cities and even states become heavily dependent on military spending—not only for the direct employment it provides but also for the consumer spending and the tax base that it makes available. Decisions to close military bases or to shift contracts to other states always meet strong political opposition and are often postponed or changed for that reason. And new weapons systems [...] are supported by many members of Congress in part because such systems will provide more employment in their districts or states.

Of the weapons systems in general, one might say that it was a great mistake to let the cavalry go. It kept the colonels busy on weekends and kept them from planning war. The cavalry was also cheaper than current weapons systems. Today we have manned bombers instead of a cavalry. The bombers cost a good deal more than the horses.

[...]

When I was in the Senate, I wondered if some of my colleagues would ever feel secure. If the sky were black with bombers, if there were so many nuclear submarines in the ocean that they were running into each other, some senators would still be insecure. I hesitate to mention some of the serious weapons gaps we face, because those senators might introduce legislation to close them. We are way behind the Indians of the Amazon in blowguns and poison darts. In fact, we do not have any poison darts. Moreover, we are short of catapults, crossbows, pikes, shields, cauldrons for boiling oil.

[...]

I hope that the people will bring some judgment to bear on the direction of the military complex, on the militarization of our foreign policy, and on the influence of the military upon our domestic life. This is particularly important now because America has become a major world leader. We must decide whether we will direct this leadership toward continuing a kind of militaristic policy, or whether we will try to blunt that thrust and inject into American politics and government an understanding of our true role. This nation should not make its record by being a military power, but by demonstrating that all of those things which we claim for ourselves—the right to life, liberty, and the pursuit of happiness and a basic belief in the dignity and worth of the individual—are the real strengths of America and that these are the best gifts we can offer to the rest of the world.

A Short History of the Neutron Bomb
(*Culpeper News*, October 1, 1981)

The neutron bomb had a modest beginning in calculations made on the back of an old envelope by S. T. Cohen, known as "the Father of the Neutron Bomb." It has no known or identified "mother." The theory and calculations were soon put to the test of technology and found workable. The essential parts of the bomb were manufactured during the administration of President Jimmy Carter, assembled in the administration of President Ronald Reagan, deployed in the administration of his successor, and used by the subsequent president in the millennial year A.D. 3000. Tests in the 1970s were conducted on monkeys, never on human beings, according to Defense Department officials of the time. Estimates of biological effects of the bomb on human beings were "synthesized."

In the early experiments, monkeys were placed in cubicles called "squeeze boxes" and exposed to radiation doses similar to those that would be released in the explosion of a neutron bomb. The monkeys used in the test had been trained to run on a treadmill.

The radiation, according to the testers, did not pain the monkeys. Five seconds after the exposure, each animal was put back on the treadmill. Results varied from monkey to monkey, but 80 percent became incapacitated within eight minutes of the exposure. All of the monkeys eventually died.

Some scientists then held that the results of exposure found in monkeys could not with certainty be directly translatable to human beings. "Clinical information," they said, would be the only way to determine human reaction.

Later studies under more natural conditions (a contained monkey farm) achieved results more applicable to the human condition. Monkeys exposed to

---

Threats to Democratic Government and Society (*Short Takes*)

A military establishment of great economic, political, and military power (the Military Industrial Complex, of which we were warned by President Eisenhower and by Alexis de Tocqueville)

Major areas of government, whole agencies, in which basic constitutional rights and liberties are not honored, as in the Internal Revenue Service, in which privacy, due process, equal protection of the law, and the principal of innocence until proved guilty are not protected, and in which actions traditionally disapproved in the United States, such as "informing," and practices bordering on "bounty hunting" and "tax farming" are used.

Nongovernmental institutions beyond society or government control, in our case, principally major corporations, national, international, and multinational, which exercise independent powers of sovereignty

A monopoly press, or a depersonalized one, controlled by corporations of great size and power

It's dangerous for a
national candidate to say
things that people might
remember.

the heavy blast reacted much as did the monkeys in the squeeze box. For those outside the range of heavy dosage, death did not come quickly. There was evidence of discomfort, if not pain, and much vomiting. The monkey house itself was unharmed.

Monkeys at the outer range of the enclosure did not appear to suffer any immediate effects, but succeeding generations of the exposed monkeys began to show mutations. Tails grew shorter, and finally disappeared. The amount of body hair decreased. Forelegs grew shorter. Eventually there was a generation that stood up and walked on its hind legs at about sixteen months of age and began to say words such as "da-da" and "mama."

Some grew up and were trained to be tank operators. In the millennial war of the year 3000, their tanks were targets of the neutron bomb. Those that were in tanks at or near the center of the blast were incapacitated within eight minutes. All of those eventually died, continuing until the last moment to drive the tanks, which, even after the death of their operators, continued to run on until stopped by walls, or rivers, or lack of fuel. Operators outside the central area of the blast died more slowly. They showed evidence of discomfort, if not pain, and vomited profusely.

Others, farther removed from the blast area, did not appear to suffer any immediate effects, but succeeding generations began to show mutations. They began to grow tails. The amount of body hair increased. Their arms began to grow longer. They stooped more, and eventually began to walk on four feet, to speak a different language, and to spend more and more time in trees. They had a strong attachment to treadmills.

Censorship
(*The Hard Years*, 1975)

Most discussion of censorship in recent times has dealt with efforts to limit or halt the use of pornographic material after it has been produced.

More serious in a democracy is the selection and control of political information and ideas before they are even spoken or published.

Who determines what persons shall speak and write, since not everyone can speak or write? Who selects what is to be recorded and transmitted to others, since not everything can be recorded?

There is danger in the concentrated control of television and radio stations; danger, too, in government efforts to regulate broadcasting. There is danger in concentrated ownership of newspapers and some danger in the development of nationally syndicated columnists. There is danger in standardized education and in the concentration of selection by book publishers and reviewers.

[...]

The problem of government control over information seems more dangerous and more difficult to counter. In the name of national security, the government justifies the withholding of almost any item of information and, beyond that, even the making of false statements.

The problem of government control was intensified during the Eisenhower administration, in part because many of its appointees were drawn from big business and from the military. The procedures of those institutions are not democratic, nor are they ordinarily conducted with the safeguards of the Constitution. Neither of them has anything comparable to the "balance of powers" concept.

Consequently, the Eisenhower administration took on many aspects of a corporate-military structure. The President and his Cabinet resembled the top executives of a corporation or the high officers of a military establishment. They set policy and administered it largely on their own initiative; they resisted external review.

The Congress was treated very much like a corporate board of directors, or junior military officers—occasionally gathered for a briefing, given permission to ask a few questions, but not necessarily given full answers. Congressional recommendations were politely received and conveniently filed away. The general understanding was that the senior officers had more complete knowledge and thus were in a better position to determine policy.

The people, of course, were at the lowest level of the structure. They were comparable to corporate stockholders or army troops. The general policy toward them was to withhold information which might discourage them or might cause them to lose heart, and to tell them only those things likely to encourage optimism.

At the time it seemed that this model might be only a temporary departure from tradition. But subsequent administrations not only copied the Eisenhower model, they made it worse.

One official of the Kennedy administration suggested that news generation by the government "is part of the weaponry"; he also suggested a government's right to lie. The Johnson administration withheld much significant information and distorted or even fabricated other information. The "credibility gap" became an everyday phrase to describe that administration.

The Nixon administration continued the pattern. During President Nixon's first term, a Senate Foreign Relations subcommittee studied United States military commitments around the world. The subcommittee, chaired by Senator Stuart Symington of Missouri, encountered great difficulty in obtaining information from the administration. Even in cases where the administration provided information, it often insisted on deleting the information from the public transcript. Much of this censorship evidently had nothing to do with national security. Rather, it was used to avoid embarrassment to our government and to some foreign governments. The Nixon administration also gave false information to the Congress with reference to the bombing of Cambodia.

In 1971 Daniel Ellsberg released to major newspapers the documents known as the Pentagon Papers. These traced the development of American activity in Vietnam in great detail and proved deception of Americans by their government over a period of many years. Though the Nixon administration itself was not covered by the Pentagon Papers, it sought court orders to prevent *The New York Times* and *The Washington Post* from printing the papers.

It was not only the government that indicated a failure to understand the Bill of Rights on this occasion. The *Times* and the *Post* retreated in the face of government pressure; they stopped printing the papers until the injunctions were overturned by the Supreme Court. They backed off and said in effect, "We hope the Court will save us." They thus weakened their claim to freedom of the press.

They also indicated a serious misunderstanding of that freedom. It is not a private right of newspapers. Essentially it is a matter of the public's right to knowledge and to truth. The newspapers did not have a right to withhold the truth from the people; they had an obligation to publish it. The press is responsible to the people, not to the government.

Recognition of this responsibility is essential to democracy. The press must stand as a defender of the people against large concentrations of power, including the power of government. In particular, the press must stand against the notion that the people cannot be trusted with information. If the people of a democracy are to make reasoned judgments, they must have the information on which such judgments can be based.

The Fourth Estate Becomes the First Estate
(*The Ultimate Tyranny,* 1980)

FROM INFALLIBILITY TO THE SEAL OF THE CONFESSIONAL

The American "free press" is more fiction than fact. Unbridled and open communication through the press is limited, first because in most major population centers newspapers are monopolies, and second, because major newspapers, as a rule, operate within a corporate form which emphasizes economic gain and profitability as the relevant standards of success. Third, the press does not clearly understand its role in American society.

The press has apparently come to think of itself as an institutionalized Fourth Estate, with special powers and privileges never granted to it by the Constitution or by statute. The powers and privileges once exercised by the church as the First Estate in medieval society now belong to the press.

In a country without an established religion or a recognized infallible head of the church, the press claims a comparable function—to speak arbitrarily, which is to say "ex cathedra," that term here called "the editor's chair."

The press has its own form of dreaded Index according to which it censors news and gives readers only what is good for them to know. "All the news that's fit to print," declares the *New York Times.* One can fairly ask by whose determination? Fit for whom? Fit for what? As medieval inquisitors decided what people should believe, so do newspapers decide who is and is not newsworthy, who is to be made much of or little of or nothing of. The press can give the secular equivalents of "beatification," "canonization," and the "interdict"; it can "excommunicate" and even "condemn," though it still does not dare burn at the stake.

[...]

If the press were, in fact, carrying out a function comparable to that attributed to the church, special privileges and exemptions might be granted. But the record of the press over the past twenty years does not lend evidence to support the granting of such special status. The press has failed as an important influence on major social and political issues of the past two decades.

Alfred Friendly, in the *Washington Post* on February 13, 1977, attempted to explain and excuse the press for its building up of the whole anti-Communist cold-war attitude of the early fifties. Friendly acknowledged that within a month after Senator Joseph McCarthy's famous Wheeling, West Virginia, Lincoln Day speech in February 1950, it was clear that he was using fraudulent material (it was actually a rewrite of a Nixon speech given to him by the Republican National Committee). Yet, major newspapers continued to give McCarthy the kind of front-page attention usually reserved for the President of the United States.

Friendly said, "At the outset, for the first week or so, and before they could be examined, McCarthy's charges appeared to be of the most profound national security significance and might, quite possibly, be true." The Senate then panicked and held hearings. "For the press to have ignored the most newsworthy event in the Congress (however phony the thing was beginning to look), the focus of congressional and, almost at once, national attention, is preposterous." Friendly is right. No one expected the press to ignore the story. The point of criticism is its exploitation, its overpublication, of nearly every charge that was made by McCarthy. In contrast is the way the press reported Congressman Hale Boggs's charge some twenty years later that the FBI was spying on members of Congress. When the congressman did not name the people involved and publicly prove his point as requested, the press generally rejected his statement as irresponsible and untrue. Subsequently, he was shown to have been correct. One can only speculate as to what might have happened if the press had only insisted on comparable proof from Senator Joseph McCarthy in 1950.

A disastrously wounding failure on the part of the press was in its coverage of the Vietnam War. Long after there was massive evidence that the administration, especially Dean Rusk and Robert McNamara, did not know what they were talking about in stating needs, in describing events in Vietnam, the press dutifully headlined their every statement. It accepted handouts, reports of success and of progress, almost without challenge or question. All of this was passed on to the public. Most newspapers continued to support the war well into 1969 despite the reports of reliable reporters who were covering the war in Vietnam itself.

Most of the press appeared not to have discovered the truth about the war in Vietnam until after the publication of the Pentagon Papers. Their publication was widely called a heroic act in the name of freedom of the press. The only risk faced by the press was financial, in the possibility that it would have to defend itself against the government in court, but the case was soon settled in the press's favor against a pre-publication federal injunction. In any case, there was little that was surprising in the Papers. To discover that persons in the Pentagon had actually talked against the war should not have been surprising. That there were plans to stifle criticism, and at the same time doubts and disagreements; that the whole truth was not told either to Congress or to the American people—this certainly was not surprising news. Nor was the information, if published, a threat to the national security. The publication of the Papers was billed as a great act of heroic journalism, when in fact what was contained in the reports was familiar, and almost irrelevant.

Haynes Johnson, writing in the *Washington Post* of June 24, 1973, accuses the press of lack of vigor and of general subservience to government policies and programs. The press, Johnson wrote, during the Vietnam War, "was a willing accomplice of government secrecy, official trial balloons, and justifications for policy failures. It was, for the most part, a staunch supporter of government policies, especially in foreign affairs." He also noted the dangers to a reporter in letting himself or herself be taken into the inner ring. "Journalists," he wrote, "came to like the informality and the close association with the cream of Washington officialdom. Out-of-town publishers and editors relished having their men in

Washington set up meetings with major figures, including an occasional presidential session."

White House invitations, preserved in permanent plastic, mounted on the mantels of editors' homes or on the desks of their offices, should be seen as signs of surrender rather than achievement. A few truly professional newspersons refuse to participate in "background meetings." [...]

In radio and television coverage of political campaigns, reporters and correspondents (it is better to be a correspondent, although no one explains what the difference is) are assigned to candidates—as a rule, early in campaigns. A reporter who covers the successful candidate for President usually becomes a White House correspondent after the candidate is installed in office.

[...]

The press generally has taken deep bows for the coverage of the Watergate case and the resignation of Richard Nixon. In fact, the pursuit of the case was almost an accident at the start, and afterward it was an act of continuing perseverance by two reporters, Bob Woodward and Carl Bernstein, sustained eventually by their newspaper editor and publisher, rather than an achievement to be credited to the press generally.

[...]

It is instructive and interesting to compare the methods used by the "plumbers" of the Nixon campaign with those used by the investigative press, as reported in the Woodward and Bernstein book *All the President's Men*. The "plumbers" used illegal wiretaps; the investigators had people listen to telephone conversations on extension phones. The "plumbers" bugged their subjects; the investigative reporters eavesdropped and used confidential sources. The "plumbers," or the administration, had the FBI check long-distance phone calls with the telephone company; the investigative reporters persuaded sources in the telephone company to give them similar information.

The "plumbers" and their principals were found guilty of obstructing justice; the investigative reporters narrowly escaped prosecution on the charge of tampering with a grand jury.

The "plumbers" broke and entered; the investigative reporters used false identification or misrepresentation of their professional role to get interviews.

The "plumbers" rifled files; the investigative reporters examined, when not watched, what they could find on desks.

The "plumbers," at least some of them, demanded that they be paid off by the Nixon campaign committee; according to their book, the investigative reporters came close to blackmail by threatening to expose informants to superiors.

The "plumbers" sought to justify their actions on the grounds that they were serving a high purpose, the reelection of Richard Nixon. The investigative reporters justified their methods on comparable grounds.

[...]

The press appears to be unmindful or unaware of its theoretical function in society, and either unmindful or indifferent to the reality of the times in which it now functions. The press today proceeds as though there were a free and competitive flow of information in this country comparable to that of 150 years ago, when there was no television or radio, and when technological limitations restricted the largest newspaper runs to about 5,000 papers a day. The reality is, in Lyndon Johnson's words to Spiro Agnew after the 1968 elections: "Young man, we have in this country two big television networks, NBC and CBS. We have two news magazines, *Newsweek* and *Time*. We have two wire services, AP and UPI. We have two pollsters, Gallup and Harris. We have two big newspapers, the *Washington Post* and the *New York Times*. They're all so damned big, they think they own the country. But, young man, don't get any ideas about fighting."

[...]

Of course the media cannot report all of the news, but there are standards for selection which the media should recognize as guiding their profession. The press and electronic communications media do not have the right to suppress news that they do not want the public to know, especially when covering political campaigns. There are at least three standards for positive selection. Obviously, if someone is speaking sense and having an effect, there is an obligation to report what is being said. If someone is talking nonsense and having an effect, the press has, I believe, as a monopoly or near-monopoly, an obligation to report the nonsense (although it can and should challenge the nonsense with information and analysis). [...]

If someone is speaking sense about current problems and not yet having any significant effect, what he says should also be reported. It is in this third area that the failure of the media is most serious. As Oswald Spengler wrote in *The Decline of the West*, "It is permitted to everyone to say what he pleases, *but* the press is free to take notice of what he says or not. It can condemn any 'truth' to death simply by not undertaking its communication to the world—a terrible censorship of silence, which is all the more potent in that the masses of newspaper readers are absolutely unaware that it exists." The danger of denial is even greater when a person becomes dependent for news, not on reading, but on one- or two-minute radio or television newscasts.

[...]

The press makes fitful gestures to demonstrate fairness, balance, or concern over its monopoly position. Many papers have in-house critics, but there is no record that any such critic has had a lasting effect on his paper's news or editorial policy. This self-criticism has been described as similar to that of a monkey at the zoo picking lice or dry skin off its own chest. The act gives some relief but does not change the animal.

Letters to the editor and expansion of the Op-Ed pages are other offerings to fairness. Their effect in setting up balance in the press or an adversary presentation is minimal. Along with serious articles, Op-Ed pages usually carry others that are on the edge of the ridiculous, if not over the edge. The seriousness of the Op-Ed page is reflected in its treatment by the *New York Times*. The *Times*, by long tradition, has not carried cartoons on its editorial page. The explanation has been that it judges cartoons to be a distraction from the serious thought being presented in its editorials. On its Op-Ed page, however, the *Times* regularly carries distracting cartoons—pictures of men on horseback with trees growing out of their heads, and the like. Evidently, distraction on the Op-Ed page is not a serious concern to the *Times* editors. It does serve as a marked contrast with the seriousness of the left-hand editorial page (the official, approved commentary) for which the editors take full responsibility.

The press seems unaware of the relationship and interdependence of all of the freedoms guaranteed by the Bill of Rights, and often gives the impression (if it does not quite assert) that as long as there is freedom of the press, all other freedoms and liberties will be secure. Any person, profession, or institution protected by the Constitution has a very special responsibility to be concerned about the protection of the rights guaranteed to others. Churches, for example, which enjoy the protection guaranteed by the freedom of religion, cannot safely advocate restrictions of others' rights without endangering their own freedom. A political party protected by freedom of assembly should not interfere with freedom of others to organize. It should not interfere with the freedom of speech or with freedom of the press unless it wishes to run the risk of endangering its own security. Nor can the press, for the sake of its own freedom, safely be indifferent to interference with freedom of speech or assembly, or the right of privacy or due process, or any other freedoms guaranteed by the Constitution.

But the press has been indifferent and careless. When the Supreme Court, in 1976, held that the Federal Election Campaign Act violated freedom of speech in provisions which had generally been supported by the press, the press did not report the Court decision as a victory for freedom of speech. (Freedom of the press was not threatened by this act.) Instead they described the decision (which held that no monetary limit could be placed on expenditures of personal funds by anyone to advance political ideas) with the headline "Fat Cats Protected by Supreme Court."

Failure of the writing press, or what is called the "print media," to understand and meet its responsibilities is especially serious, for it is through the writing press that lines of thought and policy are developed on which reasoned judgment can be passed.

The writing press is not under technological pressure or the pressure of time to present a story and provide instant analysis within one or two minutes, nor are newspapers in danger of losing licenses, as are television and radio stations.

The profession of journalism is not an easy one. It must be exercised under criticism, even under threat. Winston Churchill said of democracy that it is the worst form of government, except for the other forms that have been tried from time to time. So one can, even must, say the same of a "free press."

The Corporations
(*The Hard Years*, 1975)

The corporation is today recognized as a basic force in American life but also as a major problem. It is challenged to answer for its failure to produce enough to meet the needs of the nation. It is challenged for its failure to produce safe and economical products. It is challenged to answer for its waste and its pollution of air, water, and earth. It is challenged for its influence on education, on culture, on politics, and especially on the politics of war.

This examination is long overdue, for the corporation has developed into a separate center of power. It is one which was not anticipated by or provided for in the Constitution. It is one which has not been subject to the general laws dealing with business and financial practices. And it is one which has assumed functions that go far beyond its original economic purposes.

What we have allowed to develop is a kind of corporate feudalism, one that fits the schoolboy definition of feudalism as a system in which everybody belongs to someone and everyone else belongs to the king. In its modern form, nearly every worker belongs to some corporation. Everyone else—in civil service, on welfare, on workmen's compensation or social security—belongs to the government.

A great corporation might be viewed as a self-contained feudal manor or barony. General Motors, for example, has its own financial institutions, its own distribution system, its own labor policy and social welfare program, its own security system and special investigators, even its own foreign policy. And the foreign policy of ITT in the case of Chile included an effort to have the United States government prevent the election of a certain presidential candidate in that country. Other multinational corporations run their own foreign policies.

I would hesitate to make a direct comparison between today's corporation employees and the serfs of the Middle Ages, yet there are disturbing similarities. Many people become economic captives of the corporations for which they work. Pension programs, family health plans, seniority rewards, vacation and sick leave all limit the freedom of employees to move to other corporations and other types of work. This is true not only of blue-collar workers but also of executives and people in professional fields. I have talked with newspaper people who say, "I can't quit this newspaper and take another job because I would lose my pension program, or my family medical plan. I'm an indentured servant. I'm caught." An indentured servant may be a few steps above a serf, but that is not much consolation.

The loss of freedom that goes with working for a corporation is not always accompanied by security, something that serfs in the Middle Ages did have. Many corporations, particularly those in the military and aerospace industries, stockpiled engineers and other professionals during the boom period of the 1960s. When the corporations faced financial difficulty, or when they no longer needed the professionals, they simply cut them loose to become displaced persons in our society. In recent years, a relief pitcher in the minor leagues has had more security than a Ph.D. in physics who works for a major corporation. [...]

Feudal lords had certain obligations toward the poor, something that cannot be said of our corporations. America's poor and minorities, its undereducated and underfed, are not even the serfs of corporate feudalism. They are its outcasts.

The feudal analogy also holds when one considers the relations between the federal government and large corporations. In case after case of confrontation between the two in the last fifteen to twenty years, the issues have been settled by negotiation. When the question of sending an ambassador to the Vatican was raised in 1960, I suggested that there were other centers of power at which we were unrepresented and which were far ahead of the Vatican in terms of influence. For example, a President might first send an ambassador to the Pentagon and then to several of the giant corporations: General Motors, du Pont, General Electric, U.S. Steel, some of the oil companies. The relationship was not formalized that way, but negotiation has been the rule.

[...]

The dealings of the government with the steel industry illustrate the feudal character of the corporation-government relationship even more clearly. During the Korean war, President Truman tried to prevent a steel strike by ordering his Secretary of Commerce to take over and operate the steel mills. The case was taken to the Supreme Court, which held that the order was unconstitutional. Subsequent challenges to the industry were handled differently. The Kennedy administration responded to a major price increase not by law or by appeal to courts but by public denunciation, the threat of shifting military purchases to steel companies that had not raised their prices, and even some use of the FBI.

The Johnson administration called presidents of steel companies to the White House for "jaw-boning sessions." The message was that prices should be kept down. It seemed that if the steel executives fixed prices in the White House, it was quite all right, but if they fixed them in Pittsburgh, they might go to jail. It was as though the king had called in the barons and said to them, "If you agree to these things in my presence, they are sanctioned. But if you do it by yourselves in Wales, you are in trouble."

The approach of the Nixon administration to wage-price controls reflected the same feudal character. The idea that it is all right for big government to sit down with big business and big labor to make decisions about the economy is a different concept from what the framers of the Constitution had in mind.

Most of the production in the United States is controlled by corporate management. This is largely a consequence of the special privileges and immunities given by law to corporations to make them more effective in meeting the economic needs of the nation. The grant of special privileges and immunities implied that the corporation provided the best way to produce and distribute goods and also the best way to provide employment.

How then do we explain underproduction and wasteful production in the country? How do we explain the fact that some twenty-three million Americans are poor and that over seven million are out of work? Is the explanation to be found in bad corporate management? Are the failures a consequence of outside forces which hamper the corporations in their management of the American economy? Or is the fault in the very concept of the corporation?

The answers are not altogether clear. Undoubtedly some corporations are badly run. Undoubtedly outside policy or forces, such as war and poor fiscal management by government, adversely affect the general economy and specifically affect some industries and areas. More serious, however, than these considerations is the question of whether the concept under which the corporation has developed and operated is a valid one.

I think that the concept of the corporation still has validity but that it must be constantly judged on performance. It is a concept which must prove its own vitality in practice. And if the corporation is to be privileged as it is now, if it is to control most of the forces on which the material well-being of the nation depends, then it must become more effective and more responsible, both socially and economically, than it now is. Its great power must be subject to certain limits.

There are several things we can and must do in the area of corporate reform. First, we must assure greater freedom for corporation employees. As the power of the feudal lords ended, the kings took over. Our problem is to develop systems of security without surrendering personal freedom to the government. One way to give people more freedom is to reduce risk through greater protection in unemployment and health benefits. We need significant improvement in the national unemployment-compensation program so that employees will not be as dependent on the unemployment programs of corporations as many now are. We need national health insurance to replace or supplement corporate plans. [...] The point is to reduce the economic insecurity of corporation employees while at the same time expanding their personal freedom.

Second, we must make corporations operate within the law. The most obvious laws—the ones with reference to price-fixing and pollution, for example—can and should be enforced. Continued exploitation of migrant workers should not be tolerated. In some cases it can be ended by enforcing existing laws; but where existing legal standards are inadequate, it would be naïve to expect even a corporation of some good will to move very far ahead of its competitors.

Third, we must impose upon corporations certain social responsibilities in exchange for their social privileges of limited liability and favorable tax rates.

In considering the concept of social responsibility, it is important not to be distracted by corporate advertising. If we believed the public-relations spokesmen of some corporations, we might think their principal function is charity or the support of education. At one time when I was in Philadelphia, a company was publicizing its provision of free chemicals to kill the termites in the timbers of

Independence Hall. You almost had the impression that they did it back in 1776 and that if it had not been for this the Revolution never would have happened. The television ads of some oil companies give the impression that they are refining oil just to provide bird sanctuaries and habitats for small animals. If you drive through Bayonne, New Jersey, you receive a somewhat different impression.

The concept of social responsibility must be related to the corporation's primary economic functions. We have a right to say to the corporations, "We have given you special privileges, and here is what has happened: not enough production, not enough employment, twenty-three million poor."

When full employment does not result from the more or less autonomous operation of the corporations—the case today—we must consider spreading employment through federal legislation. This can be done by requiring a shorter work day, a shorter work week, or longer vacations. We have not done anything to spread work since the Fair Labor Standards Act of 1938 and the amendments to it established the standard eight-hour day, forty-hour week, and fifty-week year. We have had over thirty years of progress in technology since then—yet the standard for working time remains the same. That Act was a result of the Great Depression and of the need to spread existing work.

Fourth, we should re-examine the political power of corporations. This, of course, is not a new problem. I recall in particular a large corporation in Minnesota. Whenever I was running for Congress on the Democratic-Farmer-Labor ticket, it would give five or six of its employees three months of paid vacation and no instructions. But instead of going to the mountains or the sea, they would always wind up in Republican headquarters.

[...]

The time has come to raise a significant challenge to the political, economic, and social power of corporations.

To accept the idea that the corporation, as a center of economic and political power, should be free of social control is to misunderstand the nature of the institution itself. It is also to accept a formula for continued failure to meet the economic and social needs of our country.

Editor's Note

A devout Roman Catholic, Eugene McCarthy attended St. John's University in St. Cloud, Minnesota, and studied as a novice Benedictine monk for one year. After college, McCarthy taught sociology at various Catholic institutions and was a member of the Catholic Rural Life Movement prior to his election as representative in 1948. A deep religious thinker, he counted Reinhold Niebuhr among his many friends. Yet in his years as representative and senator, he did not impose his religious beliefs on his constituents or the legislative process, instead using his moral background in a quiet, introspective manner to inform his thinking. Today politicians stand in direct contrast to this "quiet morality," frequently wearing their religion on their sleeve (often in a superficial manner) and using religion as a divisive tactic, in effect legislating morality. Meanwhile, the separation of church and state, a basic premise of our democracy, crumbles (remember, while most of the founders were deeply religious, they felt religion had no role in governance). Reading McCarthy's writings about religion and its role in American society, one is struck by the difference in his approach and the modern world, creating a yearning for a more inclusive, less divisive time.

Religion

SIX

Religion and Politics
(*The Challenge of Freedom*, 1960)

It is common in countries of Western Europe to apply the word *Christian* to political movements and to political parties. In the United States none have been so labeled. It is, however, popular practice to declare that there is a Christian or religious approach to politics and to identify one's own stand on issues as a Christian or religious stand.

Although most Americans accept the doctrine of the separation of church and state as a formal proposition, they do not in practical politics make the same distinctions. One member of Congress is reported to have gone so far as to declare that if the Arabs and the Jews would get together in Christian fashion, the problems of the Middle East could easily be settled.

I will here limit my comments to the question of Christian politics. But the questions and conclusions relating to Christianity and politics do, I believe, have application to relationships between other religions and politics.

The first question to be answered is this: Is there a Christian politics? Throughout the history of Christian civilization political thinkers and leaders, as well as religious leaders, have attempted to define and describe what they considered the ideal Christian state. Some have seen this ideal state in the medieval synthesis of state and church and looked to the restoration of a similar order in this our day. Others have conceived of the ideal Christian state as a monarchy, with a Christian monarch defending both faith and country. Others, including a number of modern writers, envision the Christian state as a democracy founded upon the natural law.

If the concept of Christian politics is to be justified at all, or if any historical state is to merit the label *Christian*, it must be of such kind that, as Franz Joseph Schöningh, editor of *Hochland*, pointed out in the April 1949 issue of that magazine, "fundamentally, through its Christian character alone, it differs from every other." Yet neither history nor political theory establishes any basis for the application of the label *Christian* in any absolute sense to politics.

Recognition of Christianity by the state does not make the state itself "Christian," neither does official approval of certain Christian forms and practices. Nor does the fact that all citizens of a state are Christians make that state a Christian state. A government, I suppose, might be distinguished as more or less

Christian to the degree that it has either succeeded or failed in establishing a greater measure of justice; or, a form of government called Christian to the extent that it depends upon the inspiration of the Gospels for its fulfillment, as does democracy. Such qualified application, however, sets limits—rather risky ones—to the use of the word *Christian*. It is worthwhile to consider the words of Bishop Ketteler, who points out that a Christian state is such only because the men who build it are Christian and have arrived at the height of Christian dignity. "It is not Christian because it calls itself so, or because it retains several outwardly Christian customs."

Although in a formal sense church and state can and should be kept separate, it is absurd to hold that religion and politics can be kept wholly apart when they meet in the conscience of one man. If a man is religious and if he is in politics, one fact will relate to the other if he is indeed a whole man. The United States has never demanded of its citizens absolute submission to political power. It is in essence the very foundation of our doctrine of church and state that it has not and does not. Dean Sayre's remarks amplify the Christian position admirably: "We, too, owe allegiance to the Lord, which is over and above and beyond the allegiance that we owe to the State. So, in this respect, our allegiance is divided, too."

This conflict between conscience and the unjust and all-embracing state is age-old and indeed perennial in the history of Western civilization. The list of the great, the brave, and the prudent who, exhausting all alternatives, fell back at last on the dictates of conscience goes back at least to Socrates, who is admired for his stand against the state and honored for his declaration: "Men of Athens, I honor and love you, but I must obey God rather than you." Not only do we honor those who stand on conscience, we consider a stand against injustice the obligation of the responsible citizen.

[...]

Perhaps we forget how much we owe to the men who hammered out the American solution to this ancient conflict. It is the glory of the United States that the hard and difficult choices required of Socrates and of Thomas More are not required here. We freely acknowledge that there are limitations to man's obligation in obedience and service to the state and hold that not everything done in the name of the state is justifiable. This is the negative—even the extreme negative—side of the picture. On the positive side we acknowledge that conscience and the religious beliefs of an individual cannot help but have some influence on his political action.

Despite our protestation that ours is a government of laws and not of men, the fact is that laws and executive decisions reflect the views and attitudes of men. The majority of Americans, and the majority of men holding public office in the United States, are sustained and fortified in their political judgments by the precepts of the natural law strengthened by religious faith. Most decisions made by majority vote of the Congress, by judges in the courts, or by the President in the loneliness of his office have moral and religious overtones.

What, you may well ask, can we expect in politics of Catholics, or of religious men of other Christian religions, or of the Jewish, of the Moslem, of all other faiths?

Faith is, of course, no full and automatic substitute for knowledge and intelligence, although the truths of faith should, when applied to contemporary problems, have some bearing upon the understanding and upon the solution of human problems. The religious character of a people should be reflected in its social and political institutions and actions. Geoffrey Francis Fisher, the Anglican Archbishop of Canterbury, makes the application in this way: "Everything which touches the life of the nation is of concern to the Christian. It does not escape God's judgment by becoming in the party sense 'political.' The difficulty is that when the issue has become in that sense 'political,' people are less ready to hear what the Christian judgment may be since for that, patience and a perceptive mind are required."

Knowledge of the Bible, the Koran, the Ten Commandments, or of the spiritual and corporal works of mercy does not, of course, give the religious man in politics a ready answer to all problems. Awareness of the obligation to feed the hungry will not solve the agricultural surplus problem of the United States, but it might be expected to dispose the Christian in politics favorably toward programs such as famine relief programs. The obligation to harbor the harborless does not compel full support of every housing bill that is proposed in the Congress, but it *might* be expected to influence the attitude of the Christian in politics toward changing immigration laws so as to admit displaced persons, refugees, or others suffering poverty and oppression.

Understanding of the concept of social justice will not eliminate all injustice. Such awareness, however, should be reflected in response to statements such as that made by President Frondizi of Argentina when he spoke of the obligations of rich and powerful nations toward less favored and impoverished ones. The Christian's regard for the dignity of the human person should incline him to oppose segregation and racial injustice. His regard for the brotherhood of man should open his mind to international co-operation and common effort. His understanding of the mission of Western civilization should strengthen his interest in making NATO more than just a military instrument.

What are the marks of a Christian politician, citizen, or officeholder?

The ideal politician is a good man, an informed man, and a man skilled in the art of politics. Such a combination is hard to find. A man may be good indeed, and thoroughly informed, but failure and inadequacy in the art of politics should disqualify him as a politician.

The ideal Christian politician is not necessarily the one who is seen most often participating in public religious activities, or conferring with religious leaders. He is not necessarily the one who is first and most vociferous to claim that his position is the Christian one and who attempts to cover himself and his cause with whatever part of the divided garment that is within his reach. He is not necessarily the one who makes of every cause a "crusade," presenting himself like Carlyle's crusader as "the minister of God's justice, doing God's judgment of the enemies of God." He should himself avoid unwarranted appeals to religion. He has a very special obligation to keep the things of God separate from those of Caesar.

The Christian in politics should be distinguished by his alertness to protect and defend the rights of individuals, of family, school, church, and other institutions from violation by the state or by other institutions, or by persons. He should be the first to detect and oppose a truly totalitarian threat or movement and the last to label every proposal for social reform "socialistic."

The Christian should be distinguished by the methods he uses and must, of course, hold fast to the moral law, remembering that the precepts of morality do not themselves change even though the way in which they are applied to concrete acts may be modified as society regresses or is perverted.

The Christian in politics should speak the truth. He should make his case in all honesty, aware that any other action is, as C. S. Lewis states, to offer to the Author of all truth the unclean sacrifice of a lie. He should not return calumny and slander in the same token, but combat them with truth and honesty, risking defeat for the sake of truth. He should not resort to the common practice of labeling, which by its falseness violates justice, and by its indignity offends charity. Powerful personalities may be able to stand against these forces. The weak are likely to be destroyed. It is these who must be the concern of Christians.

The Christian in politics should shun the devices of the demagogue at all times, but especially in a time when anxiety is great, when tension is high, when uncertainty prevails, and emotion tends to be in the ascendancy.

On the basis of moral principles, he must strive to separate good from bad even though the line may be blurred or shifting. He must remember and honor in action the rule that the end does not justify the means. He should carefully avoid confusion such as that which was manifest in the attempted justification of the Inquisition, and manifest also in Cromwell's reply to Wharton's protest at Pride's Purge and the execution of the king. "It is easy to object to the glorious actings of God, if we look too much upon the instruments. Be not offended at the manner. Perhaps there was no other way left."

The Christian should be humble, reflecting in his actions his awareness of the great mystery of redemption and the shared mystery and dignity of all men.

The Christian in politics should be judged by the standard of whether through his decisions and actions he has advanced the cause of justice, and helped, at least, to achieve the highest degree of perfection possible in the temporal order.

Altogether these seem to be difficult standards and demands. Their fulfillment requires heroic virtue. There is, however, no other measure which is valid for Christians in politics or in any other way of life. As the great politician and saint, Thomas More, observed, "It is not possible for all things to be well, unless all men are good—which I think will not be this good many years."

The Need for an Established Church
(*Minnesota Law and Politics*, June/July 2003)

American colonial practice was for the most part, one that followed the British tradition of having an established church. In the New England colonies, Puritans and Congregationalists predominated, and in the Southern colonies, Anglicans and Episcopalians prevailed. Catholics and Methodists and other sects had not yet become religious-political forces requiring political attention. The men who drafted the Constitution had to choose between an established church and religious tolerance. They settled on tolerance. A mild kind of Civil religion developed which seemed to work well for politicians, some of whom were practitioners of other faiths. Those who thought religion of most any kind was useful, even necessary for democracy, accepted this relationship.

Early documents of the new republic, such as the Declaration of Independence and Washington's inaugural address, reflected a strong religious commitment. The God of early politics was somewhat impersonal and detached, described in rather general terms as "The Creator," "The Invisible," "The Almighty Being," etc.

With the passage of time, relationships between God and the politicians became more personal, manifested in the exchange of endorsements. The politicians were usually endorsing the Divine and His works (the controversy over the sex of God had not arisen), and claiming a reciprocal endorsement of the politicians' works by the Divinity. Lincoln's second inaugural address, by some scholar's count, had 14 references to God, and four quotations from the Scriptures (Genesis, the Psalms and Matthew).

Approximately one hundred years later, President Lyndon Johnson, speaking about the civil rights law of 1965 declared, "It is rather our duty to do His Divine will. But I cannot help believing that He truly understands and that He really favors the undertaking that we begin here tonight." Johnson, like Lincoln, kept the line between church and state reasonably clear, if not the line between religion and politics.

The significant blending of the two estates took place in the Eisenhower campaigns and administrations. The first Eisenhower campaign was presented under the banner of a crusade, although the significance of the cross was a little vague. One of the crusaders, a member of Congress, charged that the previous administrations had tried to "make a settlement with the devil Communism, instead of spurning him, as Christ did when tempted." The inaugural parade of 1953 featured what was called, "God's float," a late entry. The pledge of allegiance to the flag was changed during the Eisenhower administration to include the words, "under God." The postmaster general issued a stamp bearing the motto, "In God We Trust," and the same slogan was prescribed for United States money, scarcely a vote of confidence in the Secretary of the Treasury.

The Kennedy campaign and administration had a different religious thrust. It was more institutionally detached and less personal. Whereas Ike had included as part of his inaugural proceedings a prayer he himself had composed, the Kennedy inaugural included prayers by Cardinal Cushing, by Archbishop Lakovos of the Greek Orthodox Church, by John Barclay, a Protestant minister, and by Rabbi Nelson Gluek. As William Miller wrote in his book, *Piety Along the Potomac*, whereas Eisenhower had a religion which was vague but strongly held to, the Kennedy religion was strong but vaguely held to.

The fusion of religion and politics advanced noticeably in the Nixon administration. Charles Henderson observed early that Nixon was appropriating the vocabulary of religion, of the church—faith, trust, hope, belief—and that he was applying these words to the nation, and even worse, to his personal vision of what the nation should believe. He did not go so far as to say that the religion of the prince is the religion of the people, but he did say that the president was the moral leader and spokesman of the people. Nixon emphasized the collective "we," in speaking of himself and of the people of the United States, a practice which Mark Twain said should be used only by the King (or Queen) of England, the Archbishop of Canterbury (or the Pope), or someone with a tapeworm.

President Ford, when he pardoned President Nixon, was more restrained. He said that he was acting as God's humble servant.

More recent presidential candidates have demonstrated variations on the mingling of religion and politics. Jimmy Carter said that he prayed many times a day, especially when he felt a "trepidation," and that he spoke to Jesus (not to the Great Architect). Candidate Pat Robertson said that he spoke to God directly, but that he would not use those communications in his campaign. And Ronald Reagan said that he was reborn, but that he did not remember when it happened or what the experience had done for or to him.

The latest fine religious distinction relative to politics was made by Pat Buchanan, who distinguished the Old Testament from the New by declaring that the earlier testament was the direct word. Pat's politics relied on the direct word.

The problem arises from the fact that most religions in the country think they are established, and many people claim to be reborn, especially presidential candidates, in a unique way, and are therefore the bearers of a unique religion. The problem was further compounded when President [George H.W.] Bush injected the concept of "faith based issues," and when Saddam argued that he should have a nuclear bomb because Islam is the only major religion that does not have one, thereby creating a kind of nuclear weapons religion.

Three courses of action deserve consideration. A "low order" church, like the Episcopal Church, with the Queen of England serving as head of the American church, and acting as judge and arbiter, especially in cases of marriage, divorce, adultery, runaway fathers, school truancy and the like. A unique United States Established Church might be set up conforming to the standards now used by the Internal Revenue Service in determining whether church applicants for tax exemption are true churches. Appropriately, the Collector of Internal Revenue could then serve as head of the church.

A third possibility would be to look into the GI religion conceived while Robert McNamara was Secretary of Defense and was in the process of unifying the armed forces. The Pentagon reports that it has no record of what the all-purpose military-religious creed, moral code, ritual, etc., might have been. The understanding was that when the military personnel returned to civil life, they could take the religion with them, or leave it behind.

Should these options for the new religion fail, there is the fallback position of the poet William Stafford, who once proposed a proper, unifying prayer, which runs something like this: "Our Father who is in heaven, can lick your Father, which art in heaven," or possibly vice versa.

Editor's Note

While Eugene McCarthy had a very strong reputation as a domestic policy leader during his years in Congress, spearheading the creation of the Democratic Study Group and serving at the forefront of civil rights and economic rights legislation, he rose to his greatest national prominence with his presidential campaign of 1968, where he coalesced opposition to the Vietnam War, serving to knock the incumbent president, Lyndon Johnson, out of the race. Those who followed McCarthy's career were not surprised by his action on such a pressing international issue, as McCarthy understood that one of the most prominent roles of a senator was in the sphere of foreign policy. Having spent much time overseas visiting and appreciating other nations, and playing a role in shaping our policy toward these nations, McCarthy was one of the most eminently qualified legislators to speak out on foreign policy issues in the latter part of the twentieth century. Today, as the United States finds itself in a complex world, isolated to a degree from many of our traditional allies and enmeshed in an unpopular war, McCarthy's writings provide a sense of clarity. To truly understand the timelessness of his arguments, one only need replace the word "Vietnam" with "Iraq" in the following pieces to appreciate how little has changed since the 1968 campaign.

SEVEN

The U.S. in the World

Vietnam: In Dubious Battle
(*The Limits of Power*, 1967)

Vietnam is a very special problem, outside of the context of general Asian problems and outside of the context of world problems largely because of the quantitative measure of our commitment to what was until recently considered a minor if not residual responsibility and concern.

Quite suddenly and surprisingly we have found ourselves involved in the third largest war in our history and involved under terms and conditions which are different from any we have known in the past.

Vietnam is a military problem. Vietnam is a political problem; and as the war goes on it has become more clearly a moral problem.

For the first time in our history, at least in this century, we have had to raise questions about the justification for our involvement in a war.

The resolution of the question of the justice or the injustice of a war depends upon three general considerations: (1) purposes and objectives, (2) methods and means, and (3) proportion. Even if we accept that the purpose is good and that the methods are acceptable, one must still raise the practical question of whether or not the evil and the destruction required to win the war are proportionate to the good that may be achieved.

Our involvement in Vietnam must be examined in the light of these three considerations.

Our participation in World War I was certainly morally defensible, and in World War II even more clearly so. In each of these wars, also, a reasonably good case could be made for the methods and the instruments we used.

We opposed submarine warfare and poison gas in World War I. By the time World War II had come, submarines were highly respectable.

In World War II, we denounced civilian bombing when it was first initiated and expressed reservations about the use of fire bombs. But as the war went on we began strategic bombing and permitted destruction of Dresden with fire bombs. Then at least we had the defense that we were not the first to use these questionable instruments or methods. Our use of the atomic bomb, however, was of a somewhat different order and raised many questions not yet answered.

We have been fortunate in that the two great modern wars of this century were fought with the weapons of the previous war. There was time to adjust moral judgments. The danger is that the next war may be fought with contemporary weapons.

World War I and World War II were justifiable also by the rule of proportion, since the good which we could anticipate from victory outweighed the harm and the cost of achieving that victory.

What are our objectives in Vietnam? Nearly every possible purpose has been offered, at one time or another, as justification for our involvement.

It is necessary, some say, for the defense of the United States. An extreme presentation of this position was that of a recent candidate for the Senate who said that if we did not fight in the elephant grass of Vietnam, we would have to fight in the rye grass of our western states. Yet, in the early phase of this war, no one ever accepted that our defense perimeter extended as far as Vietnam.

It is necessary, others say, that we take a stand in Vietnam in order to contain China. But few if any of the China-containment men of a few years ago held that the containment of China in any way required us to commit nearly half a million combat troops in Vietnam.

It is argued that we have a legal obligation under the SEATO treaty and other commitments. But the SEATO treaty itself has not been brought into operation in the Vietnam War. South Vietnam has never requested action under SEATO, and any joint action, as provided for in that treaty, would be impossible because of the positions of France and Pakistan, and possibly Britain. The argument of legal obligation is one which the Administration sought to bolster by securing the passage of the Tonkin Gulf Resolution by the Congress in 1964, although the Secretary of State, in testimony before the Foreign Relations Committee, said that even without the Tonkin Gulf Resolution, commitment in Vietnam was defensible and did not depend on the resolution for its legal basis.

It is said that we fight to ensure the credibility of our commitments, to show the world that we honor our treaty obligations. This is the rationale of our politico-military prestige. Yet we

Marks of a First-Class Country (Short Takes)

1. It doesn't have to be involved in every war.
2. It doesn't have to win every war it gets involved in.
3. Its citizens do not have to overconsume in order to demonstrate social economic superiority.
4. It does not need colonies.
5. It does not need a domestic propaganda agency.
6. Its politics should not be restricted, especially to two parties.
7. Its president, or other leader, should not claim to be its moral leader.
8. Its character and moral tone should not depend on the example of emperor and gladiators or president and professional athletes.
9. Its foreign policy should be an extension of domestic and natural character and needs.
10. It should be more concerned over what history says about the country than what it says about its leaders.

have already demonstrated our reliability in Korea and in the protection of Taiwan as well as in Europe.

It is said that we must carry on the war in Vietnam in order to preserve and defend our national honor. Our national honor is not at stake, and should not so readily be offered. In every other great war of the century, we have had the support of what is generally accepted as the decent opinion of mankind. We do not have that today. We cannot, of course, depend only on this opinion to prove our honor; it may not be sound. But always in the past we have not only had this support, but we have used it as a kind of justification for our action.

What about the methods which we are using?

This is a most difficult area for judgment. We are tempted to take the view presented by Cromwell in his reply to Wharton's protest at Pride's Purge and the execution of the King: "It is easy to object to the glorious actings of God if we look too much upon the instruments. Be not offended at the manner. Perhaps there was no other way left."

Civilian bombing and the use of napalm in this theater of war are more difficult to defend than they were when we bombed civilians in retaliation or as incidental to our seeking out military targets in World War II, and used napalm as a sophisticated weapon against an enemy also using sophisticated weapons.

Even the discussion of the war in Vietnam calls for a new vocabulary. George Orwell, writing in 1946 about another war and another nation, in his essay *Politics and the English Language*, described the problem this way:

Inflated style is itself a kind of euphemism. A mass of Latin words falls upon the facts like soft snow, blurring the outlines and covering up all the details. ...

Political speech and writing are largely the defence of the indefencible ... Defenceless villages are bombarded from the air, the inhabitants driven out into the countryside, the cattle machine-gunned, the huts set on fire with incendiary bullets: this is called *pacification*. Millions of peasants are robbed of their farms and sent trudging along the roads with no more than they can carry: this is called *transfer of population* or *rectification of frontiers*.

The razing of villages and herding of their inhabitants into camps was called *regroupement* when the French were doing it in Algeria. Today in Vietnam we call it "revolutionary development."

The Latin word of importance in this war is "escalation." It has a self-generating power, building and growing on itself.

George Kennan, testifying before the Foreign Relations Committee in 1966, was asked whether he knew of anyone who, when we first sent advisers into Vietnam, had said that he anticipated that these would be followed by more advisers and eventually by combat personnel; whether he knew of anyone who really expected the war to go this way, or who, expecting it to go this way, was in favor of it. He said he knew of no one. It would be somewhat reassuring if we could find someone who anticipated what did happen and understood what was happening.

A second term of significance in this war is "kill-ratio." Reports of our success are given in this measurement; we do not capture hills or take towns or cross rivers. Our operations are more often "search and destroy" than "clear and hold."

The final measurement that must be applied to this as to any war is that of proportion. Three points must be raised. First, assuming that we understand what we mean by victory, is there a possibility of victory? Second, what would be the cost of that victory? Third, what assurance do we have that a better world or a better society will emerge in Vietnam following that victory?

The answers should be positive on each of these three counts. I do not believe that they are positive.

A broad warning is sounded by Arnold J. Toynbee in his work *Hannibal's Legacy*, a study of the effect of the wars with Carthage on the Roman republic. Toynbee says that the price of Rome's subjugation of the Western Mediterranean was an economic, social, and religious derangement of Roman life. The government, bent on pursuing military adventures on the frontiers, became less and less responsive to domestic problems. Toynbee draws the lesson:

War posthumously avenges the dead on the survivors, and the vanquished on the victors. The nemesis of war is intrinsic. It did not need the invention of the atomic weapon to make this apparent. It was illustrated, more than two thousand years before our time, by Hannibal's legacy to Rome.

In view of all these considerations, we should hesitate to waste our strength, economic, military, and moral, in so highly questionable a course as the war in Vietnam. Rather we are called upon to exert every effort to bring about some kind of limitation and ultimately a settlement of the war.

We have, I believe, passed several points at which some such limitation might have been possible. One was at the time of the New Year's bombing pause in 1966. Another was in the early summer of 1966 when it was evident that the significant escalation which had taken place in the preceding six months did not promise success and when there was a possibility of following General Gavin's recommendation of a modified enclave policy.

At the present time I see two possibilities: one, that we permit and encourage the United Nations to assume a much stronger role in the efforts to settle the Vietnamese war; and second, as an alternative, that we try the Gavin policy. Under this enclave policy we would reduce the "search and kill" missions. We would not seek military domination and control of the entire country, but would hold strong points in important areas of Vietnam. At the same time as efforts to achieve pacification within the controlled areas were pushed, negotiations with the National Liberation Front over the uncontrolled areas would be attempted; this would be a preliminary to a settlement with Hanoi.

Look! No Allies
(*Foreign Policy*, Spring 1978)

American government officials, from presidents on down—as well as editors, political columnists, commentators, essayists, and historians—commonly assume that the allies of the United States include most members of NATO, Israel, Japan, Australia, New Zealand, and South Korea, plus some smaller countries scattered about the globe. But the fact is that the United States has few, if any, true allies. What it has instead is a number of nations that it maintains in a dependency relationship. This is a relationship that Washington has approved and cultivated—a relationship, in fact, that it insists upon whenever any of these dependents shows any sign of independence. Some of these nations truly were American allies in World War II. Others, such as Japan and West Germany, were added to the list later because they were no longer enemies, they needed the United States, and they were willing to accept the dependency relationship.

The German and Japanese surrenders after World War II were essentially unconditional surrenders, leaving those two countries militarily and (especially Japan) economically dependent on the United States. In reality, though, it was not only its enemies who surrendered to the United States after the war, but also its former allies in Western Europe. The North Atlantic Treaty was for them not so much an agreement among allies and sovereign nations as it was an acknowledgment of the economic and military realities of postwar Europe, a treaty of dependence—almost an unconditional surrender of a different sort to the United States. That is also what was required of other nations later added to the list of dependents, including South Korea, Iran, and, in a somewhat different context, Israel.

The vestiges of sovereignty and national self-respect that survived the formal NATO agreements were largely wiped out by Secretary of State John Foster Dulles's arrogant, moralistic domination of American relations with Europe as well as with non-European friends such as India and Egypt. Dulles generally proceeded without consulting, or even caring about, the opinions of other nations. He insisted that they (especially members of NATO) accept and support American policy.

He attempted to force the European nations into what he called a "European defense community," the effect of which would have been to require them to give up their last, limited claims to military independence. To push his plan, Dulles threatened an "agonizing reappraisal" of the American role in Europe unless his plan was adopted. He denounced Indian neutrality as "immoral." He forced the British, the French, and the Israelis to withdraw from Egypt at the time of the 1956 Suez War. Subsequently, unhappy with the Egyptians because they were not antagonistic enough toward the Soviet Union, Dulles unilaterally decided—without consulting the European countries or the United States Senate, possibly without even consulting President Eisenhower—to pull out of the Aswan Dam project, thus leaving Egypt to the Soviets.

Although subsequent secretaries of state may not have acted as independently as Dulles, the presidents who followed Eisenhower showed great insensitivity to the dignity of allies. John F. Kennedy displayed indifference toward the British, especially Prime Minister Harold Macmillan, on the matter of missile deployment. Lyndon B. Johnson forced the Australians and South Koreans to send token forces to Vietnam. Richard M. Nixon ignored everyone, including the U.S. Senate, with his "incursion" into Cambodia; he and his agent, Henry Kissinger, negotiated a new relationship with China without even the slightest nod toward the obvious interests of Australia and Japan.

[...]

The first serious and open challenge to the old NATO concept—and the assertion, in fact, of a relationship much more like that of genuine allies—was made by Charles de Gaulle. When de Gaulle reemerged on the European scene in 1958, the way was open for the liquidation of France's Algerian commitment, for its escape from dependence on American aid to fight its foreign wars, and for the restoration of France in the military and economic complex of Europe. De Gaulle's return, and the recognition of the reality of France as a force in Europe—an independent force—caused concern in Washington. De Gaulle's conception of a united Europe, stretching from the Atlantic to the Urals—united not under a supranational political authority, but by free-choice arrangements among sovereign governments—challenged the prevailing U.S. idea of European unity. What Washington had in mind was political, economic, and military unity—a dependence on the United States and an alliance against the Soviet Union.

Fearful that the West Germans would move to support the French position, the United States tried to force them to make a choice between Paris and Washington. Various devices for sharing power were suggested in order to influence the West Germans to select Washington's policy. The most noteworthy was a proposal that would have at least made it appear as though there were a shared responsibility for nuclear defense in Europe and a European finger on the nuclear trigger. How the finger was to be selected was never made clear.

Note accompanying Bronze Star given to McCarthy during the 1968 election by anonymous soldier (spelling retained from original):

I received a medal for vallor in Vietnam. But vallor is a corollary of morality and this war is not moral. It has corrupted the men who fight it. It has divided the nation which conceived it.

I cannot begin to recount the number of distasteful tasks, I witnessed American soldiers perform, including the beating of women and children and the corruption of an entire population.

Therefore I cannot in clear conscience retain this reward for actions which in essence served to supress the freedom of the Vietnamese people.

Europe rejected the idea of a multilateral or multinational nuclear force. The British and French particularly opposed it. Verging on the ridiculous was the American proposal for multinational forces and the mixed manning of vessels, ideas urged especially by Secretary of State Dean Rusk. One ship was sent out on a highly publicized voyage to demonstrate the feasibility of the concept. But this was undertaken even before there had been an agreement on whether the cuisine and the chef should be French, German, British, or American, or on who would select the evening movies, let alone on more weighty matters.

De Gaulle's announcement of his intention to withdraw the French forces from NATO's integrated military command was not an announcement that he was leaving an alliance, but rather a repudiation of dependency. As Andre Fontaine wrote at the time of de Gaulle's action:

The arrogance of the president of the republic is disagreeable and even incomprehensible to his allies, but it is not the arrogance of an isolated man, otherwise it would be only ridiculous. It is the arrogance of a man who is not resigned to anything which writes *finis* to a nation about which history has spoken without a break for a thousand years.

Four years earlier, in 1962, Raymond Aron, if anything an anti-Gaullist, had explained:

It is an illusion to believe that the problems raised by General de Gaulle
will disappear when he no longer "graces the scene." The privileged
position of Great Britain in the atomic field is something which will never
be accepted in Paris, no matter who may be in power ...

The immediate American response was to try to isolate France from the rest of Western Europe. With difficulty, the United States obtained agreement from the thirteen other NATO participants on a common response to France. Yet the language of that response showed not only the caution and reluctance of the Europeans about agreeing to the American proposals for isolating France, but also how much the United States was relying on concepts that had become irrelevant during the preceding fifteen years.

In effect, the United States took the position that its policy toward Europe could be continued without France. The threat was that Washington might actually abandon its efforts for a united Europe, rather than accept any change in the elaborate structure of "military integration." Or NATO would simply pack up and move to Belgium. Plans would be made around France. Undersecretary of State George Ball, a leader of the move to isolate de Gaulle's France or to force him to keep France within the NATO military structure, announced to the Senate Foreign Relations Committee at the time that, "the NATO crisis is over ... ." The other countries of NATO, he said, were determined to press forward vigorously to maintain the integrated military structure without France. In fact, it was much better from a military point of view to have French military power back on the continent of Europe, even though formally outside the NATO command and yet physically in Vietnam and Algeria. But not so for secular and theological legalists like Ball and Rusk.

[...]

The United States remained generally indifferent to the opinions of so-called allies about events in other parts of the world. Most Western European nationals had grave doubts about the wisdom of American involvement in Vietnam. Some openly criticized it. But Washington paid little attention to their point of view, in much the same way that it ignored Japan's attitude and its interests in that war.

[...]

During the forty years since the state of Israel was established—with the support of the United Nations and of the major nations of the world, including the Soviet Union—the United States has gradually moved to make Israel almost wholly dependent on the American government. French and English interests were repudiated at the time of the Suez War, and the United Nations was allowed to shed its responsibilities almost without protest when it withdrew in the face of Egyptian threats before the 1967 war. The Soviets, too, had more or less removed themselves, leaving the United States as the chief supporter of Israel.

Progressively, the United States began to look upon Israel as a dependent and to treat it as such. Israeli ambassadors to Washington came to be selected on the basis of their good connections in the United States. Candidates for leadership in Israel had generally argued that they should be elected because of their support in the United States—until Menachem Begin suddenly took the position that Israel was a sovereign nation, an ally of the United States rather than a dependency. Distinct

---

Extract from 2004 interview:

On War: World War II was the last happy war. We probably will never have another one like it. Both sides had roughly equivalent weapons, it was fought with some attention to the rules of war, and people were really, really happy about being involved in World War II, even the civilians. It had a human dimension, World War II. There were still some laws of war that were observed. If they weren't, why [the rule breakers] were condemned. Treatment of prisoners was generally good, there was some abuse but not much. We had Prisoners of War and CCC camps in Minnesota. They didn't have many guards and there was natural protection up there. They'd escape from the CCC camp and they knew that rivers usually run to the sea and to the city, so they'd follow those northern Minnesota rivers, but they ran north. They ran into the wilderness with the deer flies and the wood ticks and more ice and snow. They could be gone about five days, they'd come back and say, take me back, I'm not going out to that wilderness again. War still had human dimensions and reasonably rational methods, but not Vietnam, and not anymore.

from his predecessors, Begin was not elected on the basis of widespread recognition or support among Americans. Rather, he believed that the United States has a political, moral, and even military interest in the independent existence of Israel. The establishment of the state of Israel was more than a humanitarian act. It was a political act, establishing a sovereign state of special character and purpose.

Begin, not unlike de Gaulle, declared that he would take the initiative in foreign policy, that he would seek to have not defensible boundaries but a defensible country, that he would not wait for a UN initiative relative to the problems of his country, or indeed wait for American initiatives or directions.

> *Reporter:* Don't you believe we should stop Communism?
> *McCarthy:* Yes, I do. And South Vietnam is the worst possible place to try."

In contrast to its attitude toward allies, the United States has treated its enemies of the postwar years—principally the Soviets and the Chinese—with respect and deference. It confers with them. It keeps them informed on matters of critical common interest and warns them about things that might be controversial.

Washington accepts the fact that both these nations have nuclear bombs, and that Soviet nuclear armaments have been designed and justified for the exclusive purpose of countering or overcoming American military power. Yet Americans protest vigorously when nations that are defined as allies build bombs or test them, or when they build nuclear reactors for themselves or other nations for nonmilitary purposes. The protests are especially strong against developments that are thought to make proliferation of nuclear weapons easier, if not more likely.

Proliferation, as now defined, means the possession of nuclear weapons by more nations than now have them. This definition, of course, excludes the increase in number, quality, and kind of nuclear weapons by the two most active proliferators, the United States and the Soviet Union, both of whom now have more than enough nuclear power to destroy each other. A nation that is asked not to develop its own nuclear weapons might well inquire as to what the Americans and the Soviets intend to do with the bombs they do not need for deterrence or retaliation. If the Soviet Union and the United States had only enough nuclear weaponpower to offset each other, the argument for nonproliferation would have far more strength among other nations.

If one sets aside the substantive, historical, and ideological differences between the Soviet Union and the United States and looks only at American methods and procedures for dealing with them, one could fairly conclude that the American government tends to treat its enemies as if they were allies. Meanwhile, American allies are treated as if they were enemies—or, at best, as highly unreliable allies to be consulted as little as possible and expected to accept U.S. policies and support U.S. programs.

[...]

Extract from 2004 interview:

Editor: What would you say if you were advising the next president on foreign policy?

McCarthy: I don't know; it's kind of a mixed case. I think I'd call on the nations that supported the establishment of Israel to come back in and share responsibility. I think almost every time I made a pro-Israel speech over the years, and at various fundraisers I included something about the Palestinian refugees. But I said, we've got to do something about the Palestinian refugees, but no one ever did much. That was a critical issue.

Essential to any alliance is a shared purpose, perceived to promote the common good of members or participating nations—a common good that cannot be achieved as effectively by one nation acting alone or by two or three nations operating to the exclusion of others that have a vital interest in the goals of the combined effort. Nations participating in an allied effort need not have that perfect conformity of customs, habits, ideas, and manners suggested by Edmund Burke to be the real forces that hold nations together. But the greater this conformity, the greater the strength and durability of the alliance are likely to be. Movement toward such conformity among participants in an alliance is clearly desirable. Agreement on methods is also desirable, but even with differences and disagreements, alliances can and have worked. Certainly there were major differences, both as to strategy and as to tactics, among the allied commanders, including Dwight D. Eisenhower and Viscount Montgomery, in World War II—not to mention the major ideological differences between the United States and the Soviet Union. Yet the war was waged effectively, at least to the point of military victory.

Alliance allows for differences in function, and in physical, military, economic, and philosophical contributions. To be effective, alliance requires compromises and concessions, but only among nations whose sovereignty and integrity are clearly recognized. Without such recognition and respect, there can be no true alliance, only the appearance or the form.

Dependencies are dependencies, despite documentary declarations to the contrary. Allies are something else. There must be among them, with or without formal affirmation, a bond of intellectual and moral commitment. As Machiavelli admonished, the relationship of ally to ally is a better, more reliable, and more lasting one than that of patron to dependent or of conqueror to subject peoples. The United States needs allies, not dependencies.

The New Interventionism
(Address, St. John's University, March 1988)

Interventionism has been a mark of United States history almost from the beginning of our national existence. But up to and through World War II, interventions were generally justified as necessary to defending the nation, freeing oppressed people, or saving democracy. Most interventions were pragmatically determined and of limited purpose.

The foreign policy of the Truman administration in the post–World War II period was consistent with this tradition. Dean Acheson as secretary of state, speaking for President Harry Truman, defined United States postwar foreign policy both as to its purposes and its methods. Seldom did he make the case for either policy or program on an ideological basis, although he was not indifferent to ethical and moral considerations. He was, with presidential concurrence, a great treaty-maker, but his treaty proposals were based primarily on historical conditions, rather than on ideological assessments and projections. The NATO commitment, the Marshall Plan, the Truman Doctrine, the aid programs to Greece and Turkey, were not against Communists in the abstract, but against historically identified Communists. Nor was the Korean War defended as an involvement based upon a general policy of the containment of communism, but as an action directed toward carrying out World War II in the Asian theatre. The Acheson-Truman conception of national defense was one of a defined perimeter, described simply by President Truman when he said that any time a pig stuck its snout under your tent, the thing to do was to hit it on the snout. This foreign policy was classical, therefore restrained and limited.

Following the Truman administration, and the departure of Acheson, foreign policy came to be dominated by the ideas and historical philosophy of John Foster Dulles, secretary of state under President Dwight Eisenhower. Dulles had committed himself to foreign service early in his life and seemed to look upon that service almost as though it were a religious vocation. His approach to foreign policy was essentially moralistic and ideological. Communists were not to be treated primarily as nationalists, but part of monolithic world communism. In contrast with the limited and defined objectives of Truman and Acheson, Dulles's objectives were open-ended and global. Even "neutralism" was, in his view, "immoral." The line between non-Communists of all kinds and Communists of all kinds was clear to Dulles.

Dulles, like Acheson, was a treaty-maker. His treaties, for the most part, in contrast with those engineered by Acheson, were not limited to defined historical situations and geographical areas, but encompassed things that had not yet occurred, and might never occur. They transcended territorial limitations, reaching out for ideological conflicts that might arise in the future. In this spirit, and in anticipation of trouble, he supported the Southeast Asia Treaty. He advocated adherence to the proposals of the Military Committee of the Baghdad Pact, designed to put together an anti-Communist bloc in the Middle East, and was reported to have sought a combination of African nations to contain Egypt and Gamal Abdel Nasser. He supported passage of mutual, anti-Communist defense treaties between the United States and South Korea, the United States and Nationalist China, and one with Japan. Dulles was the great covenantor of modern times, combining in documentary forms both legal and moral obligations.

In addition to his bent for entering into treaties, Dulles was a great proponent of congressional resolutions—some to sustain current policies and governmental actions, others in anticipation. Whereas Truman went into Korea without special congressional support, Dulles, acting for President Eisenhower, was quick to come to the Congress for endorsements of administration commitments. Thus, he presented and secured the passage of the Far East (Formosa) Resolution in 1955, which he said put the Peiping government on notice that if it attacked Formosa, the United States would instantly be in the war.

Again in 1957, following the Suez Canal crisis, Dulles came to Congress asking for a joint resolution on the Middle East that would state the determination of the United States to assist any country in the Middle East that asked for help from threatened Communist-inspired aggression. (President Lyndon Johnson, following this precedent, sought and obtained the Tonkin Gulf Resolution in 1964.)

During the Eisenhower administration, the United States continued its policy of indirect intervention through supporting the French in Southeast Asia and by sending military advisors there. It also came to the defense of Quemoy and landed troops in Lebanon. Eisenhower's administration threatened retaliatory action against the British, the French, and the Israelis at the time of the Suez conflict, and planned the invasion of Cuba.

Meanwhile, secret, interventionist foreign policy was being carried on by the Central Intelligence Agency, directed by John Foster Dulles's brother, Allen. Independent of Congress, not limited by treaty obligations or accepted standards for judging the methods by which international affairs might be conducted, the CIA enmeshed itself in foreign policy. It took credit for the overthrow of Jacobo Arbenz Guzman in Guatemala and of Mohammed Mossadegh in Iran, and acknowledged its involvement in anti-Communist activities in Laos, Vietnam, and other parts of the world.

Interventionism in the Kennedy and Johnson administrations was conducted under the guidance and inspiration of the secretary of state, Dean Rusk, a kind of Cromwell to Dulles's Calvin. Under Kennedy, the invasion of Cuba was attempted and some 17,000 special forces were sent into Vietnam. The CIA continued to be active in Southeast Asia and in Cuba.

President Johnson escalated the war in Vietnam into a major military engagement and sent troops into the Dominican Republic to "stabilize" the government. The doctrinal justification was based on a kind of amalgamation of the Monroe

Doctrine and the Eisenhower Middle East Doctrine transferred to the West.

President Richard Nixon carried the Vietnam War several stages beyond the level that it had reached under President Johnson. New tactical and strategic measures were introduced, including what was called an "incursion" into Cambodia—the first incursion in our history, or certainly the first use of that word to describe a United States military action. It was an interesting choice of a word, since there is no verb form for incursion (as the verb *invade* goes with the noun *invasion*). One cannot incurse. An incursion is therefore existential, a kind of happening.

The Carter administration demonstrated its anti-Communist zeal and willingness to intervene by embargoing grain sales to the Soviet Union and by keeping United States athletes out of the 1980 Olympic Games because of Russian intervention in Afghanistan.

Reporter: It was reported that New York Governor Nelson Rockefeller had a four-point program for peace in Vietnam, with both allied and Vietcong withdrawal from occupied areas as a starting point. Do you have any comment on this plan?

McCarthy: No. I am generally against four-point programs. Three points are about right; but when you add that fourth point, why, I think you are over-refining it just a little bit.

Although the Reagan administration has proceeded with a massive military buildup, and uses the violent language of cold war, its actual military interventions have been modest, although numerous. Libya was bombed. A few shells were fired into Lebanon by U.S. warships. Marines were sent into Lebanon, with no very clear mission, and subsequently withdrawn. Navy vessels, one of them the frigate *Stark*, were assigned to protect oil shipments in the Persian Gulf. Grenada was successfully invaded. Currently the United States government, or part of it, is supporting the Contra troops in Nicaragua, the Iranians, and possibly also Iraq in the Iran-Iraq War.

In *Democracy in America*, Alexis de Tocqueville observed that democracies find it very difficult to start a war and also very difficult to end one. His observations may be right about major wars such as World War I and World War II, or close to right, but they are not sustained by the U.S. history of military involvement since the end of World War II. In this period our military engagements have been marked generally by quick entrance and quick withdrawal, followed by prolonged diplomatic and economic conflict. These differences from de Tocqueville's theory are explainable.

The United States gets into war or military conflict more quickly than might be expected of a democracy because the preconditions for involvement are in place, ready and waiting for conflict. First, the ideologically defined basis, essentially anti-communism, elicits a response comparable to those political-religious conflicts of the past—between Muslims and Jews, Christians and infidels, Catholics and Huguenots, Puritans and Cavaliers.

Second, ideologically differing positions are sustained by treaties and agreements. Thus, President Johnson held that the Vietnam War, and our participation in it, was based on our obligations under the Southeast Asia Treaty Organization (SEATO). Doctrines and resolutions already in place further limit the need for presidents in office to make hard historical judgments before committing the United States to military action. In the Eisenhower intervention in the Middle East and in the Johnson escalation of the war in Vietnam, legality and obligation, it was argued, were based on historical decrees. The first case was supported by the Eisenhower Resolution on the Middle East; the other, by the Tonkin Gulf Resolution passed in 1964, long before the escalation, and also before the 1964 campaign in which candidate Johnson declared that he would not send American boys into Asia to do what Asian boys should do for themselves.

Third, presidential decisions may be further justified, and also insulated from historical reality and from congressional review, by the intrusion of presidential "doctrines," some sustained by congressional approval, others only by tradition or by the popularity or power of an incumbent president.

The two presidential doctrines that have had the clearest bearing on foreign and military policy are the Monroe Doctrine and the Eisenhower Doctrine, operating separately or in variable combinations.

The doctrinal approach to foreign policy began with President Monroe's statement of December 1823, when he declared that the American continents were not to be considered subjects for future colonization by any European powers, that the political system of the European allied powers was essentially different from that of America, and that any attempt on their part to extend their system to

---

Extract from 2004 interview:

Editor: A few years ago you were the subject of a documentary titled "I'm Sorry I Was Right." Could you explain that statement a little bit? Why do you feel the need to say you were sorry? And why did you feel right?

McCarthy: I don't know where I got it. [The director] said what should we call it? [I replied] why don't we just say it? It will make some people mad, but it's a pretty good commentary to say "I'm Sorry I Was Right." I said somewhere that if you're wrong, you say you're sorry and they forgive you. If you're right and say, I'm sorry I was right, no forgiveness. He [the director] said, do it anyway because it's a good title. And, it was a pretty good response. Well I *was* right about Vietnam. But I said, if it will make you feel better, I'll say I'm sorry I was right. Because all these other guys were saying they were sorry they were wrong, McNamara and others, all these guys were being sorry for what they had done wrong. I said, I'm sorry I was right. It caused me all kinds of trouble. If I had been wrong, I would have said, look I was wrong.

any portion of this hemisphere would be considered dangerous to "our peace and safety." The statement also promised that existing colonies or dependencies of any European power would not be interfered with and that in matters relating to European wars and other matters involving the European powers, "we have never taken any part, nor does it comport with our policy so to do."

Commentators and critics point out that the Monroe Doctrine was a mere declaration of presidential position, which in itself could not prevent intervention or commit the country to war without congressional declaration and support. Although the critics were undoubtedly technically and constitutionally right, the declaration subsequently took on doctrinal force, encouraging any number of succeeding presidents to interfere or threaten to interfere in South and Central American affairs. They did not seek congressional support, and they carried out their interventions with little fear of criticism or effective opposition.

The "doctrine" has been modified and has taken on new and more comprehensive meanings with the passage of time. President Eisenhower, with the passage of the Middle East Resolution in 1956, was credited with having established a doctrine that stated that the United States could intervene militarily in the Middle East if it was asked to do so by a government threatened by Communist takeover. The doctrine was not long confined to application in the Middle East. It was combined with the Monroe Doctrine as a preliminary justification for the planning of the Cuban invasion and for the Bay of Pigs venture. The basic political plan was that once a beachhead had been established in a country, that government would invite the United States to come to its aid because it was being threatened by a Communist or Communist-inspired movement—in this case, the Castro government. An extension of the Monroe Doctrine accepted that a foreign *ideology* could be treated as an actionable threat, whereas a century or more earlier, the threat had to be a foreign *government*. [...] The Russians announced their version of the Eisenhower Doctrine in the Brezhnev Doctrine, which justified their invasion of Afghanistan because, by report, they were invited in to prevent the takeover of a Communist-controlled government.

[...]

A fourth proposition that gives support to continuing intervention (once it has been initiated) attempts to justify (and insulate from challenge) presidential or governmental military actions on the grounds that the president in office is continuing policies and programs initiated or carried on by a previous president or presidents. Although President Kennedy never offered continuity as an official or personal defense for the Bay of Pigs operation, some of his supporters occasionally pointed out that the plans for the invasion had been prepared by and for the Eisenhower administration. President Johnson used continuity as a defense of his escalation of the war in Vietnam. He was, he said, only supporting and advancing a policy that had been supported by three presidents who preceded him: President Truman, who had helped the French indirectly by giving them aid under the

Bad Ideas Whose Time Keeps Coming (Short Takes)

"Politics stops at the water's edge." A prescription, which, if followed, insulates presidents from critical challenge for unwise and irresponsible foreign and military ventures.

"My country right or wrong." A cover for excluding foreign and military actions and proposals from moral evaluation, and usually means: "My party, right or wrong."

"Let there be war in my time so that there may be peace in the time of my child." A remark attributed to an Irish patriot that is a formula for continuing war, as each generation in power must show its concern for the next by protecting it in advance.

NATO program and the Marshall Plan while the French Indochina war was in progress; President Eisenhower, who had sent in advisors; and President Kennedy, who had sent in special forces and had given other help to the South Vietnamese. President Nixon endorsed the concept of continuity, saying that he was pursuing a policy that had been supported by four previous presidents.

Intervention is also continued in a fifth way, during postwar periods, in countries where wars or military involvements have not ended wholly to our satisfaction. Thus, in the defeat of Chiang K'aishek by the Chinese Communists, although we were only indirectly and moderately involved on the losing side, we avoided acknowledging failure by setting up and supporting a government in exile on Taiwan for twenty years and refusing to recognize the government of mainland China for nearly thirty years. In much the same way, after the failure of the Bay of Pigs invasion, the United States has refused to acknowledge diplomatically the existence of Cuba, and for nearly twenty-five years has maintained an embargo of Cuba's goods, thereby leaving that country's economy largely dependent on Russian support. [...] If the China quarantine of thirty years is accepted as the standard, openings to Cuba may be expected in about five years and to Vietnam in fifteen. If things do not turn out as we would like in [in adversarial parts of the world], that country may expect to be under ban for thirty years, the subject of continuing harassment and direct or indirect interventionism. That could change if we begin to make both military and other foreign policy decisions with more relevance to historical realities, rather than to ideological distinctions and inherited doctrines, resolutions, and vague treaties.

Afterword
(A Colony of the World, 1992)

ROME

A way of looking at the condition of the United States, that is not as a colony to the world, is to compare it to the Roman Republic in its years of decline.

Polybius, the Greek historian of the second century B.C., observed that a state can perish from two factors, internal and external. Charles de Gaulle noted the threat to France from the second, when on withdrawing from Algeria, he said that foreign involvements like those in Vietnam and in Algeria were threats to the integrity of France.

With the threat of war with the Soviet Union gone, and our preoccupation with communism as a threat to democratic ideas and governments ended, the danger that we are likely to perish or even decline because of external forces or distractions is minimal. The threat to our institutions, our stability, and our position of leadership and example to the world is internal. History never actually repeats itself, but there are lessons to be learned from the past. It may be later than we think, but it is not too late for us to look to the warning signs.

Sallust, a Roman historian of the first century B.C., reported on Roman society in the process of change. He noted that the earlier, defined divisions of Roman society into partricians and plebians (the common people) and a middle class of small, independent landholders, had changed into something more complex. The middle class had increased in numbers and in influence and had become more complex, made up of businessmen, financiers, manufacturers, builders, tax gatherers (the civil servants of our time). The army had become a permanent, mercenary professional body, made up of people of little or no wealth, rather than a volunteer army, representing in its composition, the classes of society. There were great numbers of unemployed. There were many poor, living on free grain distributions. The rural areas were being depopulated as people from the rural areas of Italy and from the provinces moved to Rome and to other Italian cities. Bread and circuses were offered to quiet and sustain the poor. Farmers and businessmen were in great debt. Serious work was performed principally by slave labor. The burden of veterans' benefits was oppressive. The cost of wars and of maintaining an excessively large military establishment was a great burden. Taxes generally were oppressive. The wealthy were indifferent to the conditions of the country. Politicians and demagogues proposed equality of all as the goal of political action.

Tacitus, writing a century later in the first century A.D., described a society marked by unrest, violence, intrigue, corruption, decline of morals, cultural confusion and disregard for the law. The Roman senate was distinguished by wrangling. Assassinations were frequent. Greed was the market of business and commerce, usury the rule of finance, and as Fletcher Pratt observed in his book

Hail Caesar, written in 1936: "The supply of trained leaders began to run out just at the moment when the Republic by virtue of its imperial position was most in need of administrators with minds large enough to embrace the problems of millions and long enough to envisage the problem of decades."

How does the United States of today compare with the Rome of Sallust and of Tacitus and of Polybius?

First to be noted is that there is no middle class in the United States, although columnists and political analysts continue to use the term. Rather, we have a small group of very rich, some five percent, and another of the very poor, some ten percent. The great number of Americans is a classless group made up of a varied assortment of skilled laborers, white collar and managerial personnel, professionals and para-professionals, farmers, small businessmen, government employees, etc.

There has been a massive movement of workers from rural areas and from other countries into the cities of the United States. Approximately seven percent, nearly eight million potential workers in the United States, are unemployed. According to a recent report, more than 20 million persons, one out of every 10 Americans, are receiving food stamps, the bread of Rome, with television-watching the substitute for circuses, and special celebrations of military victories as added entertainment or distraction.

While unemployment and under-employment mount, more and more work is performed by a modern equivalent of slave labor—robots and automated equipment, migrant workers, legal and illegal, and by new immigrants and by low paid workers, child labor, and even prison labor in other countries.

[...]

Wars and military actions are now carried out by a volunteer army, which is in effect a mercenary army, with citizens generally exempted from military service. Powerful institutions, principally major corporations, national, international and multinational, operate beyond social or governmental control. Major governmental agencies, notably the Internal Revenue Service, the Federal Communications Commission and the Federal Election Commission, disregard basic constitutional liberties, rights and guarantees.

There is public indifference to politics, as indicated by the fact that in presidential elections nearly one-half of the eligible voters do not participate. There is great disparity of wealth, with the upper ten percent of the population controlling and holding an estimated 70 percent of the personally held wealth, while the remaining 90 percent hold 30 percent. The burden of debt, both private and public, is overwhelming, with federal government debt approaching four trillion dollars, which, assuming 100 million potential taxpayers, would put a debt burden for federal alone, of $40,000 dollars per taxpayer.

Inflation is running near seven percent annually, while interest paid on basic government debt is below five percent, thus offering as an incentive the saving of a two-point annual loss of savings to inflation rather than a seven percent loss. Corruption in the business and financial institutions is widespread, and usury is common.

Our culture is agitated by demands for multiculturalism and bilingualism and multilingualism, and language is under attack from the deconstructionists. The media more and more emphasize the immediate and the sensational, and on critical issues are subservient to popular trends and to government policy, with television operating somewhere between greed and fear of government regulation or loss of license. The Congress is in disarray, with the president disdaining or disregarding constitutional and traditional relationships, and who now is in the market selling arms, possibly military services, selling citizenships and a new offering of pollution rights.

Albert Schweitzer and others have warned that if a people fail to foresee and forestall trouble, whether in the natural order or in the political and social order, they are headed for trouble. The warning signs are numerous and clear. It is not too late to forestall threatening troubles.

Editor's Note

Like many of our nation's founders, who were well-versed not only in politics, law, and rhetoric, but also science, art, literature, and the classics, Eugene McCarthy is a true Renaissance man. Through a varied career, he has worn many hats, among them theologian, teacher, semiprofessional baseball player, philosopher, historian, politician, and probably to his most personal satisfaction, poet. Characterized by his trademark wit and ability with words, McCarthy has published several volumes of poetry, and counted among his fans Robert Lowell. Using his life and political experiences as the basis for his writings, McCarthy the poet not only provides us with aesthetic pleasure, but forces us, through his lyricism, to search within ourselves for deeper meaning.

EIGHT

Lyricisms

Abe Lincoln: A Politician and Also a Poet
(*Complexities and Contraries,* 1982)

There is a long-standing tradition in America of scoffing at poets, especially if they show any interest in politics.

Few of the scoffers are familiar with the statement of Lytton Strachey: "It is almost always disastrous not to be a poet." Or with the words of Georges Clemenceau, great French political leader of the early twentieth century, who said that whereas poets and philosophers should not control government, politicians and political leaders who ignore what the philosophers and poets say do so at great peril.

Nor do the scoffers seem to know that Abraham Lincoln, considered by many to be the greatest American President, was a poet.

Lincoln was not a great poet. He did not need to be one in order to make his reputation as a writer. His prose was sufficient for that.

Lincoln wrote at least three poems of some length, seriousness, and quality—one of forty lines, one of sixty, and a third of eighty-eight lines. He was very strict and precise in the form within which he wrote. Each poem is divided into stanzas of four lines, the first and third line of each stanza having eight syllables, the second and fourth having six. The last syllable of the first line of each stanza rhymes with the last syllable of the third, and the last syllable of the second line with the last syllable of the fourth.

Lincoln's first known poem was written about 1845 and is called "My Childhood Home I See Again." With modesty, in a letter to a friend, Lincoln explains how he had come to write the poem: "In the fall of 1844, thinking I might aid some to carry the State of Indiana for Mr. Clay, I went into the neighborhood in that State in which I was raised, where my mother and only sister were buried, and from which I had been absent about fifteen years. That part of the country is within itself as unpoetical as any spot on earth: but still, seeing it and its objects and inhabitants aroused feelings in me which were certainly poetry; though whether my expression of those feelings is poetry is quite another question." This stanza is typical:

> I hear the loved survivors tell
> How nought from death could save
> Till every sound appears a knell
> And every spot a grave.

Lincoln's second poem is called "The Maniac." It was written about a young man named Matthew Gentry, who at the age of nineteen became insane. The poem describes the madness and then goes on to reflect on the why of it, and on the mystery of the mad boy's continuing to live while other persons, not mad but gifted, were taken by death.

The third Lincoln poem that has survived is on a lighter theme; it is called "The Bear Hunt." In the poem, he first describes the frontier:

> When first my father settled here,
> 'Twas then the frontier line:
> The panther's scream, filled night with fear
> And bears preyed on the swine.

Then he describes the hunt and, finally, after the bear is caught and killed, the argument over which hunter is to get the skin. While the argument is going on, one hound that had little to do with the catch arrives and

> With grinning teeth, and up-turned hair
> Brim full of spunk and wrath,
> He growls and seizes on dead bear,
> And shakes for life and death.

Lincoln ends the poem with a stanza of commentary, perhaps with political implications:

> Conceited whelp! We laugh at thee
> Nor mind, that not a few
> Of Pompous, two-legged dogs there be
> Conceited quite as you.

When Lincoln's friend A. Johnston (not the future Vice-President) suggested that he try to publish the poems, Lincoln agreed, but on condition that his name not be used. "I have not sufficient hope of the verses attracting any favorable notice to tempt me to risk being ridiculed for having written them," he wrote.

Lincoln's interest in poetry is shown in an earlier letter he wrote to the same Johnston, who had mistakenly attributed authorship of some other writer's poem to Lincoln. "Beyond all question, I am not the author. I would give all I am worth, and go in debt, to be able to write so fine a piece as I think that is," wrote Lincoln, the politician-poet.

Ares

(The Hard Years, 1975)

god, Ares
is not dead.
he lives,
where blood and water mix
in tropic rains.
no, NNE, or S
or W, no compass —

only mad roosters
tail down on twisted vanes
point to the wind
of the falling sky
the helicopter wind
that blows straight down
flattening the elephant grass
to show small bodies crawling
at the roots, or dead
and larger ones
in the edged shade, to be counted
for the Pentagon, and
for *The New York Times*.

ideologies can make a war
last long and go far
ideologies do not have boundaries
cannot be shown on maps
before and after
or even on a globe
as meridian, parallel
or papal line of demarcation.

what is the line between
Moslem and Jew
Christian and Infidel
Catholic and Huguenot
with St. Bartholomew waiting
on the calendar for his day
to come and go?
what map can choose between cropped heads

and hairy ones?
what globe affirm
"better dead than red"
"better red than dead"?
ideologies do not bleed
they only blood the world.

mathematical wars go farther.
they run on ratios
of kill and overkill
from one to x
and to infinity.
we are bigger, one to two
we are better, one to three
death is the measure
it's one of us to four
of them, or eight to two
depending on your
point of view.
12 to 3
means victory
12 to 5
forebodes defeat.
these ratios stand
sustained
by haruspex and IBM.
we can kill all of you
three times
and you kill all of us
but once and a half—the game
is prisoner's base, and we
are fresh on you
with new technology.

we sleep well
but worry some. We know
that you would kill us twice
if you could, and not leave
that second death half done.
we are unsure
that even three times killed
you might not spring up whole.

snakes close again
and cats do, it is true
have nine lives. Why
not the same for you?
no one knows about third comings
we all wait for the second, which
may be bypassed
in the new arithmetic.
or which, when it comes
may look like a first
and be denied.

the best war, if war must be
is one for Helen
or for Aquitaine.
no computation stands
and all the programmed lights
flash
and burn slowly down to dark
when one man says
I will die
not twice, or three times over
but my one first life, and last
lay down for this my space
my place, my love.

Lament of an Aging Politician
(No Fault Politics, 1998)

The Dream of Gerontion is
my dream
and Lowell's self-salted
night sweat, wet, flannel,
my morning's
shoulder shroud.

Now, far-sighted I see the distant
danger.
Beyond the coffin confines of
telephone booths,
my arms stretch to read, in vain.

Stubbornness and penicillin hold
the aged above me.
My metaphors grow cold and old,
My enemies, both young and bold.

I have left Act I, for involution
and Act II. There mired in
complexity
I cannot write Act III.

The Song of Hate

A sixth-century Poem, by a Celtic monk, Cadoc the Wise.
Adapted and applied to modern politics by Eugene McCarthy.

I hate: chiefs who do not guard their subjects
                nations without vigor.

I hate: landless clans
                lands untilled
                and uncertain boundaries
                houses without dwellers
                fields that bear no harvest.

I hate: a man without a trade
                a laborer without choice
                a society without teachers.

I hate: lost learning
                the agents of error
                the oppressors of truth
                fables in place of teaching
                knowledge without inspiration

I hate: a country in anarchy
                journeys without safety
                the scribe who loves war
                a country in anarchy.

I hate: lawsuits without reason
                the judge who loves money
                faults in counsel
                a false witness before a judge
                justice unhonored
                those who make strife among friends.

I hate: the undeserving exhalted to high position.

—Cadoc the Wise

Hope Amid the Despair
(*Boston Globe*, November 6, 1984)

After an absence of nearly two weeks, I returned to my house in Rappahannock County in mid-May of last spring. I was apprehensive that I might have missed the best part of the month.

I found that I had missed some things. The apple blossoms evidently had come and gone while I was absent, for the trees were now in green leaf. There was no sign of redbud at the edge of the woods, or of wild cherry. The dogwood was still in bloom, however. Golden ragweed was thick in the pastures, as were the buttercups.

I found the wild azaleas blooming where they should have been, along Route 618. The grass in the pastures was nearly as high as the knees of the cows. It hid the spring calves. The hay in the meadows was ready for cutting. Goatsbeard and wild phlox and sweet cicely and poppies bloomed at roadside. A few May-apple blossoms still clung to the stems beneath the umbrella leaves.

So encouraged, I bought tomato plants at Burke's store when I went to the post office to pick up my accumulated mail.

I decided to check through the mail before planting the tomatoes. I was in for a shock. There was no springlike optimism, not even hope, in my mail. Evidently the prophets of gloom, the managers of direct-mail programs, know not how the seasons run.

First, I opened a letter from the *American Sentinel*, warning me that American children are being brainwashed and that unless the process is stopped, and our nuclear-arms buildup continued, we and the children may eventually be destroyed by Soviet nuclear weapons. Offsetting this letter was one from the Community for Creative Non-Violence, suggesting that the only way we can escape nuclear destruction is to stop building nuclear arms.

Next I read an appeal, endorsed by Katharine Hepburn, asking for financial and moral support of population control, in some form or other, and restating the Malthusian theory that the world would be destroyed by excessive numbers of people unless action was taken now. Countering this appeal was one from the Right-to-Life organization asserting that population control will destroy civilization. No choices were being offered. I felt trapped.

There was a letter from the Committee to Re-elect Ronald Reagan, which made dire predictions of things to come if he were not reelected. And set against this was a letter from the chairman of the Democratic party telling me that he thought I would "agree with him" that the reelection of Ronald Reagan might be disastrous for the nation, if not the world.

There was a letter from James Watt, former secretary of the interior, telling me that President Reagan was a voice in the "wilderness," which critics of Watt and Reagan said was about to be destroyed.

The Watt appeal for support in subduing the wilderness was countered by a circular from *National Geographic*, which urged me to buy a book entitled *Our Threatened Inheritance*.

Then there were three letters telling me that I could and should not trust the press, generally, but that the publications recommended for subscription in the letters were reliable.

There was an appeal from the American Heart Association asking for contributions to support research in heart diseases, "the greatest mankiller."

At that point, near despair, I was distracted by the sound of an automobile horn, and by the barking of my dog.

When I went out of the house to investigate, I found that a large green Cadillac, of some years' service, had been driven into my driveway. I thought it might be a bottled-gas salesman, or possibly someone intent on selling me a water-softener system.

It was not. It was a Jehovah's Witness, who had come over the Blue Ridge Mountains from Luray to warn the people of Rappahannock County of the signs and portents of destruction, of Armageddon, and of the coming of the Kingdom.

I listened to his message, to his quotations from the Bible, with rising optimism. I told him of the depressing mail I had just gone through and of how his words had uplifted my spirit. He looked a little puzzled. I bought three pamphlets from him, and told him that with the hope and trust that his message had revived, I was going to plant tomatoes, hoping for, at least, one more crop.

I did the planting, and last week picked the last of what was a very good crop.